BAILOUT OVER NORMANDY

Bailout Over Normandy

*A Flyboy's Adventures with the French Resistance
and Other Escapades in Occupied France*

BY TED FAHRENWALD

CASEMATE
Philadelphia & Oxford

Published in the United States of America and Great Britain in 2012 by
CASEMATE PUBLISHERS
908 Darby Road, Havertown, PA 19083
and
10 Hythe Bridge Street, Oxford, OX1 2EW

ISBN 978-1-61200-157-9
Digital Edition: ISBN 978-1-61200-158-6

Cataloging-in-publication data is available from the Library of Congress and
the British Library.

10 9 8 7 6 5 4 3 2 1

Printed and bound in the United States of America.

For a complete list of Casemate titles please contact:

CASEMATE PUBLISHERS (US)
Telephone (610) 853-9131, Fax (610) 853-9146
E-mail: casemate@casematepublishing.com

CASEMATE PUBLISHERS (UK)
Telephone (01865) 241249, Fax (01865) 794449
E-mail: casemate-uk@casematepublishing.co.uk

CONTENTS

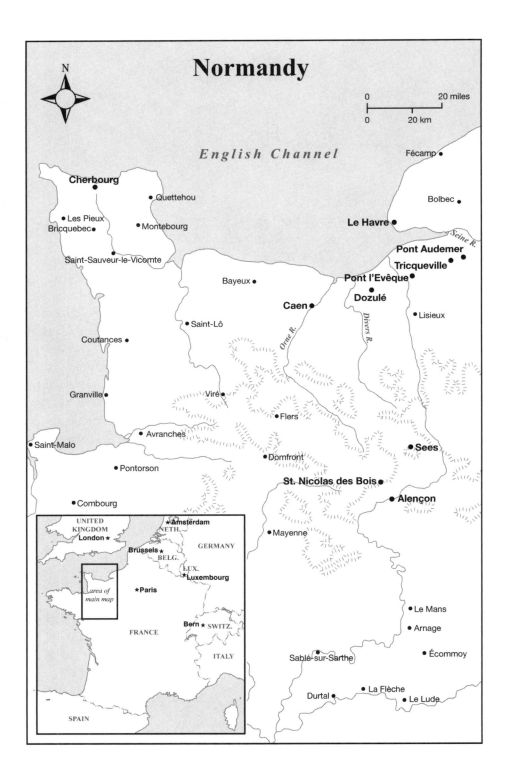

EDITOR'S NOTE

◈

My father sat down to record his swashbuckling World War II adventure tale immediately after his discharge from the Army Air Corps in 1946. He finished about one year and many cartons of cigarettes later, and then the manuscript sat on a shelf for decades, known only to family and friends. Dad didn't pursue the career in journalism that he'd dreamed of as a young college man; instead, he had a family and with his brother Fran operated a small steel mill inherited from their father. This book is a tribute to my Dad: his humor, his over-the-top love of life, and especially his unacknowledged artistic talents as a writer, storyteller, and artist. Everyone who's read the manuscript has insisted that it must be published, and I decided to do that, nearly seventy years after the events he describes and seven years after his death in 2005.

Dad's father was the archetypal "Indiana Jones"—born in a sod house in South Dakota, he grew up to become an all-around outdoorsman, an inventor with nearly 200 patents to his name, and a mining engineer who explored mines from Alaska to South America. Raised by two Northern Plains romantics on the family ranch and in Chicago, Dad was a member of the last generation to straddle the great American Frontier and the modern era.

He grew up hunting, fishing, camping, and traveling with his father, and already had his commercial pilot's license and was an avid flyer, motorcyclist, and full-fledged daredevil when he enlisted at age 22 determined to become a combat fighter pilot. With its reputation for attracting hotshots and risk-takers, that role was custom-made for him. Dad's trickster personality and comedic skills enabled him and his cohort to prank and party their way through every stage, from basic training in California to pilot training in Arizona to combat assignment in England. Those qualities enabled Dad to not just survive but also to thrive in his relationship with the backwoods French Resistance outlaws he fought and partied with—and also during his internment and escape from a German POW camp.

I thought it important to preserve the integrity of Dad's vernacular. As "unpolitically correct" as it might read these days, that was the jargon of the WWII-era flyboy; for that reason, I kept the manuscript exactly as it was written, with very little editing.

I believe that you'll find this wild ride back in time to another place and another era to be an irresistible read—and that you'll also enjoy getting acquainted with some of the more rambunctious members of "The Greatest Generation."

—Madelaine Fahrenwald

PROLOGUE

◆

A bunch of the boys was whoopin' it up, as usual. Fighter pilots all, bellied up close to the bar, boot-heels lodged in spittoons. In England this was, in a little tin hut at the edge of a grassy flying field up near the cold North Sea. The fairly indestructible remnants of a hot-shot Mustang squadron, we'd been roosting right here for a year—for we drank upon occasion, the most frequent of which being sundown.

Flying by day were we, and by night winning the bloody great war with Scotch-and-soda, and it seemed that the same rowdy crew always led off on these nighttime missions. Inevitably, as the night bombers of the RAF would string out across the darkening skies, so would Parchesi-Joe and the Gremlin, Pappy and Scotti and Mac and I trail into the musty, dim barroom of our club—lured by the wafted fumes of rare old mountain dew. And in comparison to some of these nightly affairs, combat flying was utter relaxation. The jagged brick footrest of our tiny bar was quite as much an occupational hazard as the flak lobbed up from Happy Valley or Berlin—the designers of our cozy retreat having failed to foresee the disastrous possibilities inherent in the combination of one peashooter pilot, a quart or so of ersatz Scotch, plus the inexorable law of gravity.

Booze, however, was not our sole joy and diversion. Perhaps in the course of an evening there might be a small game of chance; a reckless round of stud, wherein our hard-earned pound notes would sail through the drifting strata of tobacco smoke like snowflakes in a Dakota blizzard.

Other nights we might just crouch in the darkest corner of our lair, hashing over past aerial exploits to evolve fantastic new methods of slaughtering Jerries with a P-51. It has never been proven that there existed any liaison between High Command and our bleary-eyed council, but the most reckless of our alcoholic schemes would invariably come true. Having long since discovered the uncannily accurate prophecies that lay inscribed upon the bottom of every whiskey jug, we were thus led to believe that perhaps High Command had been fashioning our fate with the same carefree bravado as we'd been using to predict it.

But maybe we'd just drink to dear Aunt Gussie. The fairest of queens in the royal courts of old was never toasted as frequently or with such fervor as was this venerable dame. Designed and constructed according to our rigid specifications, this invisible old squaw had been brought into our cruel little world to serve solely as a salve for what we laughingly referred to as our collective conscience. The latter would infrequently cause us pangs, should we all become soaked for no apparent reason. One should always have something definite to celebrate, and Aunt Gussie's birthday was generally it. She aged rapidly.

And whenever my battered guitar would come from under the bar, then the air would well resound with a notorious collection of ballads: all those we used to know and love so well, a raucous repertoire at best. Even the Red Cross wenches could work up a blush or two at some of these delicate ditties. A fun-loving lot at heart we were, and nothing cramped our style. Each night at closing time our uproarious departure into the blackout would never fail to elicit from our true friend, Pat the bartender, the comment spoken sadly: "The Cream of American Youth. Jeeeezus!" We were sure foolin' the public.

And so tonight—that rainy night of June the 5th of '44, and the night my story begins—the squadron's evening session started out with the usual routine. After impishly pouring four fingers of rotgut into my glass, my old flying partner Mac had cried: "C'mon, Faro! Leave us have a party!"

"Why certainly," I replied. "To Aunt Gussie's 99th, bless her filthy soul!" So with a clink, a gulp, and a shudder, things got under way.

As the jamboree grew both in number and intensity, the talk around the bar became laced through with a thread of tension, for it looked to us as though perhaps our tired old war was coming at last into some sort of focus. In enemy skies of late, we'd accomplished an inordinate amount of highly specialized dirty work, and in retrospect there could be seen a certain method to our madness.

Our bomber escort work had slacked off and we'd set about strafing airdromes, racing deep into Germany to sometimes catch the Luftwaffe with its flaps down. And we'd taken our losses. Then upon our flak-addled heads there had fallen the rightful blame for the acute shortage of underwear which had developed amongst the nerve-shattered railroaders of the Reich—for we'd buzzed joyfully up and down the main lines, seeking out and punching holes into every locomotive constructed by the Jerries in the past century. After that, 8th Fighter Command had declared open season, whereupon anything that might happen into our gun-sights became a legitimate target. Indeed, one sunny Sunday afternoon we'd strafed Germany so mercilessly that Lord Haw-Haw screamed and scolded us over the radio that very night. And another time, we all left our brains in a bucket and set forth on a prolonged low-level attack on that most heavily defended of all German areas: Pas de Calais, just across the Channel from the high cliffs of Dover.

Pas de Calais we preferred to forget. High Command (we never did find out just whose High Command it was), disbelieving the profane pilot reports of a hundred previous missions, had stated its urgent desire to ascertain the degree of alertness maintained by the ten million Jerry flak batteries that bristled the French coast. So on a volunteer basis, under a hundred-foot ceiling—and with our propellers harvesting seaweed and assorted French crops every inch of the way—we'd charged squarely into the muzzle of the goddamned biggest gun in the world. Jerry had chuckled and pulled the trigger, and one helluva lot of wreckage had flown back out over the English Channel.

A lot of dirty work, but now it appeared that the time was approaching for others besides the 8th Air Force to plaster the old country with shot and shell. And today, more cause for speculation. Our P-51s had been grounded without warning and hastily disfigured by having their wings and bellies painted with broad black and white stripes. To our critical eyes, this foul bit of anti-camouflage had transformed our slim and cocky little fighters into what looked to be a mess of outsized tropical fish. A fine thing, we figured, but what the hell. Orders from Headquarters. This was, remember, the fifth day of June.

By mid-evening, thoughts of higher strategy had been forgotten to the merry tune of popping corks and clinking glassware, and our little spree was just one notch short of roaring when it was brought to a grinding halt by the appearance of a ranking paddlefoot who stomped into the bar and immediately lost what few friends he might have had.

"Patrick!" he shouted over the uproar. "Close the bar!"

We spread out into combat formation and growled in unison: "Closin' the bar?"

"The bar is closed! That's orders, goddammit! Get some sleep, flyboys, for you'll be needin' it!"

We were thunderstruck! What an unprecedented turn of affairs! But further protesting howls drew only a hearty scowl and advice to play it smart, for a change. So we bitched for a while—out of habit and to preserve our self-respect—then navigated through the drizzly gloom to our cheery little culvert-type home, and there we pondered the deliberate sabotage of our projected wingding. We'd been outranked. Something hot was on the fire. We played a few hands of stud and turned in.

I'd barely dozed off when an orderly poked his ugly noggin into our hut to holler out the old song-and-dance: "Rollout! Briefing for all pilots in twenty minutes! Maximum effort!"

Chapter **I**

AN EVEN ONE-HUNDRED

◈

All pilots . . . briefing . . . max effort: a damned poor joke on a night like this night. But we shuddered and stretched and grumbled a bit, fished out cigarettes, and slipped into our duds quickly and without much chatter.

Not much chatter, but we were all thinking hard and fast, and the same maggoty thoughts nibbled persistently through each of our heads: black night . . . rain . . . low ceiling . . . zero visibility . . . no flare-pots . . . a blind takeoff with 3,000 pounds of high-octane aboard that tiny little Mustang. To hell with it. My fingers had developed a tremor. And on the tin roof the drizzle rattled, dripping upon our heads through the twenty-seven bullet holes we'd shot there one night (whilst endeavoring to extinguish the lights without having to leave our bunks).

Mac remarked cheerily to no one in particular that, one time on just such a night as this, he had seen an elderly seagull come spinning out of the soup. More of such whimsy, until at the blast of a horn we scrambled into our jeep and took off up the road, the headlights poking into a dismal night, windshield-wipers clicking away the drizzle, cigarettes glowing nervously.

All was quiet until we slid to a halt in the mud behind Headquarters where Frascotti leaped wildly from the jeep, waved his hands to the dripping overcast, and beseeched the gods who lurked therein to clean up the forbidding skies. Slipping into his Jimmy Durante persona, he shouted out his conviction that he was surrounded by assassins. And that he should never have said—for within a few hours he was dead. We'd laughed at the time, but later wished we hadn't.

We scampered out of the rain and into the briefing room, curious to learn just what the sadists down at Fighter Command might have been smoking when they'd dreamed up a flight for this dreary, rainswept midnight. Our eyes lost all traces of indifference when we cast them onto the great chart of the Continent: for there before us was written the climax to the relentless offensive battle we'd been waging for the past year. Tonight, to mark out our mission, the confusion of red ribbons and colored tacks extended from the coast of England south across the Channel to focus upon the beaches of France.

The significance was obvious: tonight we covered the Invasion of Normandy. Paratroopers and gliders were on their way at this very moment. At 0330 hours, Allied landing craft would hit the beaches behind the cover of a terrific naval and aerial bombardment. Our mission was to run a patrol along the west coast of Cherbourg Peninsula and prevent attack from that quarter by Jerry aircraft. Every flyable ship and pilot in the 8th Fighter Command would go out tonight, to remain in assigned zones until there was only fuel enough to return to England. We would take off on instruments four abreast in tight formation, and the flights would rendezvous over the field—so hoped the Colonel as he concluded his briefing.

The Intelligence Officer briefed us as to possible enemy opposition, and the Chaplain gave us the Word. When Stormy the meteorologist came up with his terrifying weather charts and worse theories, we laughed him off the stage and headed for our squadron dispersal area.

We milled around in the pilots' hut, emptying pockets of telltale trinkets and puttering about with our flying gear, all hands busily trying to forget about the weather in which we'd soon be flying. With minutes remaining, I headed through the rain toward my good ship, the Joker, swinging my 'chute and muttering a funny little flying tune: ". . . owls and nitwits fly by night . . ." and I thought, "Goddam, ain't it the truth! But which am I?" I knew I wasn't an owl.

The Joker was crouched in the blackness of its revetment looking 200 mph standing still, so clean she was. I crawled from the wheel to the slippery wet wing and slipped into the narrow cockpit and my good crew chief helped strap me in place. He lit up a smoke and tucked it into my mouth and I waited while the sweat trickled, and then from the control tower a red rocket squirted up into the overcast. And now it was all business.

A fumbling of switches and levers and knobs to bring forth a comforting snarl from my engine, and the prop disk reflected the orange glare of the exhaust stacks. The field had come magically alive with a horde of dim red and green wing lights that flowed bobbing and twisting toward the takeoff funnel. In the ensuing long minutes of extremely difficult taxiing in total darkness, the entire outfit of some fifty ships became royally fouled-up, and I—an eager type—found myself, along with two other similarly confused pilots, in the lead takeoff position. By the darting flames of their engine exhausts I could make out the dim identifying letters painted on the fuselage of each ship. So Pappy Gignac and McKibben and I were together, and we three were hogging the slot reserved for the Colonel's flight. That, however, was tough titty, because it was too late now to monkey around trying to get organized. We ran up our engines and it was time to go, and I didn't want to push that throttle at all. My instruments glowered greenly at me like the winking, blinking, luminous eyes of a whole pack of pussycats racked up in a blacked-out bookcase.

We held brakes and poured on the coal until our ships quivered, released brakes and shoved throttles full forward, and we accelerated fast on a tight-formation instrument takeoff for what I sincerely hoped to be the opposite corner of the field and thence its black sky. Rolling mighty fast, Pappy's ship careened violently away to the left and he was out of the race. Mac and I held our course and when my ship felt light I sucked the wheels out from under her and hauled back on the stick and waited to find out whether or not an oak tree would try to stuff itself into the cockpit with me. Now airborne, I started breathing again, got the engine controls squared away, and slid in close on Mac's wing.

We banked into an easy turn to port and I glanced back to the field, and all of a damned sudden a horrible, billowing explosion half-blinded me, and I knew automatically what it was: a Mustang, a maximum load of high-octane, and one of the boys, all gone to glory in a puff of flame. I didn't know who'd bought it, but I did know that it was a pilot of my squadron. Mac and I circled the runway at 500 feet, just beneath the weeping overcast, and we watched the flaring mess die away to glowing redness.

With their pilots taking full advantage of the grisly beacon, Mustangs shot from the blackness of the takeoff position to gleam momentarily in the crash flames and disappear again as they became safely airborne. Radio silence had gone all to hell and my earphones were full of frantic chatter. We circled a couple of times in an effort to pick up the rest of our ships, but after barreling through a couple of flights which were at our altitude but traveling in the opposite direction, we gave up and struck out on the briefed course, with Mac flying instruments and me jockeyed in tight on his wingtip. Then up through the overcast and out into a lovely, lonely moonlit sky, and below us the clouds shone frosty and silver.

On up to twenty thousand, and as we neared the French coast the undercast began suddenly to take color. Almost like a sunrise it was, with a spreading scarlet glow diffusing through the clouds to then slowly diminish in intensity: the naval bombardment, preliminary to the landings, was under way. Moments later, our two-ship squadron attracted accurate, heavy flak—spectacular stuff bursting with a red flash and a lusty thud, with each burst followed by a chain of lesser explosions extending vertically downward: a signpost to announce our arrival over the city limits of Cherbourg.

After a lonely hour of sucking oxygen, we peeled down to thirteen thousand, whereupon I ripped off my mask and lit up a smoke and chased Mac around the sky. Now a fantastically beautiful sunrise boomed up through the jumbled cloud formations, and—half-hypnotized by the sight—I found it difficult to realize, in the midst of such splendor and absolute solitude, that I was flying six machine guns and five tons of hot airplane, with death and destruction the goal.

Nothing to shoot at up here, but I knew quite well that two or three miles below the beaches were a nightmare of bloody action, and I felt a bit guilty about sitting on top of a cloud acquiring another layer of calluses, when down below the walking army was getting knocked off about as fast as it was being dumped ashore. After a few hours of futile cloud-hopping, we rolled into a fast dive through a long, vertical tunnel in the soup and went shopping around on the deck, a scant few feet off the water.

The sea was rough and of a cold green color, and great waves crashed at the base of the jagged rock cliffs of the peninsula. We buzzed the Channel Islands and ran in and out of the harbor at St. Malo; but the only sign of life was a pair of coastal trawlers with their square, patched sails bellied tightly out by the wind. Nobody took a crack at us and we saw no Jerry aircraft so, a pack of smokes later, we set course for England and landed at the first airfield we could find, with a cupful of fuel between us and a crash-landing. Wedged for eight hours in the tiny cockpit, my legs were completely paralyzed and my back permanently kinked. A quick refueling and we clipped the treetops for two hundred miles back to our home base, where we learned that it had been friend Scotti who hadn't made it off the ground on takeoff. He'd taken off just a trifle off-course and had driven his Mustang "Umbriago" squarely through a brick control tower at 120 mph. Surrounded by assassins . . .

More fuel, a cup of coffee, a pair of 500-pound bombs apiece, and we went out to seek targets of opportunity down behind the beachhead. A string of Jerry trucks on a highway outside of Paris came into our gunsights and was destroyed. Home again, and out again twice more, and then I peeled off into the sack for a couple of hours' sleep. And that was D-Day for the 486th Fighter Squadron.

At three a.m. on the 7th, the orderly again caught up with me for briefing. Now the weather was completely fouled up: zero ceiling and half-mile visibility made the whole lousy mess a flier's nightmare. Only it wasn't a nightmare: it was there. We were obliged to fly. At half-past four in the morning we got into the air, with Pappy Gignac leading eight ships. That old renegade, sharing our hatred of instrument flying, led us well: winding us up through many narrow, dark corridors in the fog and up through a dozen evil little cloud decks, and we headed for France on-top, on-course and on-time, and at our estimated time of arrival peeled off through a hole and went hunting. Unable to spot any live game, we vented our rage on a small-town railroad yard and on a highway bridge—in the center of which Pappy laid a 500-pounder with neatness and precision. We clobbered a couple of lone trucks and went home for breakfast.

Not being slated for the next flight, I slept in a chair in the pilots' hut, and as I snoozed Pappy led his last squadron to France—or to anywhere, for that matter. Somewhere down around Paris, he took the boys in on a long truck convoy. They dive-bombed and then went in to deliver the coup de grâce with 50-caliber guns, and Pappy strafed an ammo truck that exploded as he zoomed over it. He pulled up into a steep, climbing turn and told his lads that his ship was afire and that he was going to jump. But at the top of his chandelle, Pappy's Mustang blew to smithereens and no 'chute was observed. It was hard news to take, for Pappy was indestructible. He'd been shot down twice into the jungles of New Guinea while flying rickety old P-39s against the Japs. But there is a bottom to one's bag of luck.

June 8th. D-plus-2. The weather still foul, but most of us had by now run out of sweat. A briefing at two a.m. to which no one paid much attention, as the mission was to be just another freelance hunt south of the beachhead. We'd revised our tactics to match the Jerries' change of pace. Constant fighter attacks had forced him from the highways during daylight hours, so he now moved his convoys by night, masterfully camouflaging his equipment at the crack of dawn. So our plan was to get into Jerry territory at night and to nail his trucks and tanks just at sunrise, before they could be concealed. We'd outfox and clobber 'em, but good.

Briefing at two in the morning and takeoff at three: so with an hour to goof around, somebody built a cheery, snapping fire and brewed up a pot of strong coffee, which lowered the goose-bumps a bit. Sipping on a bottle of good ale, I wandered about the pilots' hut and chanced to observe on the mission scoreboard that I'd flown 99 missions to date, and that this night's flight would make it an even 100.

A certain uneasiness is developed around that 100th trip. A jinxy sort of thing. But I told myself that such superstitions were a lot of crap. You bet! But then again . . .

So I shuffled past the flight surgeon and sniffed and dragged a leg, but he wouldn't take notice at all.

"Hey Doc," I squeaked, "I got a terrible cold, as any fool kin plainly see, and why not ground me until a later date?"

To which plea he remarked coolly that I was, no doubt, the healthiest peashooter in the whole damned squadron.

"Tonight I don't want to fly any more," said I, "and if you make me go you'll be sorry."

But all I got was a nasty laugh. My pal, the Doc. Finally I told him that if it was all the same to him, I'd settle right now for that after-mission likker ration. And my fellow pilots cheered me on with wild stories and vicious propaganda about various jinxed and fateful 100th missions they'd known. As a matter of record, one of our finest pilots, Bobby MacKean, had simultaneously acquired a Silver Star and a tombstone while strafing an airdrome in southern France—on his 100th mission.

So I drifted over to the booze locker to refuel my silver flask with a full charge of Channel Oil, and while I was at it, I took a quick nip. I stuffed a half-carton of cigarettes into my flying suit and announced to the motley crew that nothing mattered now: I was ready for whatever cards I might be dealt. Despite the gay line of chatter, I still thought it to be a helluva night for getting over the hump.

I wandered toward my ship, feeling the rain on my face and sniffing the soggy night wind and not giving much of a damn for anything. Good Sergeant German was slumped in the cockpit, snoring lustily. I pounded on the canopy until he came crawling out guiltily, and I swapped places with him. Came the time and I wound 'er up, but that Merlin engine wouldn't kick over: the prop ground around and around and I thought, while mentally rubbing my hands together: "Ahhhh . . . Kismet! Maybe the bastard will never start, I hope!" But my overly expert crew chief, blast his eyes, coaxed fire into the engine with a hot-shot from a handy battery cart, and the flames boiled back from the stacks. I taxied fast to catch up with the squadron and slid into position. And we poured on the coal and were airborne, four abreast in nice tight formation.

The tight sixteen-ship squadron arrowed up through low scud clouds into a dense and turbulent overcast. On top at ten thousand in the pre-dawn light, the cloud scenery was desolate and bleak and as cold-looking as Little America. We slid out into a loose, line-abreast formation. Sixteen ships, and each little Mustang looked sleek and dangerous and mean, and we were doing a thousand miles an hour as we streaked along through jagged cloud valleys, clipping hummocks and tufts and pulling up and over turbulent cloud hills.

Somewhere west of Paris we let down through the stuff and throttled back, cruising at a thousand feet, and our morning hunt was on. A loose formation, with every pilot straining his eyes in the faint dawn light, searching for targets along the roads and in the forests: Mustangs weaving and rolling and occasionally skidding gently away from the showers of tracers that would lob up from hidden gun emplacements.

The weather in France was excellent, with a thin overcast at 4,000 feet, and when the brilliant edge of the sun peeped up, the countryside was rosy and objects on the ground cast long, clean shadows. And it was just a moment after sunrise when we hit the jackpot: a long column of thirty or forty trucks crawling around the right-angle turn of a gravel road, quite obviously headed for the safety of a large patch of forest a mile from their present position.

Spaced evenly, rolling slowly, this was a target of rare quality. One of the boys, whooping bloodthirstily into his microphone, peeled off to lay a pair of bombs directly in front of the lead truck, which obligingly burst into flames. The column was stopped dead.

Cold turkey, it was, and the radio livened up with savage cries. Taking interval, we raced into a big Lufbery circle just below the overcast, and one by one our ships rolled over into their dive-bomb runs. I watched the passes and saw the strikes, and they were effective. My turn now, and a deliberate approach panned out nicely. I chandelled, kicking the tail aside so I could observe my hits.

A dandy disaster below! Trucks afire, long parallel banners of black smoke drifting across the fields, and the road all shot to hell with bomb craters. Now some of the boys were down on the deck beating things up with machine guns, and the traffic pattern was out of this world, with Mustangs streaking in fast from every point of the compass, tracers crisscrossing, ships chandelling up all over the sky and at all angles. Fighter pilots huddled in a smoky old barroom couldn't have dreamed up a tastier target than this!

Having no particular desire to plunge into that reckless rat-race, I went shopping around the perimeter of the target area. A couple of miles back down the road I spotted six or eight heavy trucks, untouched and half hidden by low hedges. With a waggle of wings, I gave my wingman the word and we pounced down onto our own private shooting gallery, coming down in trail for our first pass. My first squirt smothered the rear of the last truck with a dancing, flickering mess of incendiary strikes. Pulling out of my dive I held down the trigger, laddering my fire away the hell and gone up the road, getting a few strikes on assorted vehicles and spraying the ditches liberally. With an evasive, skidding wingover we went in broadside to the column, flying nearly abreast, each flaming our targets. My guns seemed to be perfectly harmonized, coming to a sharp focus some three hundred yards ahead of my ship; and any target caught in the focal point was automatically a dead duck.

I spotted one truck parked smack against the wall of a small farmhouse at a crook of the road and managed to get a short burst into the truck without seeing too many strikes on the poor Frenchman's house—never thinking that if the truck burned, the old homestead would go up along with it.

Streams of tracers were pestering me now, but about the only chance the Jerries had of scoring was during the six or eight seconds of accurate, coordinated flying necessary when actually firing my guns: at all other moments, during the approach, pullout, and getaway, slipping and skidding evasive action was in order.

I felt mean and ornery, hungry and tired, and I hated the lousy guts of the whole damned Wehrmacht. A roaring lust for destruction was with me now, but I was about fresh out of ammunition—and I wanted a bit to travel on. But untouched below sat the great grand-daddy of all Jerry trucks, so I thought I'd better shoot it up, just a little.

Barreling in, I concentrated on one long and accurate squirt, and a devastating stream of 50s ripped into my target. I held down the trigger until the range was point blank and the Joker was clipping the weeds with her prop. At the last possible split second I jerked back the stick. Whereupon my luck ran out.

As I crossed over the truck, the son of a bitch blew up—it having been packing an overload of ammunition. A mighty thud and a mightier surge skyward, combined with what sounded to my ear like a whole belt of machine-gun slugs pounding into the belly of my ship. A split second later I found myself to be some five hundred feet up, inverted and climbing. Half-rolling, I kept going upstairs, using my initial velocity of some 375 mph to gain a lot of altitude in a hurry. Leveling out at 4,000 feet, on course for England, I took hasty inventory.

I had control of the ship and the engine instruments were normal. My wings were bent and beat up a bit: the skin was wrinkled and a lot of odds and ends from the disintegrating truck had holed through. There was a smoke trail behind me. I thought about how Pappy had gotten it the day before, in exactly the same circumstances, and I felt lucky. My wingman slid in alongside to radio that he'd stick with me on the way home.

Having been preoccupied in cleaning my fingernails during briefing, I didn't know just where in the hell I might be, but figured that a course of due north would be as good as any. For a minute I cruised smoothly in that direction. The Jekyll-Hyde transformation induced by every good strafing attack was fading, and now all I wanted out of life was to be back at the field, to have a bit of breakfast, and to then log a little solo sack-time. I was glad that I'd not been forced to bail out in the target area, for we'd strafed unmercifully and I didn't suppose that the Jerries remaining alive on the ground would have been inclined toward kindly treatment of fighter pilots. But now the green forests and meadows of Normandy were sliding along below, very nicely. And as I was patting myself on the back, my engine instruments began to shout bad news right in my face.

That vital little coolant-temperature needle began a slow crawl across its dial toward the red danger line. I throttled back to minimum cruise and opened the oil and coolant shutters. The needle dropped back to normal temperature, then started back up again: whereupon I eliminated from my mind all thoughts of England and steered more westerly, figuring to try for friendly territory on the beachhead. The engine got hotter and nothing I could do would bring her back to normal.

The roughness of the engine could be felt first in the stick, and then the whole ship was trembling violently. I was in bad trouble, and my wing-man had to circle and "ess" in order to stay back with me. I tried like hell to keep her going—at least long enough to reach the Channel—now figuring to make it that far and then to sit in my fancy rubber dinghy while waiting for Air-Sea Rescue to fish me out. But the engine commenced to run very roughly, and quickly rougher, and I jazzed the controls in a frantic effort to find a smooth spot. The Joker was pounding violently now, with airspeed dropping away rapidly: 140 mph and 3,500 feet indicated altitude, and the ship was just staggering around the sky.

Then the whole damned engine froze up and the tired old prop, with ironic finality, stuck up in front of me like a V-for-Victory symbol. Streaming back from the cowl, white smoke turning to black with gusts of flame flashing back on either side of the cockpit. Fearing a cockpit explosion, I snapped the oxygen mask over my face, flipped my goggles down over my eyes, unbuckled the safety belt, cleared myself from the tangle of shoulder harness, and retrieved my cigarettes from their slot alongside the gun-sight—all done in a moment.

A glance at the ground, and France assumed an extremely personal aspect. I pushed the mike button and yelped out a fond farewell to the squadron in general. I hated to get out into the long tongues of smoke and those wicked little jabs of flame, but I had to make tracks in a hurry. Without debate, and automatically following a long-prepared plan of action, I pulled up to a stall, jettisoned the canopy, and jumped.

I was damned near clear of the wing when the Joker snapped off on the left wing into a quick spin, which treacherous action on the part of my aircraft scooped me neatly back into the cockpit. My right leg was wedged well up under the instrument panel while the rest of my carcass dangled outside, streamlined back alongside the fuselage, and I caught a flash of green trees coming up fast. With what seemed to require no effort, I hoisted myself back into the flame-filled cockpit and yanked my leg free. In a very few seconds I'd either be dead or alive and I knew it, but Time gave me a break and paused where it was—each fractional second seeming to allow minutes in which to think and act. I recall figuring angles and judging odds and at the same time feeling interest in one's ability to think analytically under the pressure of such intricate circumstances. Arriving at a final plan, and with no indecision, I crouched on the bucket seat and launched a desperate leap straight upwards from the ship: on up and over the top of the cockpit and over the tail. And upon seeing the vertical fin slice past beneath me, extreme elation was experienced.

Falling head down, I could see my ship close below, silver and blue against the dark forest, spinning fast, with a trail of smoke behind her. My body had too great a velocity for a comfortable 'chute opening, but I was low to the ground and I gave the old ripcord a mighty tug and felt the beginning of a powerful jolt.

Upon regaining vision, curious and simultaneous impressions were noted: I saw the unfortunate Joker strike the ground in a little clearing, to explode with a terrific orange flash; then there came the fascinating and amusing sight of a profusion of little gadgets all about me in the air—bits of rope and colored cloth, tin cans and tiny packages, as though a bomb had burst in a junk-peddler's cart below me. My dinghy had burst open, ripped from my 'chute harness by the shock of the opening, spilling into thin air all of the many interesting little emergency equipment items with which it had been packed. And I saw my red-painted ripcord falling away beneath me.

With the pounding of machine guns and the powerful hum of the

Merlin engine still echoing in my ears, this complete silence was bewildering. So utterly peaceful and still it was that I actually wondered whether or not I was still alive. I peeked up overhead and thar she was! A tightly rounded-out hemisphere of snow-white nylon: no rips, rents, or runs visible to the naked eye. And then just plain, old-fashioned joy of living filled me to the bursting point. I didn't give two hoots in hell for anything and I dug out my silver flask and took a long swig of bourbon by way of celebration.

I looked down between my dangling feet and it seemed awfully high to be minus an airplane: some five hundred feet of nothing between toe and treetops. I was drifting fast—about 25 mph, I judged—but damned if I was losing any altitude . . . just drifting quietly along like a big-assed bird. Then, in the direction of my drift, I saw a camouflaged German airdrome upon which I calculated I'd land, whether or not I wanted to. It seemed quite logical to assume that every trooper in the entire Wehrmacht was observing my downfall with sanguinary glee: the least I expected was a reception committee equipped with muskets, fixed bayonets, and a set of leg-irons. But I still appeared to be holding my altitude, and the comforting thought came to mind that perhaps I'd float right on over the airfield, a hanging target for one and all. I fished out a cigarette and lit up, feeling oddly pleased that my Zippo should function so nicely in this strange perch.

Watching the trees flowing under me, I knew suddenly that I was losing altitude, allright, and losing it fast. Indeed, I was dropping like something going through a tin horn. I dropped my cigarette and grabbed a double handful of shroud lines and tried to crank myself around so as to land facing the direction of drift, but I only succeeded in acquiring a dandy pendulum effect. I skimmed over a row of tall trees, just cleared the ridgepole of a farmhouse, careened down past the eaves of a large stone barn, and landed hard in the center of a narrow gravel road behind a big hangar at the edge of the airdrome.

A bounce and a roll and I got up running, to dive headlong into my 'chute, collapsing it. I scrambled out of the harness, bundled my 'chute with frantic haste, and looked around, wild-eyed.

Chapter **2**

"WE ARE THE MAQUIS"

◈

Twirling my head rapidly about like an owl and glaring defiantly in all directions, I was delighted to see no uniforms converging upon my position. Well, whee and hot damn! I thought, and—arms full to overflowing with great quantities of parachute—I pulled a fine bead on the nearest fringe of forest and lit out like a scared jackrabbit. I was bound on gaining the tall timber where, once in, nobody would ever see me again.

While flying low through a corner of the barnyard, I spotted a girl half-hidden in the narrow doorway of a stone pigsty. The back of her hand was pressed tightly to her lips, and I could have hung my helmet on her eyeballs. When but a few paces from her, I slid to a halt, grinned and waved, and spoke to her: "Bonjour, mamselle! Je suis aviateur Americain . . ."

The cat had her tongue. I asked her if German soldiers were at the airdrome—at the same time checking back over my shoulder to see for myself. And still no answer. For a long moment the girl stared, and then gestured me out of the bald sunlight and into the pigpen where she found her voice and began sputtering much fast talk my way. All I could get from her was that she wasn't speaking English, so I waved her down, requesting that she proceed slowly and in one-syllable words: so now, speaking my brand of French, she told me that the Jerries had all packed up and left their flying field after the last attack by British bombers. But only a kilometer from us were now a thousand German soldiers, which was all I wanted to know.

"Adieu, belle ami. Il faut partir!" One must leave, for at any moment would the Jerries be here, and that would prove to be extremely awkward for the girl and for me. So catching up straggling bits of silk and clearing my feet of the tangle of shroud lines, I peered over my clumsy bundle to again cast an anxious eye toward the deep forest. But now the girl shook her head and pulled me away from the doorway. Non-non-non-non! I must wait where I was. She would return in a moment. She cocked an ear and all outside was quiet, so she dashed away to return in short order with three people scuttling in close formation behind her. These were, whispered the girl breathlessly, "Grandmère, grandpère, and my husband, Maurice. They will help you!" I shook hands with each and gave each a smile. Well, the old folks were humpbacked and wrinkle-faced, and the old lady had an armful of tattered clothing which she thrust at me with excited gestures: I must put them on. Quickly! Quickly! So I peeled off my helmet—pausing from habit to scratch my head—then off with the Mae West and flying jacket, off with the flying suit and army shirt and pants, and then all I had to go was my pair of dapper khaki shorts. Whereupon I grinned sheepishly. The girl Helene laughed and waved: I need go no further. And as I donned the disguise, with everybody standing around jabbering at me, I tested out my new language and found it to be decidedly without fluency.

A much-patched pair of once-blue overall pants and a faded brown shirt I now wore, and a little old threadbare suitcoat with sleeves six inches too short. Maurice looked me over with a critical eye and whipped off his beret, which I draped nonchalantly over one ear. I chuckled and announced gaily: "Voila! Je suis un Français!"—Now I'm a Frenchman, as though by magic. And I hadn't been on the ground for five minutes. Quite a system . . .

The old geezer, bless his thoughtful heart, had come to greet me clutching a bottle and tumbler which he now offered to me, friendly-like. With thanks I poured out four fingers of what I assumed to be white wine and tossed it off with one long, open-throated gulp. Later—and quite unnecessarily—I was told that people just don't guzzle raw Calvados moonshine. They sip it. For high-octane fuel and a jet of flame had combined in my throat to explode with a dazzling flash in my gut. My breathing apparatus was rendered temporarily inoperative, and I knew immediately that I'd been duped; but with truly remarkable control I succeeded in keeping a straight face, and while the old man gazed at me with awe, I whispered hoarse thanks and passed around my cigarettes and lit everybody up with my Zippo. The old woman snatched a smoke, took a couple of gleeful, pucker-mouthed drags, then snuffed it and tucked the butt carefully away in a little tin box she'd fished from her apron pocket. Then she scolded me: tobacco like that was much too dear to be offered so freely.

Fumbling nervously, Maurice stuffed my chute and flying gear into a gunnysack, and now he trotted for the woods with the stuff slung over his shoulder. I scuffed about in the manure to dirty my army shoes and thus complete my disguise. Now I was the one and original hillbilly, French-type, dismounted.

To our ears came the sudden, faint sound of an approaching motorcar, and instantly our little gathering broke up. Alone in the malodorous stable, I scurried to the darkest corner and crouched against the wall, pulling over me like a shield a rusty sheet of corrugated iron. And there I squatted for perhaps five minutes . . . my heart thumping audibly, the applejack percolating over the slow fire in my belly. And when the old man returned, croaking, "Aviateur! Aviateur!" I came from hiding and asked him what might be the score. An auto, he said, with German officers and soldiers had stopped at the farm to ask questions, for a parachutist had been seen to fall in the neighborhood. Guess who?

When my friends had all reappeared, I thanked them again for their help and again stated my belief that it was wise I leave them without delay. For should the Jerries come upon us now, there would be a little massacre, with four Frenchmen and one American as raw material. My friends were well aware that I spoke the truth, for the Germans were notoriously ruthless in their efforts to stamp out such resistance by the people of France. Maurice considered my little speech for a moment, then smiled and jerked a thumb toward his house. He was taking a long chance, and it took courage. The old man crossed himself, muttered something to his wife, and they bade me adieu. They scuttled across the farmyard and away.

So I made my first public appearance, walking across the little yard, and every step of the way I fully expected a heavy hand to clamp onto my shoulder. When we gained the kitchen, I was glad.

An ancient wood-burning cookstove was in the kitchen, and a hand-hewn table and chairs, and a broom made of twigs. A curly-headed baby girl lurched over to me, looked me up and down with her brown eyes, and peeped out: "B'jour, M'sieu." The kid was about three, I guess, and a cute little rascal, so I found a bar of candy in my pocket and gave it to her. Helene snatched off the American wrapper and burned it. The baby took a serious nibble, looked up at us, and cried "C'est indescriptible!"—which was quite a two-franc word to come out of such a small child, and I chuckled. But Helene nearly wept when she explained that her baby had never seen such candy.

Helene dusted off her best chair and I sat at the table. Maurice fetched a bowl of fresh milk and a chunk of black bread. When that was gone, Helene set out a basket of cherries and a slab of salt pork, and I apologized for having eaten so much: I'd missed breakfast and had had a busy day. I looked at my watch. It was 8:30 a.m. on the eighth of June. Just four hours had passed since I'd climbed into the cockpit of the Joker back at Bodney, England. Now I sat in a farmhouse at the edge of a German airdrome, talking French to Frenchmen. With a flock of gestures and a complete slaughter of their native language, I told my hosts of the events of the morning's flight that had led to my vertical descent upon their farm. When my tongue would mire down, I'd grab a pencil and make myself clear that way. By the time I'd finished telling war stories, I had a couple of sheets of paper covered with an amazing quantity of tiny stick-men, little P-51s, big explosions, and a variety of other quaint symbols. My friends were intrigued.

Maurice and I retired to an attic room for a pow-wow, and I now discovered that I was situated some fifteen kilometers from the Channel south of Le Havre, and on the edge of Tricqueville Airdrome. And I was damned glad that my engine had given out when it had; for a few more minutes in the air with my bum navigation and I'd have been dropped right into the mouth of the Seine, subject to the guns of Le Havre. So I was quite a ways east of where I'd thought I'd been, but what the hell.

As to the Invasion, Maurice was in the dark—knowing nothing about it except that it had happened. I sketched up a map of the coast and showed him how it had begun and where the Allies were now fighting: the Americans on the west flank and the British on the east. The latter, under command of the much-advertised General Montgomery, I explained, were most likely slated to clean out the Channel Coast between Caen and Le Havre. In this event, Tricqueville should be liberated within the fortnight.

My plan of action, I told Maurice, was to hit the trail without delay: to walk to the general vicinity of Caen, to penetrate the German lines there, to meet the British and so proceed to London. All I'd need was a map of the Normandy coast and a little information. Maurice said he'd hide me out in the forest where I should wait until he brought to see me a friend of his who spoke English. Everything was under control!

The farm of Maurice Marais had suffered in the bombings of the adjoining airdrome. It was indeed miraculous that the house stood at all, for sticks of heavy bombs had fallen close by on either side. Fifty paces to the west were two half-demolished hangars, and fifty paces to the east was the rubble of a half-dozen flattened barracks. Every square foot of the house was pocked by fragments, and great cracks ran through the walls. Helene fingered the cross at her throat and said that there had been nights of terror, those nights when the bombers had come over.

Just before the Invasion, our bombers had flown over to drop tracts, and Maurice brought out a little sheet of paper to show me. Signed by Ike, it was a warning to all French living in proximity to likely target areas to clear out and go live with their country cousins until the fireworks died down. So I asked Maurice why he hadn't moved away from the German airdrome. Well, he explained, they'd always hated the Boches, and after the fourth bombing they'd abandoned the airdrome. He and his wife were happy to be rid of them.

Maurice sortied through the local area and returned. The coast was clear, so we headed out across the farmyard bound for the woods, each of us carrying an ancient axe and making like a couple of local boys out to chop a tree or two. Along a lane we went and over a fence, to drop to the bottom of a dry wash. Down the gully for a ways, and then up a steep and winding footpath that clung to the side of a timbered slope. Now we came upon a faint trail that we followed up the hillside until it terminated at a huge bomb crater. There we stopped and shared a smoke. Maurice faded back into the brush and I was alone.

Yellow clay and tangled roots exposed to the sun, rocks and bomb fragments underfoot, and all about the crater was thick underbrush and deep forest. Silence but for the rustle of leaves and the stirrings of rabbits and the occasional song of a bird. The overcast had burned away and the sky was deeply blue, and the sun focused hotly into the crater. I slid to the bottom and lit up a smoke. I sat and thought.

The squadron was back in England by this time, and right about now our Intelligence Officer, having inscribed a shaky "Missing in Action" after my name, was blotting his tear-stained mission report. And my old flyin' pals, chortling ghoulishly, were at this very moment busily rummaging through my footlocker—throwing great handfuls of valuables into the air and gleefully trying on my uniforms for size. I was lonesome for the bastards, but now I was strictly hors de combat.

A few seconds more, I pondered, and I'd have had that red-hot Merlin engine jammed up my chimney. So I was here and I was lucky and what the merry hell. I would milk this misdeal for all the fun there was in it. And I uncorked my silver flask to permit a trickle of bourbon to splash down into the Calvados below. I set about checking my equipment, mumbling happily as I puttered: ". . . Yer engine coughs, yer wings fall off, but youoooo will neverrrr mind!" After twenty-odd verses of that one, I carried on from there. I was so happy I could hardly stand it, what with being alive.

I wasn't badly off: three packs of smokes, a good lighter, and a damned good hunting knife; a roll of pound notes, a few shillings, and my trusty flask. Ripping open my Escape Kit, I took tally: 2,000 francs, a useless map, a hacksaw blade, two dime-store compasses, a needle and thread, a rubber water bottle and some tablets guaranteed to purify anything, a packet of benzedrine pills, and a short course in French. All that I had, plus a beat-up hillbilly disguise.

Gazing at the silk map for a while, I found it to be of too small scale to be of any value. And along the coastal regions of France was the hilarious warning: "Keep out of red-checkered areas! Heavy troop concentrations and coastal defenses!" The territory in which I now sat twiddling my thumbs was so heavily checkered that I couldn't even make out the names of the goddam towns.

I stripped and sewed a dog tag into the waistband of my shorts. The saw blade went into a seam of my shirt and I sewed into my handkerchief my spare dog tag, Air Corps ring, wings, and collar insignia. I took another little swig, then spread out my clothes and lay down on them, naked as a jaybird and feeling quite content. For days I'd been losing much sleep and now I was bone-tired; so grateful for the luxurious sunshine, I fell into heavy slumber before being awakened by the sound of laughter. I opened my eyes to see Maurice and his ever-loving wife standing on the lip of the crater above. We shook hands all around and then I dressed—already falling in with the casual customs of this fair country.

Helene carried a basket, and beneath the gay cloth was a pan full of meat and potatoes and gravy, with cherries and cider to top off the feast, and I left not a crumb nor a drop. As they turned to leave, I gave Maurice a pack of cigarettes and had to twist his arm before he'd take them.

My parachute leg straps had dealt me a treacherous blow, and my upper inner thighs had turned to a delightful shade of vomit-green. To move became a painful effort, so I cut a couple of canes with which I could pole myself from a sitting to a standing position or vice-versa. I sat and thought and dozed with one eye open, and Maurice returned at dusk to escort me to the house, where Helene led me upstairs and showed me my bed. She indicated an alternate exit from the house, which I was to use in the event of trouble. And I plunged into three feet of feather quilt—comfortable gadget after the bottom of a bomb hole.

For a while I lay awake, mulling over various fantastic schemes designed to fish my tired carcass from the fire, and then to sleep: whereupon, in about the third reel of dreams of flak and related short subjects, I was suddenly shaken awake. And I thought, Hi-ho . . . just another lousy briefing . . . but what was this babe doing in my hut? Then remembering who was in what barracks and where, I bounced out of the sack, on the alert.

Helene, with fear in her whisper, reported that les Boches were all around us! "Allez! Allez! Pas accelère!" I must skeedaddle, and right now. So with aches and pains forgotten in the danger of the night, in a moment I was dogtrotting briskly through the brush, flying blind toward the crater. I'd had a hunch that the featherbed was too good to last. Shivering, I counted stars, then watched the dawn to welcome the warmth of the sunrise; and at noon Maurice showed up to report that at dawn German troopers had searched the farmhouse and outbuildings. Right now German officers were inspecting the battered corpse of the Joker—and at midmorning two collaborateurs had approached Maurice, offering him 15,000 francs cash for information about the parachutiste allié. Not all the news was bad, however, for the English-speaking friend was on his way and we'd rendezvous with him in the farmhouse cellar.

I was soon perched upon a barrelhead in the dank and gloomy hole beneath the bomb-scarred house, wine kegs and spider webs and a musty odor all about me. Hearing the snarl of fighter engines, I peered from a tiny barred window to watch a flight of four efficient-looking Messerschmitt 109s race past at treetop level. I went back to my barrel, eager to meet the man who spoke my language. Son of a gun! I'd be on my merry way before long. This man would have a map and a masterful plan and I'd be patrolling Piccadilly within the week!

Now overhead a door slammed . . . squeaks traveled across the ceiling. With a shuffle of shoes on the stairway, Maurice appeared and with him was a character: a guy about thirty-five or forty with thinning brown hair and a dull face but for a set of bright blue eyes which twinkled at me through thick bifocals. This was Gabriel, who spoke English!

We shook hands. Gabriel began to talk, slowly and with extreme agony, pulling out each word with a whirligig gesture of his hand. I laughed like hell and Gabriel grinned and gave up; for his English was a frightful concoction of Dutch, Flemish, French, German, a word or two of English, plus a few sounds he'd made up all by himself. Rooked again!

So out came my pencil and paper for more stick-men and maps. Gabriel was of no help whatsoever, but he was a good egg. He told me that he hailed from up around the Frisian Islands in the Netherlands, but that he'd lived for seven years in Normandy and had just married a beautiful queen. What a farmer!

I explained again: all I wanted to do was to walk to the general vicinity of the beachhead. Didn't anybody have a map? Well, Gabriel knew a man who could really speak English, and he'd bring him here to see me!

Gabriel had brought along a litre of Calvados and as we passed the jug back and forth, I told flying stories, complete with grand convolutions of both hands. By now I could understand why it was that Frenchmen always had to wave their hands when talking: it was vital if any degree of comprehension was desired. By mid-afternoon we were thicker than thieves and about halfway fried, and Gabriel was quite unsteady. He waggled a finger under my nose. "You shleep at my housh tonight, m'frien," said he, and with that he staggered away. I retired to my forest home and spent the rest of the afternoon reconnoitering the area, and at sundown two girls came along. One was Gabriel's new wife and the other was a chum who'd just wanted to see what an American aviator looked like. Politely swallowing her disappointment, she shook hands and offered me a basket of cherries.

The three of us set out through the woods, walking a little road past the wrecked hangars until we turned in at the gate to an ancient farmhouse. We kept to the shadows and slipped into the house.

In the kitchen, a cozy room lit by candles stuck in bottles, Gabriel sat by the stove nursing along a bottle of vin rouge. In line with Dutch custom, I presumed, he invited me to shed my shoes and pull up a chair. He explained that this was a two-family house and the other people were of doubtful patriotism, so it would be dangerous if I were heard or seen by them. So we talked in whispers while drinking dry a few quarts of red ink. He showed me his family album and he showed me his radio—worthless because the Jerries had cut off the power some years before. And just for the hell of it, I asked Gabriel why he was risking his neck to help a stranger. His theory was that I'd been helping France so it was his turn to give me a hand.

At midnight Gabriel led me up a steep flight of narrow stairs to a little room, and he whittled a peg with which I could wedge the door latch from within. He would knock in the morning, like so: two quick and two slow, and for any other signal I was to lay low.

At dawn Gabriel was there with my breakfast, and he handed me the tray and went away. He had a hangover and seemed a little startled at actually finding me in his upstairs bedroom. I locked the door and grinned at myself in the mirror. This wasn't such a tough racket. The morning of my third day in Occupied France, and breakfast in bed. Fried eggs, gently blindfolded; toast and coffee and a shot of applejack. I poured the booze into the coffee, improving the taste of both, and went back to sleep. At noon Gabriel hustled me back to the bomb hole. And in a little while Maurice came along with the welcome news that a banquet was on the fire. Some people were coming to see me. We were off again!

A dapper citizen by the name of "Hope-so" was waiting for me in the living room of the farmhouse. He was the landowner—Monsieur le Patron—and he dressed like it. The country-gentleman type, in plaid jacket and grey tie, corduroy britches and leather puttees, he welcomed me to Tricqueville. In his exceedingly broken English he started in on the Jerries, and his sad cry made my heart bleed. For Hope-so's main squawk was that the Wehrmacht had discovered his secret cache of 500 litres of vintage wines and had made off with the entire stock. Hope-so offered me money and information, of which I accepted the latter with thanks. He didn't have much to offer, but the old duffer was extremely courteous about the whole thing.

Now the door banged open and a guy and a gal burst into the parlor, and the woman immediately took over the meeting. Blonde, vivacious, and laughing-eyed, she jabbered some fast French at Maurice and he jabbered some right back. She pumped my hand and, speaking excellent English, she welcomed me to Normandy. She christened me "Tayo," said that her partner's handle was "Canoe," and that they all called her "The Flea" because she'd been biting the Germans for four years and the Gestapo had never been able to catch her. And right then and there I had the sinking feeling that I was involved with the famed outlaws of the Underground.

As her sidekick stood giving me the once-over, Flea spoke up: "We are of the Maquis, Tayo. There came the rumor of an American parachutist near Tricqueville, and here we are, come to fetch you! Quick work, no?" She added that she was always sent out to track down such tips, for she was the sole member of the Maquis who could speak English.

In England I'd been briefed on ways and means of escape and evasion. The Underground, it had been said, was impossible to find if one went looking for it: but that through their network of agents they would always pick up a wandering airman. We'd been advised to follow implicitly the orders of the Maquis, for they had shuttled many of our jettisoned pilots down to southern France and had put them on the tortuous trail over the Pyrenees to Spain. But the picture had changed, to my way of thinking. Spain was one helluva long walk from here. Some seventy miles to the west of Tricqueville lay the beachhead. I was completely confident that, with a good map and a few hot tips from the local patriots, I could scuttle away through the brush and gain the British lines. I was not about to spin my wheels with a wildcat outfit around here. I wanted to head for Caen, and the sooner the better. The adventure struck my fancy, dead center. And that's just the way I put it to Flea.

When Flea translated that to Canoe, he blew his top. He was a raw-boned gent, very tall and very skinny and with a sly and cagey manner about him. Now he muttered furiously, and Flea translated back to me. The sum of his muffled tirade was that my plan was crazy and so was I. To get through the German lines was impossible, and so was I. And furthermore, he didn't think that I was an American: I was too thin and too blond. "What the hell's eatin' him?" I inquired of Flea, digging out my hanky and flopping it on the table beneath Canoe's long and crooked nose.

"Canoe, he is suspicious of his own mother," Flea laughed. The Gestapo had often disguised their agents as parachuted airmen in countless efforts to infiltrate the Maquis organizations and to ferret out their leaders. Flea, with the light of adventure shining in her blue eyes, said that my plan was risky but possible. She would take me to see César, the chief of the Maquis. César, she promised, would advise me and would have made for me the counterfeit papers that would take me safely past the German sentries who patrolled every highway.

Well, hot damn! Now we were getting somewhere. I told Flea that on those conditions I would accept with pleasure her invitation to parley with the head man.

Everyone having had his say, we sat down to the banquet prepared by Helene. Fried bunny, excellent salad, and plenty of bread and butter: and Hope-so had evidently discovered a bit of wine overlooked by the thirsty Jerries, for the table was loaded with bottled goodies. The corks began to pop. "Vive la belle France!" I proposed.

So we toasted, in rapid succession, l'Amerique, l'Invasion, la parachutiste par accident, and vive le Maquis César! And after each toast, a round of hand-shaking.

With a tasty rabbit leg poised for the initial bite, I heard the squeal of brakes and nobody had to tell me to shove off; for before anybody could make a move I was out the back door and flying low across the yard, and I took a headlong dive into the first big bush I came to. Upon closer examination, this thicket I saw to be nettles, and I sat and scratched until Maurice came out looking for me.

A truckload of soldiers, it seemed, had stopped to ask road directions, and my quick departure had pleased even Canoe. I saw, alas, that my place at the table had disappeared—these Frenchmen no doubt thinking of the awkwardness of the situation should a suspicious Gestapo officer find six places set at the table with but five visible guests.

Since I was to leave the farm of my good friend Maurice, I had him lead me to the place where he'd concealed my flying stuff. I wanted a souvenir. So I cut out a panel of my 'chute and took along four or five stout shroud lines, figuring they might come in handy sometime. Recovering my army uniform, I put it on beneath my civilian disguise. Unable to part with my helmet and goggles, I stuffed them into a pocket of my flying jacket, which I also put on, and finally I had everything but my parachute draped around my thin body.

Now Flea gave me a short course on how to act like a Frenchman—an amusing briefing on Gallic customs. Canoe inspected my disguise—tucking a bit in here and hitching up a bit there, and he scuffed up my shoes a little more. Flea sewed up a few rips in my tattered suitcoat, through which my uniform had been exposed, and then it was time to put our show on the road. I had Flea relay my gratitude to Maurice and Helene, and to her flowery speech I added my handshake and a few words.

Canoe hauled from his hip pocket a snub-nosed .38 revolver, and he looked down the barrel and twirled the cylinder. Flea laughed gaily and nudged me, and damned if she didn't reach into her brassiere and snake out a little .25 automatic. Well, whee! I was knockin' around with the one and original pistol-packin' mama!

The arsenal having been checked and stowed away, we strode boldly out into the brilliant afternoon sunshine, opened the barnyard gate, and trudged away down the blacktop highway. For the first hundred paces I was a bit leery, but that wore off. I couldn't see any Jerries and the countryside appeared to be peaceful enough. As I thought things over, a gay humor bubbled up in me. This was a hot one! A raunchy old throttle-jockey, kicking gravel along a country road in the middle of enemy country, and with two Grade A characters for companions. I looked at Canoe and chuckled. He stared at me and wanted to know why I was laughing so much. I had Flea tell him that I was always laughing at something, and for him to forget it. But Canoe was a comical sight. As he walked, his seven-foot length of skin and bone inclined forward like a poplar leaning before a gale; and he continually darted furtive glances from port to starboard and over his shoulder.

I laughed at Canoe, and then—reflecting upon my own appearance—laughed again. Hiking under a 90-degree Normandy sun, I was dressed for a trek to the Pole, and a steady trickle of sweat dripped from my chin. Over a woolen uniform I wore a flying suit—for which I'd laid out twenty-five bucks in NYC and wasn't about to abandon—and over the flying suit, an alpaca-lined, fur-collared flight jacket. Overall, my corny disguise topped off with a rakish beret. To further the illusion of innocence, I carried a wicker basket covered with a flowered cloth, and beneath the edge protruded the long necks of three wine bottles. Had not Canoe such a desperate air about him, we would have resembled nothing more than a rustic trio en route to the hayfield.

An hour out and we left the tar road in favor of the country lanes. Past fields and farms and through cool little patches of forest we trudged, resting once atop a quaint arched bridge above a musical creek to roll cigarettes and to kill off a jug of wine.

Flea and I by now were comrades. I'd indulged in wholesale flattery during our hike from Tricqueville, figuring that it would be to my advantage to have her on my side during the forthcoming negotiations with the Maquis chief. I'd guessed Flea's age as twenty-eight, admired her frock, and praised her wine: I'd extolled the beauties of the countryside, told her how much admired in the outside world was the brave and dangerous work of the Maquis, and when she'd asked me about my squadron, I'd spun a string of war stories and modestly accounted for some two-thirds of the Luftwaffe. Flea was mightily pleased, too, but suspicious. Canoe was still shooting shrewd and sidelong glances my way. I laid in wait, finally, to meet his next surreptitious look with a deadpan wink.

We angled steadily eastward, passing a few groups of farmers and pausing once while Canoe drained his crankcase—chatting all the while with Flea in the best of Continental fashion. Being no Frenchman, despite my costume, that beat the hell out of me. It could take a little practice.

At last, and proceeding now with caution, we gained a height commanding a view of the picturesque village of Pont Audemer. We stumbled and slid down along a narrow, eroded gully to emerge on a hillside cobblestone lane some three hundred yards above the main drag. Passing a cemetery gate and a few little shops, we were close to the intersection when a blue-uniformed gendarme stepped suddenly into view, saw us, and stopped to stare, his thumbs hooked into his pistol belt.

"Vichy!" whispered Flea, and our expedition stalled out. I was already window-shopping, having become deeply engrossed in a fine collection of tombstones displayed behind the glass of a little store. A hurried, whispered scheme was evolved. Canoe sauntered on down the lane, while Flea and I moseyed slowly back up the hill and ducked into the cemetery gate, to wait while Canoe engaged the gendarme in innocent chatter and led him away from the area. Flea explained that half the local police were Vichy and the rest good Frenchmen: we'd run afoul of a Nazi.

Our lanky desperado soon returned, drifting through the cemetery gate with such a guilty look about him that I fully expected to see a platoon of Jerries trailing him. Canoe, slinking past our bench, gave us a sidelong look and with a slight jerk of his head motioned us to fall in behind. A little gnome-like citizen, perhaps eighty years old, now brought up the rear of our procession. He was the caretaker of this marble-orchard, and he was in on the conspiracy. He smiled at me and nodded and rubbed his gnarled old hands together and led me over to a little corner plot where there were a dozen white crosses, each with a little bouquet of fresh flowers.

On each cross was carved "Aviateur Americain-inconnu" or "Aviateur Anglaise-inconnu," with the date of each airman's death. Flea told me that the Maquis had collected these people, and that always fresh flowers were brought to their graves. Canoe jerked a thumb toward two grey Maltese crosses that were half hidden by weeds, and he spat the word, "Boches," and then he just plain spat.

The hunchbacked old geezer went into his act designed to mislead the folks who puttered about in the graveyard. He trotted along the pathways, pausing at each grave. At each grave he'd stoop 'way over, squint at the inscription on the headstone, and read it off to us. After each stop we'd shake our heads sadly and move along to the next stone for a repeat performance. Never finding out where old Uncle Pierre was planted, we did, however, eventually find ourselves right up against the rear wall of the cemetery. The ancient caretaker cackled once or twice and took off. Canoe told us to wait while he took a looksee, and he flung his lanky carcass over the five-foot wall and disappeared.

The sky had clouded over, and with a rumble of thunder came a spatter of raindrops to drench us. Flea and I sat down upon a handy tombstone and uncorked a bottle and rolled a smoke. And between the wine and the rain we were soon wet as hell inside and out. I backed off and took a mental snapshot of myself, and when I saw the print I busted out laughing. Since Flea seemed startled, I explained that I considered the situation to be rather humorous: a fighter pilot and a blonde on a tombstone in a French cemetery, drinking wine in the rain. Ho ho ho! I chuckled merrily. Flea sighed and said that heretofore they'd always picked up bomber pilots.

Watching the wall, we soon saw a black beret appear, then two guilty eyes cased the cemetery for a moment: our dramatic friend Canoe was back with us. The coast was clear so I hoisted Flea up over the wall and followed along, and soon we were on a little dirt street that cut through a corner of Pont Audemer. The few people we passed paid us no heed, but near the edge of town I cast my roving eye upon a sexy little wench who smiled down at us from a dormer window. "Flea," I muttered, "hide me there until the liberation." But she just told me that American airmen were all alike, and we kept right on until we were out of town.

We'd been walking steadily for four or five hours, and I was getting damned tired of it. But it was after sundown when we left the road to crawl through a splintery wooden gate. We set out along a muddy wagon trail and a couple of hounds staked out in the wet meadow set up a frenzied barking. Canoe quieted them with a gruff shout. A few minutes later we approached a rambling ranch-house style building, and in the dusk an air of mystery seemed to hang over it. Invisible in the shadows of the eaves, Canoe pounded on the door.

And as I stumbled inside, it was as though I'd been whirled suddenly back-ward through Time!

Chapter 3

DRAFTED

◆

From the tapered necks of tallow-covered wine bottles, guttering candles cast a flickering light across the stubbled faces of a half-dozen citizens of the brass-knuckle variety. Clad in daggers and pistols and turtleneck sweaters, they lounged nonchalantly before a wide fireplace gazing at a great juicy chunk of meat which hung, fat popping and sizzling, on a sooty spit over the roaring blaze. Low overhead loomed massive, smoke-stained rafters, and along one side of the shadowy room was a rough plank table with split-log benches around it. Candles in bottles! Knives and pistols! Villains! Sacré bleu! I was in the wrong goddam century!

These men of the Maquis stared at me and I gave then back as good as I got. Flea introduced me: Pierre—crafty-eyed, swarthy little monkey; Maurice—crushing handshake and a friendly smile; André—dapper, smiling, a reckless glint in his eye. Retiring to a dark corner and rolling a smoke, I leaned on my elbows and kept my mouth shut, wanting a chance to size up these characters before making any overtures. Returning each glance that was cast my way, I watched through my smokescreen as they quizzed Flea about l'aviateur Americain. Flea must have relayed to them some of the tall tales I'd spent the afternoon pumping into her, for after a bit some of the faces that had been markedly suspicious became less so. Before long, a couple of the boys drifted over and offered me a drink, and then the whole outfit was gathered around. I dug out my pencil and paper and gave them the word on fighter-type aircraft. The campaign I'd directed at Flea seemed to be paying off.

The watchdogs in the meadow set up a rumpus and one of the boys ran outside to check, returning with the cry that Monsieur le Chef was coming. When a heavyset, stern-faced, brutal-looking gent limped into the room, everybody but Flea and me jumped to attention. This was César, and his nom de guerre seemed appropriate: there was no doubt as to who had the power in this outfit. He clomped around the room, patting one man on the cheek, affectionately swatting another with his cane: and when I introduced myself he flashed a couple of gold teeth, shook my hand with both of his, kissed me on either cheek, rumpled my hair, and welcomed me to le Maquis César. With formality he announced that tonight there'd be une grande fête—a big party for the aviateur. Upon receipt of this cordial welcome, I hauled out my flask and poured the hoarded remains of my bourbon into a wine glass and offered it to César. He sniffed it, savored it, and sipped it; rolled it about with his tongue and swished it between his teeth, then tossed it off with a wonderful delight. Smacking his chops, he growled that it had been five long years since he'd tasted such excellent booze.

We sat around the table and I put my proposition to César, giving him a dog tag and the passport photographs with which I'd been equipped in England for just such an occasion. César, tucking my silk map into his jacket pocket, scowled and said it was very bad to try to get through the German lines; but he summoned his chief counterfeiter, Henri, and ordered him to get to work on travel documents for Tayo. I had a hunch that things were going too well, but even if I didn't get any papers I'd be no worse off than before. So I forgot my plans for the time being and settled down to getting the most out of the evening.

I peeled off a few layers of clothing and made a bundle of my army stuff. Flea, going through the pockets of my flying jacket, came up with my helmet and goggles and the bundle of shroud lines. She leaned across the table and I could see that little .25 automatic. She suggested that I give the goggles to Canoe: "Canoe, he has the motorcycle which he rides at night on missions for the Maquis. Bugs, they hit him in the eye and he crashes into the forest because he cannot see!"

In my mind's eye I pictured Canoe barreling desperately along the pike draped over his machine with knees and elbows flapping in the breeze: he'd spin in twice as often as before if he tried straining his vision through the dark-green lenses of my goggles! So I grinned and tossed the goggles to Canoe, telling him that they were supposed to bring a pilot luck, and that I sincerely hoped they'd bring him better fortune than they'd brought me. Flea unsnapped from her bracelet a little golden charm with the number "13" worked into the design. She smiled . . . a little fetish to replace the one I'd given Canoe. We were all happy now.

During the course of this transaction, the rest of the mob had unrolled the bunch of shroud lines and chopped them into three-foot lengths, which they'd divided amongst themselves. Now fishing into hip pockets and waistbands, with a clatter they plunked onto the table as fine an assortment of small arms as one might ever wish to see: all calibers of revolvers and pistols and even a couple of little double-barreled derringers—some new, some rusted out, and some homemade. Deadpan, the boys went about affixing their new lanyards. I'd thought the silken cords might come in handy, but I hadn't figured this angle.

Sitting back, I blew smoke rings around the neck of a bottle and watched a jolly old woman putter about the kitchen. Now and then she'd bustle over to the fireplace and dump a handful of something or other into one of the blackened kettles that hung in the fire, their contents simmering. At intervals, more of the Maquis drifted in until there were a dozen or fifteen assorted characters milling around the room. And when the feast was ready, I was ready for it: rare and smoky meat, fried potatoes, and a spicy salad, with a swig of good red wine to wash down every mouthful. When the dishes had been cleared away, César tossed me a pack of German cigarettes, which I opened immediately and passed around. A mistake, that, for regardless of whether or not he might have been smoking at the time, each man took a cigarette and one for later. As I no longer had any tobacco, I bummed the makings from Flea and rolled a smoke, while all the boys smoked tailor-mades and laughed at me for being such a sucker.

We sat around and smoked and belched and swapped lies, killing bottle after bottle of vin rouge until a newcomer sidled into the room packing two baskets laden with liquid cheer. There was brandy and cognac, champagne, and two or three bottles of Calvados, and the bearer of these glad tidings was called Léonard. César pounded on the table for silence: this phase of the banquet was in honor of a mission that five of the Maquis had accomplished the previous night. Led by Léonard, they'd pulled a sneak attack on a Jerry bivouac. With pistols and Sten-guns they'd clob-bered perhaps forty Jerries and made a getaway before the camp had known what had hit them. Champagne corks ricocheted from the rafters and we all toasted Léonard. This had the makings of a fine evening.

Léonard shook my hand and I felt bones snapping. A French-English renegade, he took first prize, automatically and hands down, for being the type one would most hate to meet in a dark alley. A snarled mop of yellow hair hung down over watery blue eyes and flopped against a crooked, smashed nose. A fiery scar ran diagonally across his face, and Léonard was equipped with a fine harelip that resulted in his speaking an unintelligible, mushy French that I couldn't savvy for a damn. But as he was talking at me much of the time, I would smile and nod at appropriate intervals. Léonard was intrigued by my bone-handled hunting knife. In fact, several of the Maquis so admired my knife that they offered to accept it as a token of my appreciation at being with them. I'd scraped the guts out of many a duck and pheasant with that old weapon, and it was my pride and joy. I let it be damn well known that I was not about to part with it. All the lads now displayed their own knives and, as was to be expected, the prize weap-on—a twelve-inch stiletto that he claimed to be quite handy—belonged to the yellow-haired giant Léonard. To prove his point he snapped it across the room where it stuck, quivering, in a timber above the fireplace. As he shambled over to retrieve it, I made a mental note to encourage Leo's friendship. This whole crew, when it came to their weapons, were like a bunch of kids. In playful spirit they would whip out their pistols and point them at one another's heads, hollering all the while, "Pouf! Pouf!"—which was their quaint version of bang-bang.

We drank the cognac and the brandy and the rotgut Calvados apple-jack, and by midnight everybody was loaded. But being accustomed to this sort of thing, I was more than holding my own and doing my best to up-hold the good name of my squadron. By 2:00 a.m. I was buddy-buddy with the whole outfit and was just working up a good thirst when the booze gave out and the party broke up with an endless bout of hand-shaking and cheek-kissing. Pierre and Maurice and Philbert and I set out across-country through the blackout, heading I didn't know or care much where. I was tight and they were fried all out of shape, and it was a merry trip. Falling through fences and into and out of gullies, we came at last to a beautiful chateau, and near the chateau was an abandoned Jerry barracks wherein lived Philbert and his charming wife and child. Pierre and Maurice staggered on through the night and I sat in Philbert's tiny kitchen, talking and reading notes; and each, after I read it, was held in the candle flame and the ashes crumbled. So at about four in the morning I knocked on the back door of the old chateau, to be greeted by an old woman who wrung my hand and led the way to the top floor where she indicated the entrance to an obscure tunnel. After a bit of navigating on hands and knees, I emerged at the far end of the tunnel into a two-by-four cubbyhole that was equipped with mattress and blankets. Full of good food and better booze, I slept.

Philbert was the armaments expert of the Maquis. In the afternoon I helped him clean, strip, and oil a satchel full of rusty old pistols. My friend was a quick-moving, jumpy, wild-eyed cuss, and he seemed to be consumed by a passionate hatred of the Jerries. His wife gave me a clean blue shirt and a pair of pinstripe pants to replace the rags I'd been wearing, and in the upper leg of the trousers were five or six half-inch rips. Philbert explained that he'd been picked up by the Gestapo, and they'd questioned him in their usual manner—jabbing bayonets into his thighs and knocking out his front teeth with a pistol barrel. I'd been wondering about my friend's pathological urge to kill, but now I saw his point. At dusk a burly little thug came into the barracks. This was Athos, second in command of the Maquis: tough, stubborn, and dynamic, and nobody gave him any back-talk. Athos, in turn, obeyed César unquestioningly. And now César appeared, with Maurice and Pierre flying escort. He'd brought along a basketful of bottles, and we settled down in Philbert's tiny kitchen for a council.

Drawing a map of the French coast, I asked César to sketch in the present positions of the Allies, as best he knew. D-plus-6 this was, and now I saw that the Americans had gained a solid foothold and appeared to be driving west, perhaps with the intent of isolating the Cherbourg peninsula. Monty's British forces, however, were creeping southward along the River Orne, proceeding with caution toward Caen. I was eager to head down that way to check things over.

"Where are my papers, César?" I demanded. "Les Anglaises will be a long time in coming to Pont Audemer. One must return to one's squadron!"

Athos muttered and pounded his fist on the table. César listened to my plan, smiling now and then at my choice of words. When I'd finished, he went to work on me.

"Between here and Caen," quoth he, "there are beaucoup Boches, and it is impossible that you would not be captured or killed." He declared that on his little radio he had just contacted Maquis headquarters in London, and they had guaranteed that Pont Audemer would be liberated by the British within ten days. "Stay here with us, Tayo, and be safe amongst friends. In ten days, the liberation, and we all will have the big jamboree!" He tweaked my cheek—irritating me further—smiled, and poured me a shot of brandy.

I hated to tell César that I didn't want to be safe amongst friends. When I'd pulled that old ripcord I'd been a bit glad, for there before me lay the unalterable fact that I was on my own with the chance of a lifetime for unique adventure. I'd tumbled headlong into a different world, and I aimed to explore it. Now I craved to off-and-away on a solo tour of Normandy, and I knew well that I could get away with any reckless scheme I might dream up. I also knew damned well that the British would never be here in ten days if they maintained their present rate. But then again, I was interested in the modus operandi of this wildcat Maquis outfit. When I tired of this place I could move on. What the hell did I have to lose? Therefore I told César that perhaps he was right: I'd hang around for ten days and we'd see how far the British got.

Everybody satisfied, César gave me a little packet of tobacco, and as we smoked and guzzled I was told of the assassinations, espionage, and sabotage that his partizans had accomplished. During the past four years the Jerries had sent out troops many times in futile efforts to round up le Maquis César, and for many months the Gestapo had been one jump behind it's leader. "Ahh, je suis fatigué," sighed César, "for in two years past, I have never slept twice in the same place . . ."

Pierre and Maurice, said César, would be with me. A dandy couple of bodyguards! Maurice was barrel-chested and powerful, with arms thicker than my legs. His belly was held in with the aid of a broad leather belt and square brass buckle; and for all his beef, he was generous, considerate, and courteous—unusual traits in a muscle type. Pierre, on my port wing, was a mischievous, sly-eyed villain with a little pistol tucked into the green sash he wore about his waist. His crimson Zouave fez and rubber boots were a part of him, and he loved the life he led.

The three of us sneaked out into the night, walking a sunken trail for a few kilometers and steadily gaining altitude until we ducked under a barbed-wire fence to cross a pine-clad slope. At the edge of the woods we found a stable, and inside we found three blankets and a pile of hay waiting for us. Someone had thoughtfully provided a litre jug of Calvados, so for a while we sat in the moonlight and passed the bottle back and forth. As we chatted, enjoying the night, the distant drone of fighter engines built up into a helluva racket, and a dozen Me 109s buzzed low over the stable on-course for the beachhead. When their exhausts had become inaudible, we turned in without so much as removing a shoe.

At dawn I rolled a smoke and cased my happy home. Pierre lay curled up and snoring, a heavy black stubble covering his impish face. His nickel-plated revolver rested an inch from his nose. Maurice lay flat on his back, hands clasped over his belly, a wide, unconscious smile on his face. Over-head, a thatched roof with bits of blue sky showing through here and there. Adobe walls, reinforced with crooked, peeled saplings. The floor was muddy and there were no windows, but under the rear wall was a little tunnel just big enough to crawl through.

I leaned on the sill of the low half-door. A few paces to the west was deep forest. Fifty yards below us down a gentle grassy slope lay the farm-house, with long timbers set helter-skelter into the yellow clay walls. The roof was thatched, steep and graceful, and grass and wildflowers grew along the ridgepole. Our stable was perched high on a hillside, and in the valley below lay a panorama of tiny farms and miniature, verdant meadows and fields of ripening grain. There also lay the chateau: a beautiful estate with formal gardens and ancient trees in orderly rows. Beyond the chateau in easy curves a river flowed at the foot of a high cliff that marked the far side of the valley. A railroad paralleled the river bank, and in the dim light I could make out the point where it entered the village of Pont Audemer. Tendrils of morning mist clung to the low places, and then the sunrise slowly burned away the last traces of night. I sniffed the breeze, and the damp forest smell was perfume. It was a perfect morning.

I was hungry. I fetched a cup of water from the trough and poured it over Pierre's scowling face. The ensuing commotion awakened the big boy and we traipsed down the hill to the farmhouse. Le Patron, a happy type, greeted me cheerily. His name was Léon and he too, he cried, had in his day been a soldier. His merry face was deeply wrinkled by sun and laughter, and his squinty grey eyes always had a twinkle in them. Léon introduced me to his wife and several small children, and the tiniest girl, when I picked her up to say "Bonjour," planted on my cheek a wet, fat kiss. Madame Léon was quiet and graceful and a little on the plump side.

I knew that Léon and I would get along when he proposed that we all have a snort before breakfast: and sweat broke out on my forehead under the initial shock of that homemade applejack hitting bottom. When it had stopped ricocheting around, we sat to the table and filled our bellies with black bread and salt pork and spuds, followed by café royale and a smoke. Léon swerved off to the cowshed, singing a gay old ballad of his soldiering days. We retired to the stable.

At noon Flea came to see me bearing two corny books in English, a French dictionary, and the latest Invasion news. The latter was the same as usual: Monty was dug in on the far bank of the Orne, either fighting a holding action or being held, I didn't know which. Perhaps their task was to divert some of the Wehrmacht from the Yank assault on Cherbourg. Or possibly, what with their habit of knocking off for morning and afternoon tea, the Limeys were just a teeny bit behind schedule.

For a couple of days we kept to the dark interior of our stable, showing ourselves only to walk to the farmhouse for our meals. With his red fez cocked recklessly over one ear, Pierre slaved over the hot cookstove turning out our meals: and we ate like kings . . . rare beefsteak and fried potatoes with pints of cider to wash it all down. Henri bicycled up each day with a saddlebag full of provisions, and now and then he brought along a bottle of Calvados for the three castaways. And swapping lies during the long hours of hiding, Maurice and Pierre and I became fast friends.

Pierre was always good for an argument. One morning I became entangled in a lengthy lecture, trying to explain the principles upon which my government operated. I was slightly confused about the issue myself, but in an hour—despite my bastard French—I thought I'd made myself quite clear. Pierre, however, seized my hunting knife, pointed triumphantly to the letters stamped on the blade, and cried, "Ah oui! Union Socialiste Amerique!" Baffled, I tried to explain that USA stood for États Unis, but

Pierre refused to believe that and I let it ride. He then asserted that he had heard, from reliable sources, that les États Unis were run by a bunch of dirty capitalistes. This statement gave me inkling as to his political background so I asked him who had owned the chateau in the valley. "Une capitaliste!" replied Pierre. Where was he now? "Kaput!" said Pierre, with a grin and a wink. Whereupon I gave up discussion of the economic setup in the States and let it be known to my Comrade that there had never been anything but beaten-down wage-slaves in my family tree. The only thing that would ever pull the exploited masses from their mire of poverty would be a good healthy revolution. My theory in that little oration being a variation of the "When in Rome . . ." principle. Pierre was my friend from then on in. I asked him how he liked this Maquis business of his. How did he like hiding all day and prowling all night? He shrugged and spread his hands: "Quel difference?" He assured me that had there been no war, there would have been a revolution, so either way you looked at it he would have been doing the same thing. What a character! Maurice would pitch in and help me needle our hammer-and-sickle partner, winking at me whenever we'd get Pierre all wound up.

In practice, Pierre was not so rabid. When he had tobacco and Maurice and I had none, it was like pulling teeth to bum the makings from him. When I washed out my socks, Pierre swiped the better pair and then spent a half-day trying to get me to take off my shoes, explaining that he wanted to see how they'd feel over his new sox. Pierre was a good man to ride the river with, despite his radical views and light-fingered ways.

Spending my idle hours sketching pictures of warplanes, I'd soon infected both of the boys with the flying bug. We had ground school every morning after breakfast, during which I'd spend long hours giving my buddies the word on names, armament, and speed of various aircraft. To amuse myself, I drew up a detailed picture of a Mustang cockpit and made an honest effort to explain the functions of the assorted gauges and instruments. The skies above us vibrated from dawn til dark with the sound of planes, and whenever a flight would come near, Pierre would now dash out and report back: "Moostang!" or "Doonderbol" or "Fleeeng Fortress," or in case of a Jerry flight, "Cent-neuf!" I'd get lonesome when I'd see a P-51 outfit buzz past, and I always hoped to see my blue-nosed squadron. When the sky was blue and maybe full of fluffy white clouds, I'd watch our fighters racing about rolling their wings and having a helluva time, and I'd about kick a hole in the side of the stable. But when the weather fouled up and I'd see a bunch of low-flying Thunderbolts churning about in the soup . . . why, then I was perfectly content to be where I was, and I'd have a smoke and a nip of applejack and feel lucky to be out of the goddam war.

César came to the stable the morning of our third day there driving a one-horse shay, and he brought me some razor blades and a tube of brushless shave cream, but no war news outside of the report that the English were still on the other side of the Orne. I took a bath in a water trough and shaved. Pierre watched me closely and decided to follow suit. But he insisted upon using his old shaving brush, and when he couldn't work up a lather, he was infuriated. Quantity seemed to be the answer, so he squeezed out the contents of the entire tube and then cut himself a half-dozen times because Maurice and I were giving him such a bad time. He sulked all morning and I settled down to reading one of the English novels Flea had brought for me. I was getting damned tired of four stable walls.

The name of this book was, "Patience Sparhawk & Her Times." I had decided to read it word for word; but after ten pages I threw it halfway across Normandy. Rounding up the dictionary, I picked up one of Pierre's Parisian dime novels and was immediately and deeply engrossed. Mon Dieu! Such stories! I learned more French in three hours than I had in five years of school.

Midafternoon. There came to my twitching ears the sound of a lovely voice singing a catchy little tune. And along came a pert little gal to lean on the stable door and chat with Pierre. Pretty soon she snake-hipped over to me and said, "Aurevoir, Theo! I came to see you, but since you won't talk to me, I'm going home!" She laughed and turned a pair of great big violet eyes on me, flopped her curly eyelashes at me a couple of times, and I was done for. Riri was her name and a lovely thing she was: slim, ashblonde, and she sang like a lark. One look into those eyes and I'd had it. Léon was her uncle and he had instigated this deal, and for that I'm his friend forever.

Léon knocked off work every afternoon and we'd all sit in his kitchen and drink, keeping his oldest boy busy chasing bottles and drawing champagne from the barrel in the cellar. We'd tell stories and smoke and finally have supper; and after supper this night I walked Riri down the lane to the gate and she promised to visit me every day. She slipped me a little kiss and I prayed that Montgomery would give up any ideas he might have had about liberating Pont Audemer.

Riri came early the next morning with a gift for me: a bottle of old Benedictine. The day was one of summer's fairest, and Riri and I walked over the whole farm and through the forest hand in hand, admiring the beauties of Nature. Mmmm! A couple hundred American bombers cruised high overhead that afternoon, heading right for the mouth of the Seine. Evidently having bombed inland, they were heading home now, and I wondered who in hell might be the lead navigator that he should lead the whole outfit over Le Havre. I was well acquainted with the terrific flak over that area. I watched and waited and pretty soon the guns opened up, some quite nearby. In patterns of fours, black puffs appeared all around and within the boxes of bombers. "Touché! Touché!" Riri screamed, and a smoking B-24 peeled out of formation and exploded. "Combien des hommes?" asked Riri softly. "Dix aviateurs mort." Ten airmen dead in the sunny skies of Normandy, and Riri wept. Soon after, a great shiny ball of chaff floated down to land in the meadow, and I had a bad time trying to explain to Pierre how the stuff was dumped from the bombers with the intent of fouling up Jerry radar. He having never heard of radar either, I was forced into a technical chalk-talk.

With Riri with me, the days were too short. We'd pick cherries for Madame Léon, or Riri would sit and mock me as I chopped wood for the cookstove. Or maybe we'd stroll down the hill to the meadow to see the cows. We kept our jug of Benedictine there in the deep, cool grass, and we'd nibble on that and chat and watch the clouds drifting through the skies, their shadows moving silently over the slopes.

After nearly a week in the stable, a message came from César. Maurice led me to the chateau in the valley, taking a long, roundabout route through the forest. César had set up temporary headquarters, and in a beautiful upstairs room he and Athos lounged in easy chairs, plotting and planning. A couple of the boys and a tough-looking broad sat at a mahogany table playing cards.

"Soif, Tayo?" asked César, flashing his gold teeth at me. Grinning, I explained that it would be a chilly day in hell when I wasn't thirsty, and

César sent one of the mob down to the cellar. In short order we were each equipped with a litre of vintage champagne. César had invited me down because there was to have been another American pilot at the chateau tonight: but the smart bastard had flown the coop from under the very nose of the Maquis. "But as long as you're here," remarked César, "we might just as well have a little party." And with that, he passed around a box of excellent Jerry cigars. We had a fine time drinking up the kaput capitaliste's fine wines and brandies, and I spent an educational afternoon kibitzing on the game of Vingt-et-Un—at which the girl was winning because she was bottom-dealing.

Feeling pretty cheered by the whole thing, I removed from my wrist my government-issue chronometer and with a flourish presented it to César: "C'est pour vous, César," I hiccuped, "as a souvenir and token of gratitude for the fine way you have received me into le Maquis César!" Touched by my gesture and to return the compliment, César gave me his cigarette case and a pack of smokes: and as if that were not enough, he called over the card-playing gal and introduced me to her. Pulling her onto his lap and loving her up a little, he said, "Tonight, mon lieutenant, she's all yours in the grande suite of the chateau!" He added that the wench had peddled fifty kilometers from Rouen just to shack up with him.

This queen snatched off my beret and murmured, "Mmmm, blonde," and then asked if I was un bombardier—bomber pilot, that is. When I denied the charge she announced her hearty dislike for bomber command, and especially the RAF. Hiking her skirt up a considerable distance, she flashed a couple of jagged scars on her tree-like thigh. The damned bombers, said she, had dropped thousands of bombs upon Rouen one night and had killed three thousand people, including the Madame and three of the best girls in her house. I made appropriate sounds of sympathy, not wishing to incur her wrath: she was a big girl and could have pounded me into the ground like a tent-peg.

I thanked César for his kind donation and told him that I'd be back, probably, at around eight o'clock. He didn't know that Riri was waiting for me at Léon's, or that we had big wingding on the fire for tonight. At dusk Maurice and I scampered back through the brush, and when we arrived at the farm the celebration was just getting under way. Darling Riri was there with her grandmère; and Léon, Pierre, André, Henri and I made

up the rest of the roomful. We sat down to the groaning table at nine, and
it was after midnight when we'd finished eating. Beefsteak and salads and
pie, with each course separated from the next by innumerable bottles and
toasts.

Léon was in rare form—breaking into long ballads that defied translation. At the way his wife blushed and Riri's grandmother whooped and
Riri buried her face in her hands, they must have been songs slightly on
the risqué side. I was saddened by my lack of knowledge of the language.
The pile of empty bottles grew and grew, and one by one around the
candle-lit table each guest stood up and sang his favorite song. Riri, in her
soft, sweet voice, sang best of all. She sang "Le Marseillaise," and those
around the table caught it up, to sing with her until she burst into tears. It
was a wonderful party.

Then it was my turn to sing. I didn't want to, but André talked me
into it, requesting the patriotic songs of America. I didn't know any, but
nobody around the table knew a word of English so I rendered a long and
plaintive medley of "Jack o' Diamonds," "Red River Valley," and "The Old
Chisolm Trail"—including eight or ten filthy verses of the latter. I was a
howling success. For an encore I gave the Air Corps version of "Wreck of
Old '97." Now, I'd spent long hours teaching Riri to sing "Pistol Packin'
Mama" in English, and after a little coaxing she sang it for us now, and I
laughed until I cried at the cute twists she gave the words. Riri, flushed
with success, proceeded to drink too much champagne and she dashed
about the room, bounding from Henri's neck to Maurice's to mine, and
finally she knocked over the table and the room went dark. There were a
few minor crashes, then silence. I lit up the candles with my Zippo and
we could plainly see that Riri had spun in. Madame Léon laid her away in
the sack, and we carried on. Maurice and Pierre and I ended up crawling
on hands and knees to our stable, whereupon we went into a coma until
daybreak.

A little motor-truck churned up to the stable in the afternoon and
seven reckless types jumped from the van and crowded in with us. A
rougher-looking lot I'd never seen before: a pair of Russians, two Free
French, an Algerian, and a pair of German renegades, and they were well
armed with Mausers and Lugers and one of the Russians packed a
Schmeisser machine-pistol. All escaped prisoners of war, they had been

collected and pooled by the French Underground and were now being shuttled across France from Maquis group to Maquis group. Many loaves of black bread, wooden tubs of salt-butter, and a hundred boxes of stinking, moldy cheese were piled in a corner of the stable, and that night after sundown Pierre and I stood sentry duty until dawn. One of the Russians spoke a bit of French, and I got acquainted with him. When he found that I was an American aviator, he and his pal pumped my hand and like to've adopted me. One rolled a cigarette with his precious tobacco and handed it to me with a smile. "Cigarette pour l'Americain!" and he struck a match and lit it for me. Both were blonde, blue-eyed, and stocky, and the one who spoke French told me of the battle on the eastern front in which he'd been taken prisoner. He and his comrade had strangled a couple of guards, armed themselves, and shot their way out of prison. They were insatiably curious about America, so as best I could I told them of our farms and crops and of how every farmer has his own tractor and automobile. The one who spoke French kept trying to teach us Russian, but all I learned was "tovarich" and that meant friend. "Spasiba" meant either "merci" or "Il n'y a pas de quoi," and I never did get it straight.

During the day, Léon sent his eldest son to the stable with a note for me: "Sshhh . . . come to the house, alone!" I found Léon waiting for me in the kitchen and he whispered that, confidentially, he was dead against having his stable filled with such villains but there was nothing he could do about it. He and I would have a little party, just the two of us!

Pierre and I stood guard all that night in a cold drizzle. The following night, César drove up in his carriage to brief Pierre. And after dark we moved out lock, stock, and barrel, pussyfooting single-file to a stone barn some two kilometers distant. My Russian friends wouldn't even let me carry my blanket roll, and for a while I thought that one of them would offer to carry me. They were a couple of very nice guys, friendly to me because I was an American.

César stormed into the barn in a rage. There was to have been food waiting for us, and somebody had slipped up. Rounding up the party responsible, César raked him over the coals in a terrifying manner—shaking his fist under the culprit's nose, belaboring his shins with a walking-stick, and shouting and cursing at a high rate of speed. César, I thought, would have made an excellent flying instructor for the AAF. The guilty party, by way of amends, dashed out and returned with a case of champagne, and while Athos briefed the boys of the Maquis, the rest of us stood in the yellow light of a lantern and drank the bottles dry. I was prepared to strike out on my own, should I be sent along with this motley crew; but the band of escapees, guided by two of the Maquis, set out for parts unknown and Pierre and Maurice and I went to the chateau and settled down for the night. In the morning, I held a private little council of war.

Two weeks had passed since my abrupt arrival in Occupied France. I'd been received like visiting royalty, and inducted into the Maquis where I'd made friends faster than I could keep track of them. It had been beefsteak when I was hungry, good whiskey when dry. Life with le Maquis César was nothing but nice, especially since the arrival of Riri into my life. But the ten days I'd allotted for my stay with the Maquis were up, and the English army was still dug in on the far bank of the Orne. I was just another throttle-jockey down behind the lines, and I hardly thought that Ike would speed up the war on my account. Rested now, I craved action and I knew that once I set about it I could fish my own fat out of the fire. If I expected to pop up again in Piccadilly before the first snow fell, it was about time to put the show on the road. So I sent a message to Flea.

She came to see me and I asked her when my papers would be ready. No travel papers would be made for me, she said, for it was now only a matter of days until the liberation. She pacified my squawks, telling me that in a few days the Maquis would be moving westward to a new hideout. Well, that was right on course, so I told her I'd string along for a while and sweat out Monty and his merry men a bit longer—and I kept quiet about my own plans. At sundown I walked to Léon's farm to thank him for his wonderful hospitality. I wanted to give him a token, but I had nothing to offer him but my sincere thanks and a promise to return someday; and I said au revoir, shaking hands all around. Each of his small offspring kissed me on the cheek and I walked back to the chateau.

We gambled the night away, playing Casino until Pierre went broke. I soon acquired all Maurice's francs in a small game of chance known in France as Vingt-et-un, but which I'd learned to call "Blackjack" in Las Vegas. But the boys ganged up on me then and forced me into a fancy game of their own. It was a combination of chess and checkers played with many men and countless squares, and they made up their own rules as they went along. When I was milked back down to my original stake I quit, and our family was happy again.

After ten days in the stable at Léon's, what with the abundance of small animal life inhabiting such places, I was now kept quite busy trying to scratch wherever I itched—so this chateau life was welcomed for its comfort. The place was ancient and richly appointed with inlaid oaken floors and high raftered ceilings, and the fireplace was broad enough to accommodate a half-dozen people on the benches within it. On the walls were mounted the heads of boars and stags, with little engraved silver plates telling where and when they'd been taken. The chateau was a beautiful place, even stripped of its furnishings.

We left early in the morning to unload a captured German truck of its cargo of mines and grenades, all of which we concealed beneath the edge of a moldy haystack near the home of one of the Maquis officers. We spent the remainder of the day in the home of this character, David by name. David was right out of a dime novel—even to the fuzzy fedora and Van Dyke beard. He played the piano and liked to drink, and was killed later on in a street fight with the Gestapo.

The evening of the third day in the chateau, Riri came for me and she took me by the hand and led me to a little hut at the edge of the forest. The single room was crowded with wives and children of the Maquis men, and one of the boys was setting up a little 16mm projector. An old silent movie with titles in French hit the bedsheet screen and for a while there was a corny maze of Arabs and oil-wells and American explorers, and just as the heroine was about to become the chieftain's number-one concubine, Richard Dix drove over in an old Curtis dive-bomber and blew the hell out of the harem. It was some evening, but I saw only about a quarter of the picture for Riri was parked on my lap nibbling my ears and distracting me in general.

At noon the following day, Athos skidded into the driveway to the chateau, dumped his motorcycle, and dashed into our room sputtering that le Gestapo was en route to the chateau to set up a temporary headquarters. Action! We accomplished the fastest chateau-cleaning on record, erasing all traces of our occupancy. Pierre ran through the rooms with a bag of fine dust, throwing it into the air as he traveled, and immediately the joint looked as though it had been abandoned for years. In a moment

Pierre and Maurice and I—the three musty-steers—were charging through the forest, on the run. All that afternoon we stumbled along tortuous trails and creek beds and at last, after a long haul up a logging trail to the top of a mountain, we came upon a tiny stable perched precariously at the brink of a nearly vertical grassy cliff. Forcing the trapdoor, we chucked our blanket rolls inside and then cut a great pile of giant ferns, which we spread over the floor. With blankets over all, we had a good bed and a new home.

Fast-flying chunks of grey scud cloud had been piling up all day, and at last a dark and solid overcast covered the sky. The tattered cloud base touched the top of our mountain and the air grew chilly: then the rain pelted down, a little at first and then in a cloudburst, and we sat on a log beneath the roof of a lean-to and watched the downpour. André, bedraggled and muddy but with a jaunty wave of his hand, came puffing out of the woods with a gunnysack of provisions: soy bread, a chunk of meat, and a litre of Calvados. And the latter was a welcomed thing. We took it to bed with us.

The chattering of machine guns brought us scrambling out of our blankets at sunrise. Overhead we saw the makings of a dandy dogfight, for six Me 109s and a like number of English Spitfires had just tangled up in a tight little rat-race; and they really mixed it up for a few minutes, wheeling and dealing at eight or ten thousand feet. The light rattle of British machine guns and the deeper, slower pounding of Jerry 20mm cannon came to us: then, magically—as is the way of all good dogfights—there were suddenly no aircraft in the sky. Four slowly drifting parachutes were scattered at various altitudes, miles away, and Pierre pulled out his pistol and gave a shout and ran headlong down the cliff. As I expected, his short legs couldn't keep up with his body, and he tumbled head over heels for the last half of the long, steep descent. He got up running, still clutching his gun and on course for the nearest 'chute. Four or five hours later he returned with a cocky young Maquis named Guy.

"Ou est la parachutiste, camarade?" I inquired. He said he'd found only one, and that one had been a Jerry. And where was this cent-neuf jockey? Pierre smirked and patted his revolver, so I presumed that another unfortunate 109 driver had come to the end of a promising career.

Guy brought glad tidings. Flea had rounded up an English aviator and was bringing him to the mountain stable to keep me company. I was overjoyed at the prospect of finding someone with whom I could converse in connected sentences. But when Flea had failed to show up by dusk, Guy invited me to his home: a chateau at which his parents were caretakers.

We cut off through the woods and approached the place carefully. Nearby Guy showed me the spot where a British Wellington bomber had augered in while attempting one dark night to drop munitions to the Maquis. Guy, who had witnessed the crash, said that the ship had roared in low over a hilltop and caught a wingtip on a tall pine tree, to cartwheel into the creek bed where we stood—killing all five airmen. Very few of the weapons had been salvaged, said Guy bitterly.

His mother was a very old and gracious dame, and she told me to follow her to the attic for a surprise. There in the faint light of a single candle sat her husband, his white head glued to the speaker of a modern Zenith radio. I never knew what the hell to expect next in this country.

The old man turned the radio over to me. With trembling fingers I tuned in BBC, and into the attic came the dramatic, scalp-prickling beat of the kettledrum: "Boom-boom-boom-boooooommm! London calling!" The Voice of Liberation, beamed on Occupied France. The news—first English and then in French—and then I knew for sure that I was not long for the Maquis; for it appeared that the Channel Coast would be forever free of the threat of British invasion.

Guy's old mother came creaking up the steps to offer me a bowl of strawberries and cream, and at that point the unreality of the situation struck me: rain drumming on the roof close overhead . . . my tattered disguise, wet and clammy against my skin . . . the flickering candle . . . the old man's evident fear as he stood at the top of the steep staircase, hand cupped to ear as he listened intently for the dreaded footfall. All that, and a dish of strawberries and cream.

I dialed around and picked up Axis Sally's program, in hopes of hearing a good record or two; whereupon, from this little American radio, came the lonesome voice of Dinah Shore singing: "When you're a long, long way from home . . ." For a moment I was elsewhere, and the last strawberry wedged itself alongside the sizable lump that had suddenly filled my throat. I switched off the radio to find, however, that I was still a cockeyed fugitive from the Wehrmacht. So I thanked the old lady and the old man and motioned to Guy, and we had a merry time making our way up the rainswept mountainside. When we crawled into our blankets we were both sloppy wet and scratched by briars, but to me the evening had been well worth it.

In the morning we saw Flea and Athos and a stranger slogging toward us along the muddy logging trail. Flea called out: "An English comrade for you, Tayo!" I hollered, "Hello, Chum!" and the stranger shouted back, "Hi, Pal"—each of us talking the other's language. And I shook the hand of young RAF sergeant Freddy Giles, gunner-navigator of a Lancaster bomber shot down two days before by a Jerry night-fighter. Freddy, sole survivor of his crew, was still suffering from shock; and being both in the same kettle, we hit it off together. He spoke not a word of French and was welcome company, if just for that.

Freddy wasn't too quick on the uptake, but now and then he showed a flash of Limey wit. Discovering that he had bailed out near Tricqueville and had met Maurice and Helene, I asked him if he had, perchance, met a character by name of Gabriel. Freddy, thinking a moment, replied brightly: "Gabriel? Blimey, Yank! You must have been up a ways!" He'd made a joke, see?

I felt for Freddy, for this backwoods life was strictly out of his line. His life had been sidewalks and taxicabs and the double-deck buses of London town, and to him a tree was something with a little iron fence around it. My shiftless life, on the other hand, had been such that this way of living was second nature. I'd been lucky. From the time I'd been old enough to carry a gun, I'd hunted and fished and prowled the woods and mountains and deserts of the forty-eight States, and I loved and understood the ways of Nature. Plagued by an unquenchable wanderlust, I'd drifted endlessly, always seeking something-or-other, in quest of adventure, always wondering what might lie beyond the next hill. So now I was at home and happy. And in adopting the ways of these partizans I found no difficulty, for their ways came naturally. For example, in eating—without having to contend with the painful frills of poor, inhibited Emily P.—I could suck soup with greater rate of consumption and far finer sound effects than the best of these Maquis types. Taking a firm tooth-hold on a slab of beefsteak, I would now reach to my belt for my skinning knife and with a skillful swipe, slice off as much as I thought I could chomp down without strangling. To eat a square meal with a good knife as the sole utensil was a pleasure. After dinner, a rub of the blade on a sleeve and the dishes were done. Then a shot of applejack, a pleasurable belch, and a cigarette. Such lack of folderol inevitably enhances the pure enjoyment of good food.

Poor old Freddy. We gave him a sack of tobacco and a packet of papers. Two hours later he still had his sack of tobacco—slightly depleted—and at his feet was a pile of wrinkled and torn papers. Thereafter we took turns rolling cigarettes for him.

The fourth day at our hilltop stable was cold and rainy. A courier came along with an urgent message from César: the countryside was being combed by German patrols and we were getting hot again. We would proceed at midnight to another hideout, and the move would be to the west. Had it been the other way—away from the beachhead—I'd have taken off, for I was increasingly eager to move to within taunting range of Monty's dugout. So we gathered up our food and extra bottles and made packs of our blankets. At midnight we slung our packs and left the shelter of the stable.

In the pelting, driving rain we skidded and tumbled and fell down the cliff and into the valley, slunk past the German-occupied chateau there, and crept through a tangle of underbrush until we came upon a flooded creek. Guy popped up out of the weeds where he'd been awaiting us, to whisper excited instructions: silence was to be the watchword on this expedition, for the night woods were full of Jerries. After the monotony of the past weeks, this affair was entirely enjoyable; and as usual, my Maquis comrades afforded me a never-ending source of amusement. Dearly loving their outlaw role, their every act was always accompanied by a dramatic flourish or two, and this rainy midnight scene was right out of a horse opera.

Here was a sodden bunch of citizens huddled in the dripping thickets, clutching assorted muskets, clubs, and bottles. Maurice and Guy, in a bitter tête-à-tête, whispered savagely at each other—about to come to blows over possession of our only honest weapon, a Mauser rifle. Pierre stood aside, whistling tunelessly, twirling his stubby revolver on his trigger finger with unassumed nonchalance.

I peered toward Freddy, then poked Pierre and pointed. I wanted to share my delight at the spectacle, but Pierre was caught off guard and his shrill "Hee-hee-hee-hee!"—followed by convulsive gurglings—rang through the night and echoed off the Jerry chateau: for Freddy was a living caricature of a French-type Wearie Willie. An oversized beret was slung wetly down over his ears, and a soggy woolen scarf was wrapped around his long, thin neck. His six-foot, round-shouldered frame was inclined forward to counterbalance the weight of an amazingly sloppy packsack that hung so low that it bounced against his arse whenever he moved. And Freddy, a rapidly disintegrating loaf of black bread hugged under one ragged arm, stood with his back to the slanting rain, dismally poking holes in the mud with his crooked walking stick. A miserable sight he was, yet so purely comical that I hardly dared think about it.

Arguments all settled, we trudged away in line-astern formation with Guy in the lead followed by Freddy, Maurice, and me. Pierre brought up the rear. Wading waist-deep through the fast-running creek, we followed a sunken trail for an hour or so, moving silently as ghosts with but occasional exceptions, which were slightly dangerous but increasingly humorous. All would be quiet but for the swish of wet clothes through wet grass. Then from up ahead would come crashing through the silence a grinding "CRONCH-CRONCH-CRONCH . . . SPLASH!" which would be Freddy lumbering across a patch of gravel and into a deep puddle with his Number 12 flying boots. Several times we called a halt to warn him against unnecessary noise, but to no avail. For if there was bit of gravel or a pool along the way, Freddy would unerringly find and taxi through it. With the thought in mind that perhaps the leading elements of our column might at any moment be challenged, I dropped back to walk with Pierre. We thoroughly enjoyed ourselves, what with whispering and chuckling and, as we had a monopoly on the bottles, taking a nip now and then. And before long I was navigating under a lopsided load, for I'd started out with a bottle of red wine in each coat pocket, and now Pierre had just hurled one empty up to the head of the column—thusly giving Guy and Freddy quite a fright.

Having just circumnavigated a pair of sentries who stood at a crossroad, and after tiptoeing across a concrete highway, we were surprised by the quick approach of a Jerry one-lung motorcycle that bore down upon us. We pressed ourselves into the wet hedgerow that fenced the highway and a helmeted Hun putt-putted past us a scant five or six feet away. Pierre, muttering "Pouf! Pouf!" under his breath, tracked the target with cocked revolver.

A squadron of Ju 88's snarled overhead at treetop level with exhaust stacks glowing, engines droning their unsynchronized beat, and I had to admire their pilots' guts to attempt a low-level attack in such dirty weather. I for one was goddam glad to have my feet in the mud. An infrequent jangle of horse-drawn equipment came to our ears, and once the nearby shouts of soldiers; but that was all the enemy had to offer. For many kilometers we made our way along rough and sloppy woodland trails, pausing once to empty another bottle of wine and again to quench our thirst at a tiny hillside spring. And just before dawn we climbed the high stone wall encircling a chateau. Forcing open the door, we fumbled around by match-light, located a half-dozen straw mats, and fell asleep with no further chatter.

Scattered about the chateau were many German army bulletins and propaganda sheets; and in the straw mats we found lice and Jerry coins and other signs of animal life. The chateau had been a German SS headquarters for a couple of years, and my theories as to the fate of the unfortunate Frenchmen who'd been questioned here were fed by horror stories from Pierre and Maurice. Pierre spat upon the big SS insignia that had been carved into the plaster wall of the master bedroom, and he superimposed the Croix de Lorraine—symbol of the Franc-Tireur Partizans.

At last my status with the Maquis had crystallized: I'd been drafted. I was presented with a musket: a double-barreled shotgun that had been handmade by a plumber in Marseille during the days of Charlemagne, or before. Also tendered me were six cartridges, which fit tightly into the rusted Damascus barrels of my weapon. Each "cartouche" had a firing pin protruding from the topside rear; and when struck by the curly-cue hammers of the gun, these pins would be driven downward, thusly blowing up the cartridge and, I ventured, probably the gun too. The shells were hand-loaded with buckshot and equipped with plexiglas wads cut from the cockpit of some crashed aircraft. Knowing Maquis methods, I assumed that they had plenty of the wrong kind of gunpowder packed into them. I took a rather dim view of my weapon, but for friendship's sake I showed great delight in the acquisition. I had the big picture of me dueling against a burp-gun with my trusty fusil.

Still biding my time with the Maquis, I did my share of the chores. I peeled spuds and chopped wood and hauled water from the deep well, stood my tour of guard duty by night, and ran around with the boys on their "missions." While the others squawked about standing guard, I looked forward to my three-hour tour in the wee hours of the night, for it gave me a chance to be alone with my insidious schemes. When it wasn't raining, the nights were made delightful by the songs and cries of nightingales and owls and the rustle of forest creatures. The deep, canopied well in the courtyard was inhabited by hundreds of small bats whose darting, whirring, amazingly accurate instrument flights fascinated me by the hour.

A sentry's orders were sweet and simple. A new password was used every night, and anyone failing to respond correctly to the challenge "Qui va la?" was to receive a charge from the Mauser.

But the nocturnal missions were altogether interesting. One, typical and highly successful, was accomplished during the second night at our latest chateau. After an evening of planning over a litre of applejack, four of us struck out through the woods until we came to a blacktop highway. Brawny Maurice then felled a small tree so that it lay across the narrow roadway, and we retired to the concealment of a brush-covered embankment to wait patiently for a customer. And the woods were cool and sweet-smelling and peaceful for an hour or so, until to our eager ears came the moan of a truck low-gearing up the grade; whereupon we butted cigarettes, cocked our guns, and held our breath, and then the dimmed-out headlamps of a Jerry truck came into view. When it halted just short of our road-block, we scrunched deeper into hiding, fingers on triggers, sweating out the ambush. The unfortunate driver and his partner climbed down to the road and commenced to tug at the tree and that was the last time either of them ever swore at anything, for Pierre muttered a vicious, "Un . . . deux . . . trois!" and we stood up and strafed 'em, but good. Pierre's revolver, Maurice's Mauser, André's buckshot gun, and both barrels of my rusty relic blasted simultaneously, and Pierre ran in to give a rather unnecessary coup de grâce. Now quickly raiding the truck, we removed to the forest many heavy, flat Teller mines and a couple of crates of long-handled grenades. After stripping the bodies of weapons, Pierre threw a can of gasoline over everything and touched it off with my trusty Zippo. A burst of flame in the night and we loped through the heavy, dancing shadows and away. Halfway back to the chateau I turned back to look, and the low overcast still reflected the lurid glare of the burning hijacked truck.

Doubling our guard, we retired to the kitchen with a fresh litre of brand new Calvados and celebrated the night's dirty work. Mainly, I was celebrating the fact that my fusil had held together. And in the morning we spent many hours relaying the loot back to a hiding place in a tumble-down shed near the chateau.

We lived well here. Soon after our arrival the Maquis panel truck, with "Secours Nationale" painted on the side, pulled into the courtyard and a fat, protesting calf was unloaded. I looked at the mournful critter and licked my chops. Freddy patted it on the head, talking to it as though it had been a pet dog. I think it was the first calf he'd run across, and he was quite horrified when Pierre and I led it into the garage for the massacre. Pierre, red fez tilted dangerously, found a small ball-peen hammer and with it swatted the calf atwixt the eyes a half-dozen times, with no appreciable results. I grabbed a length of four-by-four and hauled off, and our supper went down for the count. Pierre had it skinned before it had stopped twitching. For four days thereafter we had steak for breakfast, lunch, and supper, and at the end of that time we had consumed one entire calf includ-ing hooves, head, and tail, with which items soup was made. My last sad memory of this calf was that of a furry head bobbling about in a seething cauldron, mournful eyes staring into space.

My idle hours were profitably taken up by friendly little games of chance. For a nominal fee I'd taught Freddy to play Casino, and we played countless games. When I had all his escape-kit money, I gave it back and we started over again. Pierre was always good for a few francs, and I took a sizeable wad from him during an all-night session of blackjack. He wouldn't speak to me for nearly a day.

We were never without sufficient booze, for we manufactured our own—often drinking it while quite warm from the still. The Maquis had its own still which they called "le machine." It was mounted handily upon an ancient two-wheeled cart and when the Maquis moved, the still followed along, and we all took turns operating it. A more relaxing job of work I have yet to find.

At sunrise one could look off across the valley from the chateau, and down in a timbered creek-bottom could always be seen pure white wood-smoke filtering through the treetops. That was le machine getting under-way for the day's production. And the scene at the still was a cartoon of old Kentucky moonshiners, except that instead of peaked-crown, wide-brimmed hats, these characters wore berets on their heads. Pierre and I worked le machine for a couple of hazy days, stoking the fire and feeding the kettle and now and then tapping the coil for a tin-cupful of yellowish, fiery 'shine—Calvados by name. Now and then during the days, a local hillbilly would pop into the clearing with a litre bottle which we would fill, accepting 100 francs in return. A pleasant way to run a war.

I probed continually for information on the Invasion. Flea would tell me that les Anglaises were still roosting at their old stand along the Orne, but always she would assure me that they'd liberate us in ten days. And whenever I'd so much as suggest that I might take off to walk westward, César would pat my cheek and say, "Alors, Tayo . . . you're just restless. You stay with the Maquis, eh?" Then I'd catch him briefing Pierre and Maurice to keep their eyes on me. And I played along, agreeable on the surface, but always gathering information and biding my time. Henri had a very good map of the Channel Coast, which I would acquire when the time came. I would need it more than he.

With a lonely eye to the skies, I watched for the slim blue-nosed Mustangs of my outfit. It made me itch to get back, watching our fighters weaving around upstairs—their pilots still in the twentieth century and an hour from England, while I, somehow entangled in the middle of the seventeenth century, stood in the courtyard of a fancy chateau dressed up like a clown and grabbing the ground like an intelligence officer.

And I lay on my back to watch many a good dogfight, squirming and breaking into cold sweat when the boys would get into tight spots—as though I instead of they were strapped into the cockpit—and it was satisfying to note that the Jerries invariably came out clutching the dirty end of the stick. When a ship would plunge into the forests we'd grab up our guns and run for the wreckage. Several times we found abandoned Jerry 'chutes, but never a live pilot.

One morning I stood watching an American P-38 that was flying straight-and-level on course for England at about ten thousand feet. Her pilot had his head up-and-locked, for a lone diving Me 109 closed in swiftly from dead astern and then cut loose at point-blank range with all guns. There was a sudden orange flash alongside the cockpit of the Lightning, and that was all. The "fork-tailed devil" just nosed down gently, then vertically, with a dead American flyboy pushing the throttles full forward. The P-38 went in at terminal velocity, the howling crescendo of her engines filling the whole sky. The 109 did a couple of sloppy victory rolls and went away.

So passed a week at the chateau. Came the Fourth of July, and it developed into quite a day. In the afternoon we all watched a dogfight that was something right out of Hollywood. The sudden roar of fighter engines revving up and down and the chatter and thud of machine guns and cannon brought us out of the chateau on the run. Low overhead was a lone RAF Mosquito giving battle to twelve Focke-Wulf 190s. One against a squadron . . .

The sky was about half-filled with low, scattered clouds and the rat-race was in and amongst them, and in five minutes of the damned fanciest flying I ever hope to see the lone Mosquito shot down four Jerry fighters and then made a getaway. The last we saw of the RAF ship, her pilot was blasting for England at full throttle, darting from cloud to cloud, the eight surviving 190s giving chase and filling the air around the Mosquito with countless black puffs of self-destroying 20mm cannon shells. There went a man I'd like to know, that RAF pilot, and I sort of think he made it home intact. I suppose nobody believed his story when he did get home.

My French comrades, knowing that the Fourth of July was for me comparable to their own Bastille Day, thoughtfully flung another grande fête complete with crêpes suzettes, red wine, and great quantities of Calvados. At the end of the evening, Pierre stood at one end of the kitchen hollering, "Viva l'Amerique" at me, and I stood at the other end hollering, "Vive la France!" right back at him. But what a head in the morning . . .

Now, on the fifth we had an unusual day, which began with a great hullabaloo in the morning. Athos appeared bright and early to brief us. We were to post ourselves in the thickets around the chateau, covering all entrances. We would wait for and permit to enter one auto with three people aboard. Any vehicle following was to be strafed and the occupants assassinated. These instructions were simple enough so, lugging my wretched fusil, I toddled off to the main gate and took up a comfortable stand behind a screen of brush where I sat and smoked and peered off across the valley in the best of Maquis style. Before long, jouncing along the rut road came a tiny sedan with César at the wheel, Athos on the far side, and a gal in the middle. I opened the gate and admitted the car, then followed it up to the chateau.

All the Maquisards had drifted in from the brush to rendezvous on the top floor, and César then announced that this wench was a horizontal collaborator, and plus that she was suspected of being a spy for the Nazis. The Maquis had kidnapped her from the local cat-house and had brought her to the chateau for a little interrogation. How droll!

In the room were a square oak table, three chairs, four bottles of vin rouge, a dozen glasses, a bottle of ink, some paper, a quill pen, and an alarm clock. Young Guy was appointed sergeant-at-arms. He stood in the doorway, the Mauser under his arm, while the others of the Maquis formed a serious circle about the table. Athos shoved the girl into a center chair. Everybody glared at her for a spell. She looked from one man to the next, seeking a trace of sympathy where none was to be found. She was quite poised, appeared to be about thirty years old, and was fairly attractive in a run-down, haggard sort of way.

César beat on the table with his fist and shouted, "SILENCE!" Now sauntering over behind the victim, he tilted her face upwards with the palm of his hand, looked into her eyes, and asked her politely to start writing her confession. She shook her head and shrugged: she had nothing to say, she was guilty of nothing. César sneered around the room and remarked sarcastically, "Hah! She has nothing to say!" And his face began to flush and the veins of his forehead began to bulge, for César, as I have insinuated, was a man of quick and violent temper. Now with a terrifying scowl on his hard face, he bent over the girl and told her again to start writing. She just smiled nervously, whereupon César straightened up and gave her the full swing of his open hand. She kept her smile. Athos reached over, stripped off her wristwatch and diamond ring, appraised them suggestively, and tucked them into his pocket. The wench was frightened by this action, all right, but still showing plenty of spunk she again denied her guilt. César, however, grabbed a handful of her hair with a mop-wringing grip and swung his free hand back and forth for a while: poppety-pop, poppety-pop. When the girl's face began to be a bit red and puffy, César released her, plunked the clock down before her, and delivered his ultimatum: she had ten minutes in which to start writing. Out of the corner of her eye she watched Athos as he pulled out his revolver and sat idly twirling the cylinder. The clock ticked very loudly.

As she fingered the pen, César poured a round of drinks and smilingly offered her a glass of wine. As she sipped, she meditated on her predicament. Coming evidently to the logical conclusion that she was nothing but trapped, she picked up the quill and began scratching industriously, with César perusing each page as it was written and now and then prompting the girl to give every name, place, and date involved. In an hour or so she'd completed her manuscript and César and Athos witnessed her signature. From his pocket, Athos now produced a pair of barber's shears which he waved briskly under the girl's nose, and that pulled the final prop from her tottering morale, for she now wept and cried, "Pas ma chevelure!" Athos shrugged, grinned and replied, "Your hair, hell! Perhaps your life!" And they escorted her roughly to the little sedan, threw her in and drove away. No more was ever said of the gal or her ultimate fate, but I don't think she went back to work. No sooner had the sedan disappeared down the trail than a horse-and-buggy clattered into the courtyard with lanky Canoe at the controls. Flea was at his side, and half-hidden under the canopy were two strangers. I took one good look and let fly with a rodeo yell: "Yeeeeohoo! Hello, Suckers!"

And I was right the first time, for I got an immediate and disgusted reply in my own language: "Suckers is right, Pal! Let's blow this goddam trap!" Hot damn, I had me a Yank at last. Out of the carriage jumped a couple more parachutistes par accidente.

The lad who'd answered my gleeful cry was a reckless-looking citizen, thin and gaunt and with a heavy stubble of beard and a crop of ragged black hair. The other was of medium build, neat despite his ill-fitting disguise, and clean-shaven but for a genuine Royal Air Force moustache. Flea introduced us, and when the raggedy Yank heard me introduced as Monsieur Tayo, he burst into hysterical laughter: "Tayo? Why you sad sonuvabitch, I'm sick of hearin' about you. All I hear in this part of France . . . people tellin' me about some crazy bastard named Tayo who bailed out of a Moostang and drank the country dry!" I was pleased to learn that I'd acquired a reputation of sorts since my arrival in Maquisland.

From Joisey City, this feller was. His name was Lou Lynch and he'd been born a little off his rocker, since then having been further addled by a few close bursts of flak. A B-26 bombardier, his ship had been blown up by flak over Pas de Calais early in May. The local Resistance group had stashed him away in a little house in Amiens, right under the nose of half the Wehrmacht. He'd been trapped in one dinky room for the past six or eight weeks, part of which time he'd been forced to hide in a little old chimney while Jerries were billeted in his room. Lou, as I, had been stalled off on our escape plans, and what with being so walled-in he'd about lost his mind. So he slipped away and headed westward, beamed on the beach-head, but had been rounded up by Flea and Canoe and persuaded to have a chat with César—who in turn had delivered him to the chateau. I was so damned glad to have an American to talk with that I pumped Lou's hand for five minutes.

Flight-leftenant Brian Lester Taylor III, RAF, was a retired Lancaster pilot. A quiet type, he was a perfect complement to Lou, who was quite wild and always ready to leap before looking. Brian had been en route back to England after a long night raid on Friedrichshafen, across the lake from Switzerland, when a Jerry night-fighter had growled up dead astern and shot the Lanc down in flames. At dawn, unable to find any of his crew, Brian had acquired civilian clothes and had struck out boldly along the highways. Just the day before his arrival at the chateau, he'd been strolling happily along the road when an elderly Frenchman had accosted him with the blunt statement: "Vous êtes Anglaise!" You're an Englishman!" Where-upon the old man had chuckled and gone his way, leaving Brian speechless and slightly in doubt as to the perfection of his disguise. Picked up by Canoe, he'd met Lou, and now Brian said that he was still puzzled as to how "That bloody old French-type" had identified his nationality at a glance. I explained that I, for one, had yet to see a Frenchman equipped with a straggly Royal Air Force cookie-duster.

So we were four airmen, sans avion, in hostile territory. Fliers tend to get along with others of their breed anyway, and in this set of circumstances our friendships were welded instantaneously. Wasting no words, I told the boys that it was the intent of le Maquis César to keep us until the lib-eration, but that I was about to launch a spearhead toward Piccadilly via the front lines. I would enjoy their company, but they could either remain in the comparative safety of Maquisland or string along with me, as they saw fit.

Lou, jumping to his feet, wanted to hit the road right then. Brian said he'd jolly well like to give it a try, but not until he'd had a bite to eat. Freddy, a little against his better judgment, said that he'd do as we did. So it was definite: the four of us were leaving. Because I spoke a little better French than did the others, and because I had the inside track with the Maquis, it was agreed that I would be the spokesman and leader of our little band. I was to try again, at the first opportunity, to get counterfeit visas from the Maquis and to ask for information and a guide. We had nothing to lose by asking again. If the Maquis should see it our way and furnish the poop, our expedition would be that much easier. If our requests were refused, we still had one another!

César and Flea came to the chateau that night and a meeting was called. César announced gravely that on his little TSF he had received a message from London headquarters. General de Gaulle had proclaimed the Maquis to be officially recognized by the Allies as the French Forces of the Interior. Henceforth the German Army would recognize the FFI as a legitimate French army—the theory being that captured Maquisards would now be treated as prisoners of war instead of being executed as outlaw partizans. Remembering the Germans' record of savagery in the disposal of captive Maquisards, I thought that the good General de Gaulle was being a trifle optimistic.

"And," quoth César, "as of now this Maquis is gonna be run like a military outfit. Attention! Form ranks! Fall in, goddammit!" After a while three ranks were formed: a half-dozen Frenchmen in each of the first two and four airmen in the rear, all slouched in various conceptions of attention—the most common version being a hip-shot stance with thumbs hooked into belts.

César issued his orders. Of the Maquis detachment to be stationed at the chateau, Guy was named as in command. Pierre and Maurice were next in the chain of command, and so on through the list until it came to me and my fellow conspirators: we were now buck privates in le Maquis César and would obey the orders of Guy (so said César). That last crack I let ride without derisive comment, knowing that we wouldn't be around much longer anyway. Guy was the hot-headed patriot of the bunch, but quite juvenile, and with a poorly controlled temper that smothered any reasoning ability he might have had. I wouldn't have trusted his judgment as far as I could have thrown the whole chateau.

Upon César's departure, Guy swelled like a pouter pigeon and called another formation. Allez-oop! We were in the army now, and now was the time to start drilling. Lining up his men, Guy showed them how to hold their muskets on their shoulders like soldiers of the king. He ordered my gang to line up in the rear rank, but I told him to shove it. After four years in a goddam military school and three more in the Air Corps I wasn't about to shuffle around in an old chateau with a rabbit gun over my shoulder under command of a dead-end kid. Brian remarked that he too thought the idea rather absurd. Lou, however, with a fiendish gleam in his eye, announced to Guy that the aviateurs would take over instruction duties for the evening. Guy blustered a bit. He would tell César that we had mutinied, and we would be shot for same. But we just laughed and laughed and went about trying to teach the Maquis to walk, at least in a cluster, and to handle their weapons with some semblance of method. Brian taught the British manual of arms and the British salute and British-style drill, while I taught the American manual of arms, the Air Corps salute (an entirely different thing than that of other branches of the service), and I didn't know how to drill so I left that all to Brian. Lou, with malicious delight, invented some fantastic ways of getting a rifle from one shoulder to the other and then to the ground. And his mischievous mind could dream up some humdingers.

During this orgy of militaristic maneuvering I slipped upstairs and requisitioned Henri's map of the Channel Coast, upon which I'd had my eye for days. Lou and I that night walked sentry duty together, and by match-light went into a huddle and laid out a tentative course, selecting as an objective the Channel town of Houlgate which lay north and a little east of Caen.

Came the dawn and the Maquis set their four prize privates to work hauling water from the deep well, peeling spuds, and gathering wood for the kitchen fireplace in which all cooking was accomplished. Using a heavy log as a battering ram, we filled the order for a lot of wood by the simple expedient of tearing down a nearby abandoned Jerry barracks. For all Lou's wailing about our not getting underway, he was having a wonderful time employing his insatiable, hot-foot-variety sense of humor, and his wild laughter rang out from dawn to dark. The Maquis boys were a little afraid of him, for I know that they believed him to have made the turn.

Lou, however, was only having fun in his own quaint way—and in particular with one of the lads who, blessed with a negative I.Q., had taken a great shine to him. "Moron," as Lou fondly called his protégée, was eager to become bilingual. Endlessly pestering Lou, he would for example pick up a butcher knife and wave it under Lou's nose, crying, "Couteau, couteau!" and, with his mouth hanging open, Moron would wait for Lou to speak out the English equivalent. Never at a loss, Lou would nod and point to the knife and say, "Sonuvabitch!" Then Moron would pace the floor, memorizing "Sonuvabitch, sonuvabitch, sonuvabitch!" When finally he had learned the truly delightful names of a dozen different objects, Moron would string them all together, thusly reciting a long, unbroken, unconscious blue streak of high-grade profanity. Lou would then compliment him: "Trés bien, Monsieur Moron!"—and then he'd gaze innocently at me until I'd break down completely; whereupon Lou would run the scales with mad laughter. And the Frenchmen would look at one another and at me, making circles around their ears with their pointing fingers. One night I shook hands with Moron and he, grinning his pride at being able to say goodnight to me in my language, replied to my "bonsoir" with: "I yam flak-happy, Monsieur Tayo!" I was caught off guard and shrieked involuntarily right in his face. It was impolite, but I couldn't help it.

This business of saying goodnight had become quite a chore, now that our numbers had increased. Everybody in France shook hands upon the slightest provocation, and by now I was an old hand at the racket. Upon awakening in the morning I'd shake hands with Pierre, Maurice, Henri, André, and the rest of the Maquis just as though we were congratulating one another on pulling through the night. Before breakfast and afterwards would we shake hands. Upon meeting for supper, as though we hadn't seen one another for months, another round of it. And then again before retiring. In a crowd, it was etiquette to take on two people at once, with both right and left hands in operation at the same time. With a circle of people saying goodbye or hello, sometimes the illusion of a game of ring-around-the-rosy was gained. For a joke, now and then, I would stick out a thumb or even a little finger, and somebody would shake it every time. I had even seen Pierre, while taking a casual leak, thrust his free hand behind him for a farewell handshake by Henri. It was, however, a nice custom, making for fraternal feeling.

One morning there occurred another incident that tended to speed my departure. We were all at breakfast when one of the Maquis came in from walking the final sentry tour. This meat-head, playfully pointing the Mauser in the general direction of where Pierre and I sat smoking and picking our teeth, hollered, "Pouf!" And the Mauser cracked out, "POUF!" as it sent a steel-jacketed slug crashing through a windowpane some three inches to the side of my head and on a level with the bridge of my nose. The stupid bastard with the rifle stood paralyzed until Maurice jerked the gun from his limp hands and then booted him halfway across the court-yard. The Maquis, to appease me, banished the culprit from the chateau for a day. A bit later, Pierre slyly pointed his pistol at me and whispered, "Pouf" and I grabbed the first thing I saw and threw it at him. It happened to be a bucket of water and Pierre was quite angry and very wet, but the rest of the Maquis backed me up, pointing to the bullet-hole in the window as a clincher to my argument. And even after that episode, some of the boys were still unconvinced that I thought a rifle to be a weapon and not a toy. We stood around the courtyard while Guy demonstrated the manual of arms. Then, jacking a cartridge into the chamber and with finger on trigger and the safety off, he shoved the muzzle into my middle and mur-mured, "Pouf! Kaput!" If he was just trying to get a rise out of me, he suc-ceeded. For the first time in a long time I lost my temper and twisted the gun from his hands in such a manner as to land Guy roughly upon his back. I jacked the cartridges from the gun and put them into my pocket, then threw the Mauser as far as I could. It landed muzzle first, jammed deeply into the soft turf. Guy was furious but outnumbered, for all present again backed me up. It took Guy quite a while to clean the gun, and even longer to swallow his pride sufficiently to enable him to come begging to me for his shells.

Athos—tagged "Scarface Al" by Lou—showed up in the afternoon and according to plan I approached him with the remark that perhaps his four aviators might soon be leaving for London. I suggested that he tell César to hurry our papers along, for we'd be needing them. As I knew he would, Athos informed me angrily that we were going nowhere: we would stay with the Maquis. I didn't press the issue. As he left, Athos ordered Guy to keep les aviateurs always in sight: none of us was to walk away from the chateau unless escorted by one of the Maquis.

Deciding to run a check on the Maquis to find out how serious they might be about guarding us, we slipped away one by one to rendezvous in a ramshackle old mill some hundred yards from the chateau; and there we lay low, playing a quiet game of Casino and sucking on a jug of raw Calvados. In a half hour, attracted by a sudden turmoil from within the chateau, we peered through a crack in the wall and with some amusement noted a half-dozen Maquisards—all armed to the teeth—come stampeding out the kitchen door. They galloped off in all directions to cover the various trails the aviateurs might have taken. When their cries had faded, we strolled into the kitchen and resumed our game of chance. In an hour or so, winded and red-raced from their exertions under the hot sun of Normandy, the Maquis returned. Upon finding their quarry in the kitchen of the chateau, they looked at one another quite sheepishly and Guy, to complete our merriment, cussed me of all people for being the ringleader. "What's all the excitement about, Guy?" said I. He said that they'd thought they'd seen a parachute falling and had run to investigate. And unwilling to allow him to save face in such a clumsy manner, I remarked that we had just gone for a little walk in the woods.

The Maquis and I had drifted apart. Now, instead of being one of them as of old, I was one of a tight little clique of English-speaking fliers, and the Maquis boys didn't like my turnabout. Upon the arrival of Lou and Brian and Freddy, I'd ceased my stumbling efforts with the French language in favor of endless sessions of hangar flying with the airmen. It was delightful to just start in talking again, without having to lay out each sentence in advance. Only Pierre and Maurice were as friendly as they'd been before, and each called me aside to ask me to abandon les autres aviateurs. "Let the other aviators leave, Tayo," said Maurice, "for before they came everything was pleasant. Now, c'est pas bon!" And I smiled and told him that he and Pierre were two good friends.

The Maquis sincerely believed it impossible for four foreign airmen to penetrate the lines without being captured or killed, and in refusing to let us go they were considering our safety. Secondly, however, they were considering their own. I, for one, knew too much about them. Were I captured, there was a chance that either inadvertently or under torture I might let slip information that would result in the immediate extermination of le Maquis César. And the French had reason for their chronic distrust of people. Right in their own hometown, half the people were patriots and the rest collaborators: and if the people of the Maquis couldn't even trust another Frenchman, I didn't blame them for distrusting a stranger with information worth their lives. I could see their point, but I knew also that combat airmen had enough savvy to keep shut their mouths.

If I stuck out my neck and drew back a stub, that was no one's affair but my own. I had the whole damned French coast in which to poke around and I didn't figure on getting caught. But I knew that if the Jerries did get their hands on me, they couldn't hold me for long. As for walking in civilian clothes, well, I'd take a chance and rely on a dog tag and a lot of fast talking in the event of capture by the Wehrmacht. The adventure of trying to outwit the bastards appealed to me so strongly I could hardly wait to give it a try.

Then too, I was a trifle fed up with being strung along by the Maquis. I'd been sucked in and drafted, but mostly I was irritated with myself for not having headed west the moment my feet had hit France. There was no doubt in my mind that had I done that, I'd have been in London by now. But then again, I'd not have met Riri. It came out even.

I set about planning a non-spectacular getaway. To leave the chateau by night was the deal, but I didn't want to double-cross the Maquis by leaving them unguarded in their sleep. The best way for us not to have to desert while on guard duty was for us not to be on duty, so that evening when Guy read off his guard roster I piped up and told him that it was tough, but les aviateurs couldn't be sentries any more. It was against the rules of war! Guy threw his rank around in a helter-skelter fashion for a while but we just gave him the old razz, and he sent a courier to advise Athos of the latest mutiny.

Athos wasn't long in coming. We sat around the table while he bellered and blew for quite some time. Freddy sat by the fire and bit his fingernails. Brian watched the show with amusement. Lou lounged at my side, hands in pockets, scowl on face as Athos and I got into a helluva feud. I knew of no alternate rules of war to cover the situation, so I formulated a few to fit the bill. Athos hollered and beat on the table when he saw I wouldn't scare. He stopped for a breather and took a drink of whisky before he carried on:

"You are in France now. You are of the Maquis. You will take orders from me, Athos, who takes orders from César, who takes orders from General Koenig, who is Commandant of the FFI. You are soldiers of the FFI and will obey us or else. Compris?"

"Non!" I replied: hell no, I wasn't taking orders from General Koenig, or from César, or from Athos either. I was a hot-rock of the Huitieme Chasseurs, Armeé de l'Aire, Etats Unis—8th Fighter Command, AAF—and took my orders from nobody but old Monsieur le General Ike himself. I added that his four airmen were about to hit the trail for Merrie Olde England and we'd appreciate a little help.

Making like he hadn't heard me, Athos stomped over and stabbed a forefinger into my chest: "Tomorrow, Tayo, you go with me in the auto. We execute the collaborator and you, mon ami, will pull the trigger. Tomorrow!"

I'd just as soon have done the job for Athos, but he was getting away from the subject, so I told him I couldn't quite see it. "C'est contre les regles de la guerre!" What the hell did I know about the Rules of War? Nothing.

Athos went away mad, after enlarging upon previous orders that the Maquis would keep us under strict surveillance. Well, we'd overplayed our hand. Our mild uprising had resulted in too violent a reaction, so we went into a huddle and quickly revised our plan. I sought out Guy and announced that we had reconsidered: we would be sentries for the Maquis after all. International affairs were again smoothed out. Our revamped plan now included the utilization of the ancient alarm clock used by Guy to awaken his guards.

The Maquisards were quite conscientious about keeping an eye on their charges, so Lou and I put our heads together and worked out a little deal that we believed would solve that angle. Our foursome would wear the Maquis down to a frazzle. After a few days of our treatment, we'd have the boys tuckered out to the point where none of them could stay awake long enough to guard us properly. So we briefed Freddy and Brian and put our hare-brained plan into action at once.

None of us went to bed that night, but stayed instead in the kitchen and flung a little party. The Maquis boys, smelling an overgrown rat, stayed with us and all night long we drank and sang and took our turns at walking the walls with the Mauser rifle. And nobody got a wink of sleep. People were a bit fatigued the next day, but as the Frenchmen would drag off upstairs to try to get a little shut-eye we'd stomp about and whoop and holler, and there was no rest for the Maquis. After a night and a day of this, our team was just getting into the swing of things. The second evening Brian and Lou built a helluva blaze in the kitchen fireplace and we sat all that night swigging great quantities of Calvados, talking flying and singing ribald songs in bad barbershop harmony. The Maquisards, a bit bewildered, joined in and we all had a dandy time. Nobody got any sleep. And the following day, due to our combined efforts, the Maquis remained awake while singly we caught up on our rest in the cellar of the old mill. We were primed for action. We would leave tonight!

Early in the evening Henri came to the chateau with a horse-cart laden with beefsteak and wine and a portable phonograph. As he carried in a big stack of records, he said that tonight we'd have a feast and a dance. Although I didn't see how the Maquis lads would be able to do much dancing, I was all in favor of the shindig. A good brawl would knock the props out from under the lot of 'em, so Henri's surprise party fitted right into our goofy scheme. Comrade Pierre had somewhere acquired a tall chef's hat to replace his red fez, and he fried up a batch of steaks that were done to perfection. After having eaten, the little Maquis detachment of the chateau was one big yawn, with each man equipped with a small pouch that hung beneath each eye. But after a litre of Calvados had been consumed, fatigue was a thing of the past and we swept the floors and combed our hair, pretty-like.

And the guests arrived: an old grandmère and an old grandpère and two young and tender queens—and if looks could have done the dirty work, those little gals were pregnant before the door had swung shut behind them. (Smartest thing that old grandpère ever did was to come to that party . . .) Now, inasmuch as somebody had possession of Lou's favorite chair by the fireplace, he cast armful after armful of wood onto the fire until the blaze was so ferocious that folks had to move away; whereupon Lou slid into his chair and settled down to full enjoyment of the evening.

We all had a drink and Henri set up the juke-box. The records were mostly tangos and boleros, but there was one in English that Brian played at every opportunity—the Lambeth Walk, and what a mess it was. These Frenchmen liked their jive fast and they had the old phonograph's governor screwed wide open so that the records played at maximum rpm. The dancing was intriguing, to say the least, and the lad known to Lou as "Snake" did a pretty mean job of it. Snake, with his glittering eyes, slick black hair, and striped turtleneck sweater, latched onto one of the charming little gals, clamped a sweaty paw behind each of her slim hips, and embarked upon a terpsichorean interpretation of that sport for which France is far-famed. He "danced" with that poor kid for twenty minutes and his feet didn't travel more than an inch. Lou's vulgar laughter drowned out the music.

Full of green whiskey, Brian and Freddy and Lou and I soon fell into the mood of the fête. Lou, quite fried, bowed low to the wizened granny, seized her, and jitterbugged the old woman all over the chateau, and she had a high old time of it, her excited cackles ringing out above the honky-tonk shrillness of the phonograph. Brian, also well oiled, tried a dozen times to lure one of the queens into various dark corners, each of his efforts being thwarted by the eagle-eyed old man.

Under cover of the merry-making I prowled the chateau, requisitioning various items I thought might come in handy on the long trek: a litre of Calvados, a loaf of black bread, a hunk of salted butter, a handful of sulphur matches, and a couple of packets of tobacco and papers; then pulling out my good knife I chopped from a big chunk of beef in the storeroom four or five pounds of raw meat, which was stuffed into the big pocket of my flying jacket. And after greasing my shoes with a slab of suet, I stepped outside for a weather check.

I made a joke about ducks to the Maquis sentry as he came trudging past, soaked and shivering in the cold rain that was pounding down from rumbling night skies. An occasional bolt of lightning ripped a hole in the inky sky, showing in its flashes the edge of the somber forest in which we would soon find ourselves. And Nature's reckless mood only blew on the coals of the smoldering, reckless feeling that had been building up within me.

Rejoining the party and contacting the boys, I told them we'd drink the Maquis to sleep and take off when all was quiet. I was boiling away inside, eager to put the expedition on the trail.

For the remainder of the evening Lou's ear-to-ear grin never faded, and between giving the hot-foot to unwary patriots and bouncing around the dance floor with one or the other of the gals, he was indeed the very life of the party. Then when the fire had died away to a friendly glow, Henri picked up his concertina and squeezed out a very sad ballad, singing off-key and punctuating his lines with well-timed hiccups. Pretty soon, of course, they sang Le Marseillaise with tears and toasts, and then Lou shouted, "Vive la Joisey City!" and we drank to that. When I vive'd Chicago, Pierre la revolutioniste came back with a wistful, "Ahhhh! Sheeeca-go! Beaucoup gang-stair, oui?"

The clambake broke up at midnight and the exhausted Maquisards stumbled dazedly upstairs, and to allay suspicion Brian and Freddy went along to feign sleep. At a prearranged time they would rendezvous with Lou and me behind the old mill. And since I was slated for sentry duty from midnight to one a.m., with Lou to follow my tour, the two of us had a legitimate excuse to remain in the kitchen. To be forced to leave my truly good friends of le Maquis César without so much as a handshake and au revoir was not a good thing, so I wrote a message to César explaining why we were leaving and thanking him for hospitalities extended, and I assured him that were we captured we'd never reveal our connections with the Maquis. After including a little stuff about it being our duty as officers de l'Armée de l'Aire to make every effort to return to our respective squadrons, I rolled the paper into a tube and stuck in into the muzzle of the Mauser, then hung the rifle on a peg. At five minutes of one I set the alarm clock to sound off at one-thirty, then pussyfooted upstairs to place it close to Guy's ear. That half hour would give us a fair enough head start, and would leave the Maquis detachment unguarded for but a short time.

Lou and I downed a mighty swig of applejack then shared a last dry cigarette. When I pulled open the heavy door, a gust of wet wind poured in to snuff the candle. The chateau was blacked out. We figured we might as well get the hell going, so we slipped out into the night.

Letter to César

"César my Friend—
1. Do not worry about us. We will never give any information to the Boches if we are captured.
2. It is our duty as officers of the American and British Armies to try to return to England with no further delay.
3. According to the orders given us by our Commanding Officers

in England it is absolutely not possible for us to stay with and assist the Maquis.

4. We are very grateful to you and your men for aiding us, as you have done. You have fed us well and hidden us from the Boches, and for that we thank you.

5. I, Théodore, wish to thank you, César, and the men I've been with for so long. Especially Maurice and Pierre. You are all good soldiers and brave Patriots of France. I can never thank you enough for aiding me as you all have. My memories of Normandy will always be of the brave Frenchmen living there.

6. When Eure is again Free I wish you would all write to me and I will answer all your letters.

7. I think that you, César, as a soldier, will understand why it is necessary that I leave you now.

Au Revoir my friends—and Good Luck.
Théodore Fahrenwald
1st Lieutenant
United States Army Air Force

Vive la France
Vive l'Amérique
Vive l'Angleterre"

Chapter 4

A HOMING PIGEON NAMED TAYO

Fast-flowing rivulets gurgled across the courtyard, frothed by the steady drumming of the rain. A dozen tiny waterfalls cascaded from the gutters of the ancient chateau to tumble musically onto the cobbles, and my comrades and I were drenched before we'd taken a dozen quick steps. Now feeling our way to the rendezvous point, we sat out of the rain and I chomped at the bit until the Englishmen showed up—Brian having managed somehow to retain his debonair look, while Freddy as usual looked quite wretched. But I was as purely happy as I've ever been and I led out, following a premeditated route through the wet meadow grass that would leave behind us no trail. A cautious detour around a slumbering watchdog, a quick crawl beneath a fence or two, a few minutes of skirting nearby grain fields, and we were well away.

Standing at the edge of the gloomy black forest, we paused to uncork the silver flask and chuckle over a snort of Calvados, all of us content with the knowledge that our skullduggery had panned out well. We were on our merry way to the front lines, and I didn't give two hoots in hell for what might lie ahead: it was just nice to be on the move again. We nipped on the jug and laughed, heh-heh, for now the alarm would be sounding in the chateau; which, as the Maquis were aroused, would no doubt be the scene of bitter recriminations as each of the mob would blame the others for permitting les aviateurs to make their getaway. Guy would soon be trembling through a little vis-à-vis with a wrathful Cesar, and I wondered who would next be in command of the little detachment.

We'd walk line-astern with ten paces between men, and we'd take our turns at leading the column, for in this manner should the leader blunder into a Jerry patrol the others would have their chance to peel off into the brush, avoiding capture. So I picked up a compass course of due west and struck straight into the woods, and I had to chew a twig to keep from singing.

One faint trail led to another, always angling westward, and for a couple of hours the only sounds were friendly: the soughing of the rainy wind through the dripping pines, the dull plop of an occasional soggy twig snapping underfoot, or a thud and a muffled curse as one or the other of us would catapult headlong over an invisible snag. At last, zig-zagging down a treacherous, muddy path that terminated in a rushing creek at the far edge of the woods, we waded the creek and became no wetter in the process. But now we came upon a concrete highway that ran in our direction, and following the road we came to a bridge—and during the next quarter-hour, had any stranger chanced to peer beneath the bridge, he'd have seen four bedraggled trolls sitting in a row puffing sodden, wrinkled cigarettes and passing a jug of whiskey back and forth. And we held another low-voiced pow-wow. We'd walk the highway until dawn or until it no longer took us westward, whichever should come first. After the ordeal in the dense forest, it was a downright pleasure to set foot upon a hard-surfaced route, and for the next couple of hours we made up for lost time. But when we came upon the outlying houses of a little village, we were forced to call a halt.

"So do we walk through the son of a bitch or do we go around it?" inquired Lou impatiently. A weighty question, that, but before anyone could make answer a fast-moving auto bore down on us and we dove instinctively into the roadside ditch as a Jerry staff car hummed past, tires whining on the wet highway. We climbed back to the road, not quite knowing whether to laugh or to cuss for, while our amazing disappearance had been comical, the handy ditch had proven to be full of water and thick with nettles. But I was much reassured by the fast reaction demonstrated by my fellow fugitives.

Lou and I grabbed the bull by the horns and strolled into town for a looksee, and by the first traces of this cold dawn there was nary a soul to be seen in the rainswept streets of this bleak little hamlet; so we sent up a flare to the Royal Air Force and the Englishmen tiptoed along behind us. Just beyond the town the highway veered southward, and since daybreak was close at hand I craved the comforting camouflage of the woods. My tactics failed to meet with unanimous approval, but objections from the rear fell upon deaf ears and I jumped the ditch to pull myself upward through the tangled wet growth of a pine-clad hillside. Grumbling mightily, my partners followed along. I had the only map.

So up and over a long and tortuous hill to slide then into the valley beyond; then up again and down, over windfalls and through great, close-knit patches of giant ferns. And the woods were sweet-smelling, grey clouds scudded lowly, and the rain, in slantwise sheets, poured down. There wasn't any sunrise, but the world gradually became less dark, and then I was highly pleased to find myself engulfed in such wilderness.

Now across a flooding creek on a fallen tree, and up a grassy slope steep enough to force us to hands and knees, and then one long sigh of relief: for the forest was behind us and ahead lay a level stretch of farmland. But we'd sighed too soon, it seemed, for the going instead became more difficult. Each tiny field was tightly fenced and hedged and our trail became painfully circuitous. Tempers grew raw after we'd grunted and snatched our way through a dozen hedgerows, so nursing the cuts and scratches donated by the evil vines and brambles, we slopped our blistered heels gratefully along a country road, pausing only to kick the gumbo from our shoes. We having bunched up for companionship, before long the rabbits in the meadows along our trail perked their ears in amazement as they heard our fine quartet rendition of ". . . them blues I don't lose when it rains . . ." But despite the deluge pouring down onto our beret-clad heads, there was never a more lighthearted outfit than ours.

Every so often I'd squint knowingly at the map and check our course with the compass, but I was totally disoriented. At last, in reply to Lou's increasingly vulgar and suspicious questions as to our present position, I advised him that he'd probably never realize his luck in having as navigator a homing pigeon named Tayo. Further advice to the effect that he should stick with me if he cared to wear diamonds big as you-know-what just brought a growl from Lou: "Diamonds hell! We'll be wearin' bracelets!"— and he held his wrists together, making like handcuffs. Brian, realizing that even if we did know our position we still were lost, just murmured, "How droll!" and went on singing his filthy flying songs. I didn't know where in hell we might be, but I was damned if I'd acknowledge the fact. And when we approached a familiar row of bombed-out hangars, no one was ever more surprised—and showed it less—than I. How we ever got to where we were, I'll never know, but the opportunity to rub it in was perfect.

"Heh heh!" I remarked to Lou in a nasty way, "On our left we have Tricqueville Airdrome, the home of my good friend Maurice Marais. You don't think I'd have left the country without sayin' goodbye?" And when that patriot's house loomed ahead of us, no further aspersions were cast upon my navigation. Had the lads been able to have read my mind, however, they'd have tossed in their chips and surrendered.

Leaving a soggy trio crouched in the rubble of the Jerry barracks, I sneaked to the house and beat on the door, which soon opened just enough to permit an eye to peer out. As I was recognized the door was flung wide and I hastily explained the deal to my old friend Maurice. He agreed readily to my request that he not mention having seen us, for he and the Maquis were at slight odds; they demanding that he join their outlaw crew and he refusing, preferring to work his farm, feed his family, and to accomplish his good patriotic deeds quietly and anonymously.

Time was a-wastin'. Here I'd been a month in Occupied France and I was now within ten paces of where I'd bit the dust. I'd had a peachy time, though, and was slightly reinforced now. Reasoning that the Maquis would likely come to Tricqueville in an effort to track us down, I declined Maurice's offer of breakfast and just took what information he could offer as to the whereabouts of local Jerry troop detachments. Helene gave us bread and cider and two cigarettes to add to our provisions, and she ran out into the rain to greet Lou and Brian and Freddie. We walked away and I turned to wave and she called out, "Bonne chance, Tayo, bonne chance!" Well, good luck to Helene and Maurice, too. They were fine people and didn't deserve the break they got when Tricqueville was liberated, months later: their baby was killed by an artillery shell when the Marais farm became a battlefield.

In a couple of hours we holed in out of the rain in a tumbledown shanty atop a high hill, and we made breakfast: raw steak, bread and butter washed down with cider, a mighty gulp of Calvados, and a cigarette. We wrung out our clothes, catnapped for an hour, passed the jug, and headed west again with the rain stinging our faces and our spirits zoomed to a new high. Our first objective was the Pont l'Évêque area, some forty or fifty kilometers away as the crow flies. And we walked without a break for many a wet kilometer.

Four or five hours later, tired and hungry again, walking in pairs and now not even bothering to navigate around the deepest mud puddles, we trudged along a rut road. Passing a well-kept farm, we sneaked off the road and ducked into one of the outbuildings for to have a dry cigarette and a little rest. The boys sprawled out on the dusty floor and I sat in the saddle of a Model B John Deere tractor, and we smoked and listened to the rain and talked quietly. Then a middle-aged farmer walked past our open shed, glanced at us, and went on into a stable.

On his return trip he cast a baleful look at us, so I spoke to him: "Mauvais temps, oui?"—lousy weather, eh? I thought he might fulfill his part of the old saw and reply that, "Oui, it was good for ducks," but he just grunted something to correspond with "yup" and went about his chores. I remarked to the boys that I could stand a square meal, and that I'd fix it up for the lot of us, providing they were willing to take a slight chance. They being entirely agreeable, I trailed the old boy into a little shed where I found him patching a harness that needed no patching. Silently I watched him tinker for a spell. I rolled a smoke and tossed the makings onto the bench beneath his nose, and he built a smoke, took a light from my Zippo, and said, "Merci . . ." I uncorked my silver flask and he took a swig and I took a swig and we were still casing each other. I asked him if he was the patron of this fine farm and he admitted the fact—cocking an eyebrow at my fantastic mistreatment of his language. Now tiring of the fencing match, I dug out my handkerchief and, unfolding it, showed the farmer my wings and insignia and dog tag, and confessed that we were two American and two English aviators. And the farmer smiled and shook hands, and when I said that we were thirsty and maybe had a little hunger, he told me to round up my comrades and to follow him to the house.

In triumph we traipsed across the farmyard and into the house, but as I closed the door I checked back across the yard to make an uneasy mental note of a young feller who was now leaving the farm, and he was leaving at a dead run. My instinctive urge to take off was, however, smothered by the sight and smell of kettles simmering on a redly glowing cookstove; and when the farmer introduced us to his wife and to the hired gal, the sight of the latter made us remember our manners, for she was slim and dark and she tendered each of us a charming smile. As the girl began carrying chairs from the parlor to the kitchen, Brian bowed and exclaimed, "Permettez moi, cherie," and he took the chair from her, being rewarded with a demure flopping of curly eyelashes. Lou, snatching the chair from Brian, grinned wofishly at the poor girl and cried, "Permettez-MOI, mamselle!"—and he murmured an aside to Brian: "She ain't yer type, leftenant."

Well, we'd struck it rich, for it so happened that we were just in time for supper. All told, eight people sat to the table, and we four hungry derelicts, not wanting to gobble our friends' entire meal from under their noses, helped ourselves politely to small portions of meat and potatoes. But the Frenchmen refused to take anything at all for themselves, insisting that we eat our fill; and—it not being required that our arms be twisted twice—we cleaned house. When the platters were clean as an old hound's tooth, our courteous host hauled out a carafe of fiery booze and poured us each a goodly jolt. We'd eaten so damned much that I thought I'd risk offending the farmer by offering payment, but he just smiled and refused. Brian slipped a hundred francs into the sugar bowl when nobody was looking.

"Monsieur," I queried, "the English, do they advance?"

The farmer smiled, walked to a kitchen cabinet, and slid out a little drawer. There in a nest of batteries lay a tiny radio and when the farmer flicked a switch, a voice boomed into the room. "London calling! La Voix de la Liberation!" I was flabbergasted. And we followed the news commentary, checking the latest Invasion news against our map: and we soon realized that as far as we were concerned, the situation was that of D-Day.

I smelled a rat. The deal at this farm was too good. We walk a night and a day. We are cold, wet, and damned hungry, so we drop in and panhandle a meal. We eat well, drink well, and tune in on BBC for the suppertime news. In Occupied France, there were heavy penalties for unauthorized operation of radio equipment, and this farmer's radio had not been skillfully concealed. Could it be that these people had been permitted to retain their radio in return for services rendered? How the hell was I to know? And I'd seen the young citizen dash from the farmyard when we'd entered the house. Four allied airmen were worth 30,000 francs per head to the collaborator who betrayed them to the Nazis—a tidy sum for any greedy Frenchman.

These were vague suspicions, but they added up to enough to make me wish I were elsewhere, so I told the farmer we had a long road to travel. His insistence that we stay with him, at least until it would stop raining, only crystallized my uneasiness into action, and I gave the boys the word. With hasty thanks, we retreated into the rain to scamper southward along a gravel road. A few minutes later, as we were about to strike out into the brush for fear that someone might have already contacted the Jerries, Freddy let out a startled whoop: "Blimey! They're after us!" And so they were.

Quite a caravan was dead astern and closing in fast. Hot on our tail were two one-hoss shays, each loaded with citizens and bristling with gun barrels. Four or five cyclists pedaled furiously behind the trotting horses, and to bring up the rear of this strange procession were a half-dozen characters running along afoot. Lou looked at me and I looked at Lou, and we groaned. It could be only another Maquis outfit. Holding a hasty council, we voted unanimously to resist being recruited by this oncoming horde.

Soon we stood with our backs to a log fence, surrounded by a villainous mob of young Frenchmen—each complete with beret, pant-legs tucked into rubber boots, turtleneck sweater, and waistband—into which was stuffed a knife or pistol or both. A few Mausers were brandished gaily beneath our noses and I groaned again and rolled a smoke. Lou's expression of desperation had returned. Brian stood cleaning his fingernails, while Freddy had his own chomped halfway up to his elbows. We waited.

A fugitive from a hayseed-circuit Shakespearean road-show jumped from a carriage and came toward us. His long grey hair was swept back, puffed out over his ears, and curling at the nape of his neck. Piercing eyes were framed by two pendulous pouches below, and above by bushy eyebrows that joined over the bridge of a classic hooked nose—from each nostril of which there sprouted a little tuft of fur. To complete the picture, this type wore a tan trench coat, ascot scarf, and no hat, and he carried a knotty walking stick. Lou, with his penchant for hanging appropriate handles on characters, grinned at me and muttercd, "The Great Profile!"

Profile looked down his nose at us. By way of greeting, I spoke up: "Howdy, neighbor!"

"Who are you?" he demanded in good English.

"Who are you?" I countered in good French.

"Keep your hands where we can see them," Profile suggested, adding that he was chief of the local Resistance group. "The farmer who fed you says that you are two English and two American aviators. Prove that to me."

He inspected our dog tags and interrogated us carefully, and I answered his tricky questions evasively, naming no names or people or places, but always in generalities. And at last Profile told Lou that he was satisfied that he was an American, but he was equally sure that I was not. When I asked him why the hell he took that attitude, he said that while Lou spoke like an American, I didn't. Forced now into an impromptu discussion of accents as found in various parts of the States, I explained that Lou spoke the peculiar low patois common to the tribes of clam-diggers found on the eastern shores of Continental USA. My dissertation started Lou off on a series of return compliments, and pretty soon the whole Maquis was gathered around us, smiling and making jokes. So with the aid of a little machine we'd borrowed from Pierre, we bummed some tobacco and rolled enough cigarettes to go around.

The kid who'd run from the farmyard was in the group and Profile told me that the farmer had given the kid the word, the kid had steamed over to Maquis headquarters to sound the alarm, and the gang had converged on the farm. The farmer had shouted, "They went thataway," and then we were in the net. My uneasiness had been legitimate, for the farmer could easily have been the wrong variety of Frenchman, in which case these people who now surrounded us would have been Jerries rather than Maquisards.

Profile was laboring under the illusion that we would be happy to join his Maquis, but I put him straight. I said we'd go with his outfit only if he would promise to help us travel westward; and surprisingly enough, he took me up on the deal. "Gentlemen," he said immediately, "I am delighted to help you. You leave tonight by auto, which will take you to the other side of Pont l'Évêque."

Well hot damn! Maybe thirty kilometers, and traveling first class! That trip would take us past a very difficult and dangerous stage of our route, for Pont l'Évêque was more or less of a front-line replacement depot, and the area swarmed with Jerry units of every type.

So we joined the Maquis again and, trudging back toward the little farm, I had a chat with Profile. A landowner before the war, he'd been educated in England and once had traveled to America. He apologized for having questioned us so severely, explaining that in the Pont l'Évêque area were known to be a number of Gestapo agents disguised as fugitive allied airmen. Profile added sadly, "A pity, but today one must be suspicious of everyone in France." I agreed.

Lodged now in the dry hayloft of the friendly farmer's barn, we were told to stay there until dark. The farmer brought a litre of champagne and Profile tweaked and twisted the cork until it flew to the rafters. "Vive la France!" Clink!

Before leaving us, Profile asked if there was something more we desired. I pulled my head out of the loft window and spoke up: "Why, sure . . . but she's sweepin' the kitchen right now!" Brian said, with a wistful sigh, "Ah, for a cup of tea . . ."

Profile strode away, hands plunged deep into pockets, hair flowing grandly in the rainy breeze. The charming demoiselle of the farmhouse soon appeared in the loft with a snack of eggs and milk and a come-on smile for the four castaways. Launched with a chorus of evil whistles, there now ensued a cutthroat competition for her favors. I was just beginning to make a little time with the gal when Lou stalled me out with a word or two: "Monsieur Tayo, he has a gros wife and trois petites enfants en Amerique. Also he has one fat wife and infant deserted in England. That is why he parachuted into France." And my good friend Brian added his two francs: "Oui, c'est vrai"—Lou had spoken the truth. My stock plummeted to an all-time low, and I was finished in that league. But as Lou began to make a little headway, Brian whispered in the young chick's ear for a moment, whereupon she blushed, pounced upon him to deliver one resounding smack, then dashed from the barn. Pausing on the doorstep of the house, she blew a kiss to the three raffish faces which peered and leered from the loft door, and she called out: "Au revoir Brian!" Lou and I were baffled. Brian, however, explained it all to us: "Some blokes got it and some ain't. You ain't."

We dozed fitfully and I awoke to hear Lou mumbling in his sleep. As Brian and I stared at him in amusement, Lou cried out plaintively, "J'ai froid! J'ai froid!" I kicked him hard on his leg and awakened him to remark that he'd sure as hell made the turn when he came to the point of talking

French in his sleep. Brian added that cold or not, there was very little excuse for that sort of thing.

Long before dark, Profile returned with the news that our auto was ready and waiting: and he smiled at Brian, unwrapped a parcel, and handed the English pilot a thermos of hot tea—gesture of rare charm and courtesy, that. "Simply wizard of you, ol' boy!" cried Brian, and as he sipped my friend was back in England for the moment.

In all haste, Profile led out across-country. The rain had stopped, but the sky was bleak and a chilly wind whistled through my soggy clothes. We trudged past a flea-bitten old sheepherder who sat with his sheep alongside his gypsy wagon. When the bewhiskered galoot waved and shouted a cheery, "Bonjour!" Profile chuckled. Our disguises, he said, were admirable but almost too perfect—for we looked exactly like Parisian blackmarketeers.

At a tiny crossroads settlement where a few pretty little houses nestled amidst the hedges and orchards, a dozen happy Maquisards lounged around a tiny black sedan that stood dejectedly at the edge of a tar highway. Profile introduced his four airmen to three young Frenchmen, then he shook our hands and bade us adieu. Where our chauffeurs were taking us, I sure as hell didn't know, but I thought it should be an interesting trip.

So Brian and Lou and Fred and I crawled into the rear cockpit of this diminutive machine, and the seat was so narrow that we were wedged together in an awkward huddle. The door was slammed and a bicycle lashed across the roof of the auto, to be securely fastened in place by wires which were strung down and twisted about the rear door handles. Taking stock of our position, I got that old, creeping, trapped feeling again. The three Maquisards squeezed into the front seat and one of them leaned back to hand me a .38 Smith & Wesson revolver. I looked down the cylinder and saw that it was loaded.

The starter ground dismally and failed, so a bunch of the boys put their shoulders to the car, gave a mighty shove, and we were off to the races. We sped at full throttle along that narrow road, and the poor bald tires shrieked for mercy at each and every curve. The way was slippery and winding, and the brainless jerk at the controls could not drive worth one good goddam. His attitude toward shifting gears was that of the old sledgehammer mechanic: "If it won't fit, jam it!"

Wanting very much to hit the silk and start walking, I consoled myself with mental notes of the kilometers being clocked off. To have walked this route would have absorbed much time and effort. I crouched on Freddy's lap and focused my eyes on the speedometer.

We somehow accomplished a 90-degree port turn with no appreciable loss of airspeed, and now before us loomed a short, steep hill—a narrow cut with a high, vertical bank on either side. Our bold pilot, neglecting the simple procedure of shifting gears, allowed our speed to slacken and finally to peter out altogether. The engine stalled and we rolled backwards a bit before he jammed on the brakes. Despite several agonized growls from the starter, the engine failed to respond. I felt badly.

I felt one hell of a lot worse when there appeared a German armored car, which rolled ominously over the crest of the hill above us and pulled to a halt dead ahead and some ten feet from the nose of our little black sedan. Alongside the driver of the patrol car there stood a slim and capable-looking German officer who cradled in his arms one of those efficient little Schmeiser machine pistols. My poor tired heart soared upwards and wedged crossways in my throat and I sneaked a glance at my comrades. They looked quite like Death warmed over. Nobody appeared to be breathing. I eased a hand to the door handle and checked the freedom of movement of the door, but because of that worthless bicycle overhead we were trapped. So I cocked the .38.

A guttural shout from the armored car and two of the Maquis climbed from the front cockpit and walked right up into the muzzle of the Jerry's burp-gun. For five hopeless minutes a waving of hands . . . a flurry of talk . . . a righteous flashing of official-looking papers. The Frenchmen returned, climbed into the car, and I heard the sinister, metallic, double-click of a revolver being cocked. Now the patrol car rolled slowly forward and eased to a halt alongside the side windows of the sedan. Brian and I stared blankly up into the expressionless faces of the Jerries, then fumbled in our jacket pockets as though reaching for our papers, which nobody but Lou had (and his were queer as an eight-dollar bill). So we fumbled and stalled and sweat and the armored car paused for an indecisive moment, then rolled on down the hill and around the bend, out of sight. My heart flopped out of my throat and began to throb like a cockeyed tom-tom.

Our luck was unbelievable. Again breathing, I discovered that I was soaked with unearned sweat. Then the starter whirred and the engine caught and we taxied on up and over the hill and careened down the black-top—fat, dumb, and happy. One of the Maquis lads looked back at us and laughed, but in his laugh I could detect a faint note of hysteria. I was sore at the Frenchmen for taking such a long chance, mad at myself for having been sucked into such a deal, and completely grateful to the Jerries for being such a gullible lot of bastards.

Between the hare-brained job of driving and the run-in with the Wehrmacht, I was ready to jettison the rear door and head for the brush. We buzzed past a pair of miserable sentries who stood guard at a rail crossing, and after a few minutes of fast driving we whipped off down along a muddy side road. The damned auto got to bucking in and out of the ruts and shortly we spun in. The nose of the car was dug well into the embankment and I wasn't even surprised, for I'd predicted the event to Lou some few moments before. As a matter of fact I was delighted, for after we'd been unwired and were again slogging about in the mud, I experienced one grand relief; for on either side was a comfortable depth of forest, dark, damp, and inviting. I was beginning to appreciate the tall timber after having been trapped in the dinky damned Maquis sedan.

Grunts and groans from all hands brought the machine back onto the road. We climbed aboard to ricochet down a long and slippery hill, at the bottom of which our able pilot hung the auto up on a boulder. So we piled out and started walking, and night had fallen: night as black as pitch. Brian and Lou and I fell back a little and killed off the remains of our Calvados. In a half hour we came upon an isolated house at the edge of a wood.

A merry sliver of firelight escaped from the doorway. A dozen glowing cigarettes bobbed about in the yard, and amidst murmuring low talk was to be heard the occasional faint clink of tin cup against bottle neck.

Our three reckless chauffeurs led us into the kitchen of the house and announced to the crowd: "Quatre aviateurs!" A French-type stepped up and introduced himself as Charlie Blackwell, B-17 pilot. Another phony shook my hand and said that he was Major Stanley Lopka of the Royal Polish Air Corps. A third said his name was Billy: very young and slender, dark and smiling and Irish was Billy. And over a litre of rotgut applejack we swapped lies.

Charlie didn't have to tell me that he was a bomber jockey: heavy-set, slow-moving, deliberate, and placid he was. (And who the hell ever saw a fighter pilot flying in combat wearing officer's pinks?) When Charlie put on his plaid cap and lit up his Meerchaum pipe, he looked to be a butcher boy from anybody's French village. He seemed to be perfectly content with his lot in life, too. Young Billy was of the same mind, explaining that he'd been down in France for a year now, and wasn't at all inclined to leave. He'd been gunner on an obsolete old Wellington bomber that had blundered from its Channel patrol run to within range of a Jerry coastal flak battery.

The only live one of the trio was the stocky little Pole, Lopka; and we automatically liked one another when we found out we'd both been flying Mustangs. Stan had been Squadron Leader of his RAF Polish fighter outfit, and he loved that little Mustang as much as I did. In the course of our reminiscing, Lopka remarked that he'd lost track of his aerial victories after the first dozen or so. These Polish fighter pilots were famous for their lack of brains: once strapped into the cockpit, they lived only for revenge. Lopka, with equal fluency, spoke Polish, English, French, and German, and I figured him to be a dandy addition to my expedition.

Dog-tired, we were escorted to a barn full of hay where I sat and pondered the interesting day. Amazingly, it had been just twenty-four hours since we'd tiptoed through the doorway of César's chateau, and since that happy moment we'd had quite an outing: seventeen hours of sightseeing afoot, plus one inspiring auto ride. And now our assortment of dismounted aviators was increased to seven, a lot of talent going to seed: two fighter pilots, two bomber pilots, two gunners, and a bombardier-navigator. All we lacked was an aircraft. What the hell. I tunneled under a half-ton of soft hay and slept.

Came the dawn and we breakfasted in a beat-up old shack at one end of a cherry orchard. An old woman and a wee little boy lived there, and the Maquis gave them food in return for her services as cook. A cranky old crone she was, but when I slipped her a smile and a bit of tobacco on the sly, she henceforth fed me well. For the rest of the crew it was a monotonous diet of bread and milk, but for me it was bread and cream.

This Resistance group was less well organized than that of César, and I didn't go out of my way to be particularly chummy with any of the bunch. Their chief was a reckless sort of chap, always with a Luger in his belt and always dressed for the woods in flannel shirt, riding pants, boots, and a flat-crowned cowboy hat. When he told me that two of his men had penetrated the German lines and that one had returned intact, I rounded up this gent, Pierre by name, and tried to pump him as to his route and methods, but learned damned little. For Pierre was a cagey, reticent type: but Lopka, however, told me that Pierre was in good standing with the Jerries, and that by posing as a collaborator was able to travel freely among the enemy. As a fact, said Lopka, the shifty Pierre was now under a shadow of suspicion of being a true collaborator.

For a couple of days we lay around the barn awaiting the scheduled westward migration of this Maquis outfit—and a pleasant enough life it was. In our happy home there hung guns from spikes originally driven to carry harness and hay-rope and such prosaic equipment. A little auto stood patiently in one box stall, and in another there stomped about a thin heifer and her calf. Now and then the old cow would nuzzle the dozen grenades that rested handily in her feed box. We tossed countless darts in games played to the tune of an endless string of flying stories, each of which began with the old refrain: "So thar I wuz at thirty-thousand feet, on fire, flat on me back, with nuthin' on the clock but the maker's name!" And good comrade Brian kept us chuckling with his hundred bawdy RAF songs, sung in a manner most droll and made all the more comical for Brian's Oxford accents.

I ran across a stack of dime novels, complete with flashy covers portraying unattired queens in quantity and leering gangsters clutching daggers rich with gore. So to while away the idle hours, and eager as always to better my knowledge of the complicated language I'd been forced to adopt, I picked up one magazine and began the first story, casually. I immediately plunged with zest into a painstaking translation of these works. A very choice item, that first story; it would scarcely have made the grade in Boston. For it concerned itself with the vicissitudes of a pure little virgin gal from the country who journeyed to Gay Paree with the honest intent of paying a social call upon her ailing grandmére. But as she leaves the train station she is rounded up by a low-type cabby who lures her into a local cellar bistro, plies her with absinthe, slips her a Mickey, and carries on from there. Within the first five pages of the story, the poor kid has been relieved of her small change and various other items. When she comes out of her hop-dream, she decides that it hasn't been so bad after all, and she skips with gay abandon into a Life of Sin. Several chapters later, and now more than slightly deflowered, she is working the main drag when who should accost her but her sporty old grandpére. A heart-rending scene ensues, and in a childish fit of remorse, she plunges a stilletto into her monstrous bosom and expires, right in the old gutter. The obvious moral to the story being: to hell with one's ailing kin-folk, and if visit you must, best one keeps crossed the legs.

We weren't far from the Jerries here, for after sundown and then all night long there would come to our ears the constant clatter and jingle of wagon trains moving along the nearby gravel roads. The second night, Lou and I walked a quarter mile and watched from a thicket, and it was plain to see that the Jerries were running out of gasoline thanks to our strafing fighters. Many motor trucks and all gun carriages and wagons were strictly mule-powered, and the skinners hollered and swore and whacked their steeds from dusk until dawn, and Lou and I sat in our bush and savored the misery of the dust-caked enemy troopers.

During that second evening at the Maquis' barn, there occurred a little affair that broke the monotony. For the chief brought to the barn a swarthy little rat of a guy whose arms were bound at his back. An Algerian and a Nazi spy, he'd been sent out to infiltrate the local Resistance setup and he'd been caught. Papers had been discovered, of all places, concealed in his jointed bamboo walking stick, and now the chief turned him over to the boys for disposal. The spy was silent, miserable, and resigned as a couple of the lads led him away in the darkness. The trio disappeared into a nearby gully, and after two quick shots the Frenchmen returned—one blowing smoke from his pistol barrel—to report that the prisoner had run for it, but had been struck in the back of his head by two bullets at twenty paces. I thought that to be remarkable shooting, considering the total darkness.

On the afternoon of the third day, the Maquisards set about packing their gear, while we—having no kit to pack—waited impatiently. Pretty soon the whole crew straggled off across an open meadow, then plied along a tree-lined lane, and we walked westward for four or five kilometers. Bicycle-mounted scouts ranged dramatically out ahead of our sloppy column, casing the crossroads and waving frantically for us to come ahead when all was clear. After three or four hours of taking wrong turns and wandering in aimless circles, we stumbled into an abandoned farmhouse: a musty, fallen-down old shack shielded from the road by a snarl of vines and scraggly trees.

Our leader indicated that we were all to sleep in the attic of the house, but I took one gander at the layout and declined the invitation, for the sole entrance into the attic was a tiny trapdoor reached by a rickety ladder. In my mind's eye I had a big picture of ten Maquisards and seven fidgety fugitive aviators all racked up in that little firetrap at night with a squad of Hitler's Finest standing in the room below shooting blanks up toward the ceiling. I picked up my blanket and scouted out a stable that backed against a fence and a hedge, found a stall with a rear exit, tore a sizeable hole in the hedge for use as an emergency runway, and there I settled down for the night. Lou and Brian and Freddy and Stan joined me, and we huddled together for warmth.

As I dozed, Lou let out a sudden yelp. In rapid succession, Brian, Stanley, and Freddy gave a startled yell, and I joined in with a yip as the sharp little dig of tiny claws pattered across my throat followed immediately by a snaky, dragging tail. It appeared that a large and nonchalant rat had taxied over us for a novel evening stroll.

The urge for sleep having dwindled, we sat around on the grass and watched the graceful play of distant searchlights and the sparkle of countless tiny pinpoint bursts of flak up over the front lines. It was a dandy summer's night with the starry skies alternately clear and partly obscured by fast-drifting low clouds, and the moon was about half. And then the wow-wow-wow-wow of unsynchronized aircraft engines approached our area and we caught a glimpse of several low-flying Junkers 88s.

Immediately a strange sound—such as an enormous, unmuffled motorcycle engine might make—came to our ears, and abreast of the nearest Jerry bomber and perhaps a quarter-mile away from it we saw a fast-moving little aircraft that marked its course by the streak of flame behind it. And this was my introduction to that clever weapon, the Buzz-Bomb, which was named by the French "Avion sans pilote." Now a whole flock of these ingenious demons roared overhead en route to our front lines. One went haywire, described a couple of tight circles above our interested heads, and then headed back toward the Third Reich, where we hoped it might do some good upon landing.

Some of these infernal machines, possibly being radio-controlled, were paced by Ju 88s while others flew on alone; and when they would plunge into a patch of cloud we could follow their flight by the unearthly glob of flame that sped through the mists. Soon from the beachhead there came the faint feel and rumble of mighty explosions, and it occurred to us that it might tend to be a bit unhealthy for one to be in proximity to such commotion.

On this rundown old farm, somewhere between Pont l'Évêque and the Channel, it so happened that our cook was a tired old Jerry soldier. Captured by the Maquis, he'd been put to work doing all the chores. He washed clothes, swept floors, chopped wood, absorbed insults; and pitifully eager to please, he spent his idle hours perched atop one or the other of several cherry trees where he would shake the branches and collect great sacks of cherries for his hungry captors. The old bum, seemingly glad to be out of the fight, was very polite to us all, and he turned out a fine breakfast of beef and spuds and wine.

Two more ex-Wehrmacht soldiers now joined our international brigade. These young deserters, being Polish, were questioned by Lopka, and their sad cry was that they'd been impressed against their will into the German army. They'd both fought against the British at Caen since D-Day, but their true enemy, so they said, had been the Boches. During every skirmish they'd emptied their Mausers into the backs of the forward German troopers. Prisoners at Caen—being a drug on the market—were executed by the Jerries, and these two Poles had been assigned to guard a group of twenty Canadian prisoners who'd been earmarked for slaughter. During the night the two Poles had liberated their prisoners and deserted, walking eastward until taken by the Maquis. Having proven their good intentions, the Poles had been issued FFI brassards and weapons, and they now were industriously harassing their former employers.

I had a snootful of this outfit. I spent an afternoon mending my clothes, greasing my shoes, and trading with the natives. Swiping a bit of tobacco from one of the Maquisards, I traded it off to another for a pair of woolen sox. After swapping my tattered old suitcoat plus a scarf to the young Irishman for his good black suitcoat, I set about talking comrade Brian right out of his best pants. These pants twenty years ago had been excellent grey pinstripe flannels, but now they had an oval patch of a royal-blue material sewn into the seat. To Brian, with his poise and polished manners, this exaggerated horseshoe effect lent a completely ridiculous aspect. This fact I pointed out to him, laughing uncontrollably all the while, and he finally accepted my faded blue jeans as a fair exchange for regaining his tottering dignity.

Lou slyly requisitioned a litre of Calvados from the kitchen, and our original foursome plus Lopka retired to a meadow behind our stable where we spent the remainder of the evening making jokes and wiping tears from our eyes after each swig from the jug. Retiring merrily to our mud-floored box-stall bedroom, our combined exhalations built up an atmosphere so charged with double-distilled fumes that a careless spark would have blasted our stable halfway to England. And to disturb us this night, a promenading rat would be forced to pause and jump up and down on each of our faces.

Bright and early in the morn I was dumfounded to behold the men of the Maquis gathered around buckets shaving, washing their necks and wrists, and engaged in other such unprecedented tasks. This was a veritable revolution, and upon inquiry I learned that this was Bastille Day, the fourteenth of July—some thirty-seven days since I'd pulled the old ripcord and five days out from le Maquis Cesar.

The chief informed us that in honor of the holiday—which in France matches the fourth of July in the States—Monsieur le Grand Chef, the big wheel of the FFI, was coming up from Paris to make a tour of inspection of the Maquis units along the Channel Coast. He was due in here soon, and then there would be one big party.

So Lou and I borrowed a razor, soap, and towel and retired to the prendre l'eau where we "took a little water" and went to work. A quarter hour later, feeling decidedly unnatural, I tapped Lou on the shoulder: "Monsieur Fahrenwald, from Sheeca-go!" Lou shook my soapy hand and grinned: "M' name's Lynch, from Joisey City!" It was about eleven in the morning when our outposts began to shout wildly and bow low, and then a one-horse carriage clip-clopped into the farmyard and out leaped René, the hot-rock from Paris! Our chief saluted clumsily and shouted, "Attention!" and the Maquisards and airmen formed a ragged reception line where they lounged while René made a little speech and then came down to shake hands with each aviator. Now crowding into the tiny kitchen and hollering for glasses and bottles, we worked the old Jerry cook to a lather. A toast to la belle

France with a bit of anisette. America was vive'd with a jolt of Calvados, and another took care of England, and then it was a free-for-all bout with champagne corks hurtling about like so many bullets.

Lou and I were wedged into a corner and he finally shouted, "Awright! Bring on the goddam chow!" but our hosts took no offense since they savvied only French. In a while were brought out great slabs of roast beef and a huge kettle of French fries, loaves of black bread, pots of jam, and gallons of vin rouge. Knowing this to be our last square meal for an unknown time to come, Lou and I gorged ourselves shamelessly, making off with twice our share whenever a platter came our way; and when a jug of fine old cognac came within range I surreptitiously refueled my silver flask. After the banquet, René passed around a box of the finest German cigars obtainable. I cut mine in halves and retired to the shade beneath a cherry tree where I smoked with maximum enjoyment. And then I cornered the Maquis chief from Paris, introduced myself, and struck up a little chat.

René was wiry, alert, slim, and handsome with crisp black hair and snapping blue eyes, and when I said I'd been a fighter pilot he smiled happily and dug out his wallet to show me a bunch of snapshots. He'd flown fighters for the French Air Army up to the fall of France, he said, and he handed me each photo with loving care: René, clad in tunic, shiny boots, and silk scarf, posed in front of his ship; René smiling in the cockpit of his Morane fighter; René standing with an arm wrapped around the propeller (as all good throttle-jockeys have their pictures made at least once). He showed me a snapshot of a special hot job he'd flown in the National Air Races before the war: a tiny, low-winged ship with fixed gear and two-bladed prop, and René claimed it had attained a speed of around 250 with but 250 horses in the nose, and I said that that had been remarkable for those days. René and I were now buddy-buddy. And building the quick friendship to a climax, I told him of the performance of the American P-47 and P-51s, and he grinned his disbelief that I'd flown a single-engine fighter with deux-milles cheveaux in the nose. When I added that those 2,000 horses would haul the ship along at a rate of some six- or seven-hundred kilometers per hour, I could see the old stick-and-rudder itch building up in him.

When I figured René to be ripe, I sprung my plan on him, and he was the first and only Frenchman who didn't just shrug and mutter that I was crazy. His eyes lit up and he rubbed his hands together and said that my projected tour of the front might be a bit difficult, but that it'd sure as hell be fun to try. So on the grass behind a thicket we spread out our charts and plotted a course to the town of Dozulé, which lay some thirty or forty kilometers to the west. From Dozulé to Caen was but a dozen kilometers farther down the line. A main concrete highway ran east and west from Pont l'Évêque through Dozulé and on to Caen, and we would walk from the Maquis hideout southward, backtracking around Pont l'Évêque to a point south of that city. Then changing course, we'd parallel the highway into Dozulé, and upon arrival there would contact a certain "Monsieur Ash." This mysterious M. Ash would attend to the details of the remainder of our expedition. René wrote out detailed instructions and burned them when I nodded my understanding. Then he called over the Maquis leader and ordered him to furnish Lou and me with a guide to escort us around the danger zones of Pont l'Évêque.

So I'd at last found a Frenchman who thought my way, and it had taken a brother peashooter-pilot to give me the lucky break. I bounced to and fro like a wounded coon, then scuttled around the camp giving the boys the good word, and my high glee had soon infected them with the eager spirit of the thing.

I hated to say so-long to Brian and Freddy, but to my way of thinking a quartet is about three too many on an operation such as mine. I wanted a lot of maneuverability. Lou and I were going to stick together and take off right now. The others could trail along in pairs at two-hour intervals: Brian and Freddy, then Lopka and the B-17 driver. And those of us who made it through intact would rendezvous at noon of the first of August in the bar of the Regent Palace Hotel in London for a grande fête to end all grande fêtes!

I slipped into the kitchen and refueled my silver flask with the chief's best cognac, then tucked a half litre of high-octane Calvados into my jeans. I filled a pocket with lump sugar and I was ready as I'd ever be, traveling light and feeling merry.

Lou, grinning foolishly, was wandering in circles around the cherry tree, his thumbs hooked around his suspenders. I shook hands again with Brian: I'd miss that suave and dapper flyboy and his droll songs.

The guide donated by the Maquis leader was a pimply-faced young punk equipped with thick spectacles and an undershot jaw. I didn't like his looks, but figured that the chief wouldn't have slipped us a ringer. So Lou called to the boys, "See you guys in Picadilly!" and then he scowled at our guide and issued the fateful command: "Getcher ass in gear, Four-Eyes!" It was Dozulé or bust, and I was happy.

Four-Eyes led out under a fence and across a meadow, and for an hour we trekked single file through a maze of old barbed-wire entanglements and hedges. Then over, under, or through a series of fences until we pulled into a little old farmhouse wherein Four-Eyes' ancient kinfolk eked out their lives. After a cigarette and a gulp of cider, the kid sent the old duffer out to reconnoiter a main highway nearby, and we followed along a hundred paces to the rear.

The old man looked up and down the road, reversed his course, waved us an all-clear, and returned to his hut. So we immediately stepped out onto the highway. Upon observing the scenery there, had my first thoughts taken effect a mighty bolt of lightning would have roared out of the heavens and struck that old bastard right between the eyes—for in the screen of trees along the road were parked a couple of Jerry trucks and an armored car. Some twenty paces off my port wingtip were a dozen soldiers of a German communications crew, all busily laying telephone wire. But we couldn't stop and watch.

We trudged numbly across the highway and continued down the opposite lane, and just as we lost sight of the Jerries there sounded a grumble of gears as the armored car started forward. I gave a hasty hop or two and took a header into a thicket, arriving there a fractional second ahead of Lou. But the armored car rolled past and Lou and I and Four-Eyes resumed the march.

Four-Eyes was nervous as a whore in church. He led us down a narrow wagon road that had a wall of hedge on either side. After ten minutes the hedges petered out, and we stood at the edge of a broad prairie.

The nearest soldiers were some twenty feet from us. Several hundred other members of Hitler's vaunted war machine lay sprawled out on the turf playing mumblety-peg or feeding their faces, or smoking and shooting the breeze as soldiers are wont to do.

Unobserved as yet, we retreated a few yards—out of sight but not out of hearing of this Jerry army. Four-Eyes had turned so chalky white that his pimples looked like red thumb-tacks stuck all over his face. The jughead had led us into the geometric center of a German bivouac. Having turned white, he now turned yellow. A wagon turned off the road and headed down our narrow lane, cutting off retreat, and our faithful guide whispered shakily, "We are encircled! I return to the Maquis!" And with that he scampered away, leaving Lou and Tayo with a firm grip on the well-known bag.

We crept beneath a bramble bush, and the oncoming wagon—now followed by another—clattered past so close that had I stuck out a foot I'd have been trampled. I struck a cautious light to a butt and we shared a smoke, inhaling deeply, then blowing the smoke carefully into the grass roots. With one angry whisper, Lou settled the matter of Four-Eyes' ancestry: "That dirty bastard's mother and father were brother and sister . . ."

So we hunched under the brambles like a couple of goddam gnomes and we finished our cigarette. Whispered Lou bitterly, "So we sit here with our thumbs up until the goddam war is fini?"

Well, we were automatically spies in the eyes of Jerry. It boiled down to a case of our being hauled ignominiously out of a lousy bush and getting shot, or running a bluff and maybe getting away with it: so I shrugged. "Observe the turtle, Lou," I suggested. "He progresses only when his neck is out."

Lou grinned and spread his hands. We crawled silently through the base of our thicket, rolled out onto the edge of the meadow, counted to three and stood up.

Chapter 5

BEAUCOUP, BEAUCOUP BOCHES

◈

So picking our weary way through clusters of German infantrymen, we strolled through the very center of the hostile encampment . . . looking nonchalant, perhaps, but feeling like two fat goldfish in a big bowl with two hundred starving tomcats dabbling their paws at us. For long, long minutes the nasty guttural of the Jerries' jabbering filled our ears. Attaining the far side of the bivouac area, we crawled deliberately under a wire fence to fade then behind a row of trees: whereupon Lou flashed me a reckless smile and laughed, "Heh-heh!"

And we strode away smugly, to blunder immediately into a red and white sentry box that was placed before a small ammunition dump. The sentry, fortunately, was facing in the other direction, so we beat a hasty retreat and began a wide detour, making every effort to keep much shrubbery between ourselves and the sentry. But as we set about to accomplish this maneuver, a monstrous prime-mover truck came howling across the field we had picked to cross. It was, however, lurching violently in and out of the rutted road, and the burly Boche at the controls was much too busy hanging onto the steering wheel to give us much more than a cursory glance.

If the past half-hour's experiences were to be the criterion of our front line expedition, thought I, our trip should prove to be anything but dull. First the crossroad incident, then the bivouac, then the sentry box, and now a Jerry bastard had liked to've run us down with a twenty-ton truck. And now, spurred by a natural reaction to all this, we took out across country with me ahead at times and with Lou now and then in the lead, depending upon our individual bursts of speed. Then I took my compass in hand and held a course of 180 degrees due south.

The trail to Dozulé would be along two sides of a right triangle. The first leg would be straight south for some twenty kilometers to a point beyond a pattern of parallel landmarks consisting of a highway, a railroad, a stream, another highway, and a range of hills that lay beyond. Over the mountain we would find a creek flowing westward, and that would put us on the beam for Dozulé.

The birds were singing and so were we. Fair-weather clouds sailed through a sky of royal blue and, despite the fact that England lay to the north and we were hiking south, Piccadilly was getting closer with every step. Now in rugged hills and forest, only an occasional farm was patched here and there in little clearings along the slopes. In an hour we sat on a log and studied our map, trying to orient ourselves. Somewhere nearby was the railroad tunnel wherein was concealed the private train of the notorious General Rommel, according to intelligence given me by René, along with an emphatic warning to steer clear.

We trotted nimbly along a narrow sheep trail that angled along the precipitous side of a jaggedly eroded canyon, scrambling over boulders and windfalls through deep dry washes until we came then to the crest of a high hill. Some five hundred feet below on the broad valley floor lay twisting country roads and a softly beautiful patchwork of gleaming grain fields and tiny meadows, and the hedgerows drew thin black threads between each jigsaw parcel of land. A half-dozen kilometers to the southwest lay the spires and smoke haze of Pont L'Évêque, but neither Lou nor I could locate any railroad tracks, much less put our finger on the tunnel of General Rommel.

Clinging to the edge of the forest at the crest of the hill, we came to the top of a high cliff and lay on our bellies to peer over the edge. Tucked neatly into a clearing below us was a rich little farm, and to whet our thirst a creek bubbled merrily at the base of our cliff. We lost no time in sliding downward through a humid tangle of ferns. I left Lou in concealment and waded the brook to reconnoiter the farm.

Amidst a litter of sawdust and wood chips close by a shed there stood a rickety old grindstone. A small boy was laboriously turning the crank while his daddy ground an edge onto a sickle blade. Drifting over, I gave with a neighborly "B'jou!" and the man flipped me a look and continued his grinding. I rolled a smoke and offered the makings, and the man laid aside his work and sent the boy away with a pat on the back. The Frenchman built himself a cigarette with a quiet, "Merci bien," and his eyes crossed when he spotted my Zippo as I gave him a light. I knew by his ways that this bird was on the level, so I gave a whistle and Lou emerged from the brush, and as he sauntered toward us I told the farmer who we were and explained that we had a thirst: "Nous avons beaucoup soif, mon ami!" And he smiled and led us toward his barn. En route, alarmed upon spotting fresh tire tracks in the mud by the well, I spoke up in haste: "Vous avez l'auto, peut-être?"

"Non!" said the farmer. He had no auto, but the Jerries did. There were many of them around here, and several times each day would German officers drive into his yard to demand milk and butter and eggs. Just an hour ago there had been a German auto here! In the barn was a row of tremendous barrels, their spigots dripping cool cider into the dust of the floor. Taking from a peg a tin cup our friend handed it to Lou, motioned for us to help ourselves, and then left us to walk toward his house. While I kept a sharp eye on him, Lou crouched before a barrel tossing down cup after cup of cider as fast as he could draw them full. I took over and between the two of us we did a pretty fair job on the barrel. Lou now uttered a low growl: "Check this, Tayo!"

The farmer was returning pushing a wheelchair and accompanied by his daughter, who was nothing but an eyeful of undiluted sex appeal. Aboard the wheelchair was the Frenchman's father, an old poilu gassed all out of shape during the war to end wars. The poor crippled greybeard thrust out a quivering hand in greeting: "You have like my good cider, Americains?" I laughed and replied that we had consumed at least three litres apiece; whereupon the good old man chuckled with pleasure, rubbed his hands, and looked fearfully about him. Les Boches, he allowed, would execute him if they knew who now drank cider in his barn. He cackled so hard that he was seized by a fit of coughing, and the girl patted him worriedly.

"Remain here for supper!" cried the old one, "for it is not every night that I can enjoy the company of deux officers de l'Armée de l'Aire des Etats Unis." (We didn't look much like Air Corps officers!)

I looked hungrily at the slender, tender, and tall French girl who stood smiling at us and I realized that my judgment was already impaired, so I put to Lou our answer to the kind invitation. Lou—and I could have kicked his arse down the mountainside—declined with thanks, explaining that it was necessary we move on.

"Ou est le tunnel avec le train du General Rommel?" I queried, remembering my difficulties at precise navigation.

The farmer grinned and tapped his foot in the dust: "C'est là-bas!"—it's down there! I rubbed my chin and looked at Lou. We were standing on the roof of the general's private retreat, with some two hundred feet of Normandy between us and an awkward situation. And the girl added to our confusion by asking me how we'd managed to avoid the Boche patrols that constantly perused the area. I rubbed my fingernails casually across my tattered lapel and murmured, "C'est pas difficile, mamselle."

We gave the old poilu a handful of tobacco and some papers and he gave us a bottle of red wine and said au revoir. Away we trudged reluctantly, to turn and wave at intervals until we could no longer see the good people of that little hillside farm.

By the time we'd traversed the valley floor, both the sun and our morale were extremely low. Each road to cross had required careful scouting, for Jerry traffic was heavy. Following the edges of fields, we'd clung to the camouflage of the hedgerow and had cursed our way through a hundred of those snarled, interwoven, vine-and-bramble, rusty-barbed-wire bastards. I'd plow into a hedge until hopelessly entangled, rendered immobile: then using my trusty knife as a machete, I'd slash hell out of things until we could forge ahead a bit. After kicking, biting, cutting, and cussing our way across the valley, we were both crisscrossed with scratches and frazzled of clothing and temper.

But now mounting a range of hills, we tramped for an hour through a delightful forest, emerging to look down into a narrow and very, very beautiful little valley where a pair of lovely chateaux lay between two tiny villages. The sun was on the horizon and the shadows were long and chimney smoke, white against the black forest beyond, curled gently to the sky. We jumped the final ten feet off a little cliff and landed on a pile of sand that marked the mouth of a cave, and there we sat and drank our litre of wine and studied our map.

A splash through a creek and we were across the valley in a few minutes, and we headed along a footpath that paralleled the foot of the far hillside. To follow the path was a bit against our better judgment but, after the recent hysterical battle with the hedges, a level trail was too good a thing to turn down. Marked clearly in the mud along the way were innumerable prints of hobnailed boots and the fresh tracks of saddle horses; but the evening was peaceful and we were just two Frenchmen strolling a country lane at sundown. Plugging along, we talked quietly and smoked until we came without warning upon a gap in the hedge that paralleled our footpath.

A few feet away off the port wingtip, standing around a cherry tree, was a circle of young Jerry officers. Laughing and joking, they were catching cherries that a small boy was tossing to them from a precarious perch high in the branches. As the Germans faces were, like sunflowers, turned skywards, Lou and I scuttled past the opening and made haste along the trail. As we mopped our brows, wondering how long our luck might hold out, our hedge petered away altogether. On the right lay one of the villages, swarming with soldiers. On the left we were exposed to the direct gaze of a score or more Luftwaffe pilots who played about the grounds of a chateau, yelling at one another and riding fine horses and in general having a peachy time.

"Well, what d'ye know," I whispered unhappily to Lou, "we done taxied right into the middle of a Jerry flak-farm!" Lou replied, equally unhappily, that at this stage of the game he needed an airmen's rest camp one helluva lot more than did the Luftwaffe lackeys who milled about the chateau.

We couldn't retreat very gracefully or turn to the right or left so, wishing we were elsewhere, we trudged ahead, slipping back into our hillbilly routine once again. Tugging my beret to a more jaunty angle, my confidence zoomed; for that black beret was a valuable item—every time I tugged it rakishly down over one ear, I felt like a Frenchman! And we were two of them, going home after a tough day in the potato patch. No one could deny that we looked the part!

Trotting toward us came a Jerry officer mounted on a snorting bay mare. Dressed fit to kill in shiny black boots, steep-visored hat, monocle and all, he was a grim-looking type, and we stepped politely from the trail to let him pass. With the thudding of his Luger against his hip and a squeak of saddle leather he brushed past, the mare smelling rankly and her rider meeting our innocent regard with a conqueror's stony stare.

Our fateful little pathway now sloped downward to dead-end at a blacktop highway at the end of the main street of town. We were not happy, and to stall for time we slowed our walk. To the left, pacing to and fro at the entrance to the chateau, marched a sentry, Mauser slung handily over his shoulder. In the front yard of a little village house a few paces to the right of us stood a pudgy, bald-headed officer in his undershirt sloshing water noisily over his head from a white basin that rested on a tree stump. His orderly stood by, holding a towel in the ready position. There was a sentry to our right as well, pacing the entrance to town. Beyond him, milling about in profusion were soldiers, gendarmes, and damned few villagers. This catastrophic scenery being taken in and weighed at a glance, we trudged wearily to the left, away from town, past the sentry at the chateau gate, and up the road. Out of sight of the whole blamed mess, we ran into the woods for a goodly distance, holed up, and had a smoke and a nip from my flask.

Steady on-course now, by midnight we were bushed and quite hungry to boot and, with the intent of crawling in and sleeping for a spell, we approached the barn of an isolated farm. As we crossed the farmyard, a burly figure loomed up in the moonlight and for one long moment it appeared to be a trooper. But it was a civilian, the owner of the farm: and as it would have been awkward to say nothing, I hit him for a drink of cider. Neither Lou nor I liked his looks, and we didn't bother to make talk with the farmer.

Unlocking a barn door, he begrudgingly drew a glassful of very bitter, low-grade cider. I asked him if there was a place we might sleep, and he showed us into a musty, dusty, ramshackle old room in the barn. Extending into the room was a long boom and in a circular wooden trough rode a five-foot millstone, and a deep rut in the floor showed where horses, hitched to the boom, had wandered in circles for many a year. And in the mill we could sleep if we liked, said our shifty-eyed and sullen host; and with that he walked to his house. Dirty bits of straw and piles of dusty chaff littered the floor, and when we poked into a stack of cordwood rats scurried forth. The setup plus the farmer's attitude made up my mind for me, and I suggested to Lou that we make tracks. We figured uneasily that perhaps the farmer thought of us in terms of a bundle of franc notes that would be his when he turned us over to the Jerries. And without further discussion we hightailed it for the tall timber, carefully keeping the mill between our moonlit, fleeing figures and the farmhouse.

I'd run through several second winds already, and, while waiting for a third, my legs got so goddamned tired that when mounting even the slightest hill I had sometimes to grab a pant-leg in either hand and literally pull one foot ahead of the other. But for a couple of hours we made fairly decent progress, and at last from a hilltop we gazed out over our major checkpoint. Shining below us in the moonlight was a highway and a double-track railway, a wide river, another highway and beyond, a gloomy, black-forested mountainside!

We'd reached out and covered many a kilometer in the past fifteen hours, and now we felt quite cheerful but too damned tired to try crossing so many well-guarded thoroughfares at this time of night. Spying an abandoned shack halfway down the slope, we made for it.

On this hillside was an orchard, and the air was heavy with the fragrance of apple blossoms; then suddenly the night was filled with an angry droning. Fifty million bees were prowling about in the moonlight, making honey or whatever the hell French bees do at night, and every last one of them took out after me. Weariness a thing of the past, I ran like a deer, whipping my silk scarf frantically about my head to scare off these gremlins; but three of the little bastards bit me and Lou rolled about in the wet grass screaming with joyous laughter at my frenzied antics, which were desperate rather than deliberately calculated to brighten his evening.

We cased the house and with a stick pried the padlock from the door. Debris cluttered the floor, so we hauled our weary bodies into the fireplace, making ourselves at home. I tucked my scarf about my face, pulled a block of wood under my head, and went into a coma.

Having slept cold, we awakened at dawn and my back felt like a washboard, whereupon I discovered that I'd slept upon a row of loose faggots. Lou looked as though he'd just climbed off the rods at Frisco after a tough cross-country run, and the sight of him sent me into peals of girlish laughter. My morning was made cheery. Lou's clothes were torn all to hell and soot from the fireplace was rubbed well into his stubble of black beard.

Bits of straw covered his shaggy head, and as I snickered at him his face split with a foolish grin. "Leave us join the Air Corps," he muttered. "Uncle Sam Needs Pilots!"

Just after sunrise of that Sunday morn in Normandy, Lou and I picked up walking sticks and swaggered down the hill and walked across the main highway, as bold as brass, even while recounting the previous days adventures and resolving to be a little more discreet on the next leg of our journey. A hundred yards below us lay a tiny village nestled between the highway and the railroad. We pulled up short outside the town, not quite knowing what to expect at the rail crossing. As I rolled a smoke and thought, Lou crawled through a fence and faded into the depths of a thicket.

I looked up to see walking toward me from the direction of the village three people: two men and a woman, all about thirty years old. They stopped in front of me, all glowering in a most unfriendly manner. By way of striking up a conversation I asked, in my best Sunday French, if there might be a German sentry at the rail crossing. My answer from the trio was a hostile stare. Throwing caution to the winds, I shouted to my invisible comrade: "Hey Lou! You're caught with yer pants down! We got company!" And he popped his head from the bush and stared blankly at my guests.

The woman said nastily: "This is my property. What are you doing here?"

"Check that, Lou!" I called, and parroted: "What are we doing here?" And when Lou hollered his blunt, precise answer, I cringed automatically until I realized—or rather hoped—that the woman was no linguist. Lou hitched his belt and bounded over the fence to join me.

The woman stated the fact: "You are not Frenchmen!"

I gave her an indignant look. Lou bowed stiffly and in an insulted tone of voice said, "Bonjour, Madame!" and we took off into the village.

Spotting an old-timer puttering about in his garden, I hung over the neat picket fence and struck up a chat with him. He knew me to be a poorly disguised furriner of some brand, but he couldn't quite guess which brand, and when I put him wise he seemed to be genuinely delighted to meet us. A garrulous old geezer, I had to keep after him before he'd come to the point and answer my questions. The old boy volunteered much advice, which boiled down to his opinion that our best bet would be to just walk through town, use the pedestrian gate, and stroll across the tracks just as though we were bound for the meadow to search out our cows. He added in a confidential whisper that there were beaucoup, beaucoup Boches over thataway, and he waved his knotty hand in a sweep covering 360 degrees of the compass.

"Merci, mon vieux," I said with a friendly salute, and with a nod to Lou we navigated a crooked little lane until we came to the railroad. I cranked open the gate and we walked across; and upon noting that the rails were shiny and unbroken as far as the horizon in either direction, I wondered just what the merry hell our dive-bombers were doing for amusement these days.

A few hundred paces took us across a lumpy meadow—a sweet-smelling meadow still wet with dew—and then we were on the river bank, gazing across thirty feet of deep, swiftly-flowing water, and the river wound in a series of hairpin curves.

"Swim?" I suggested halfheartedly.

"Looks kinda wet," said Lou. Well, what the hell: we'd do it the easy way. We'd find a bridge and make the crossing like a couple of white men. Once across, we'd fade into the brush of the mountainside and soon be on course for Dozulé. Clumps of trees and underbrush along the riverbanks prevented us from seeing what lay beyond each bend, so we just started walking. Five minutes later I happened to glance back toward the village and I saw in a field of tall grass a lad waving his arms about his head. This character was bouncing up and down like a spaniel running through a weed patch, and such odd behavior of a Sunday morning bore looking into. So we left the riverbank and headed back to run a check on this jack-in-the-box Frenchman.

He was a smooth-cheeked handsome lad of about sixteen years, and he motioned excitedly that we should crouch in the grass out of sight. He asked us if were aviateurs Americains and I told him that he spoke the truth; whereupon our young friend explained that the three strangers who had accosted us . . . even now were they telephoning le Gestapo! Without further chatter we made tracks, running crouched down along the ditch below the railroad. With a kilometer behind us, we ducked into a tobacco shed and took a breather. And I wasn't took amazed when the lad invited us to come with him and join his Maquis!

He was courier for his Resistance group, which had headquarters fifteen kilometers from the village, and he'd been on a "mission" when he'd come through our village, had heard the rumors of our passing, had observed the collaborators, and had come to rescue us. To top it off, he offered us each a 1,000-franc note! When we declined the invitation to meet his chief and refused the money, the kid said he'd guide us across the river and put us on course for Dozulé.

This time, creeping along a hedge, we headed again for the river. Halting to pull aside a bush, the kid said, "Voila le pont!" and there was the bridge Lou and I'd been seeking. It was an old wooden bridge: and seven German soldiers stood at the approach, and now I could hear their voices. As we peered through the concealing leaves, an old man driving a few cows crossed over coming our way, and the sentries stopped him and examined his papers.

Lou and I had fallen into another cesspool and had—as usual—come out gold-plated!

Borrowing a couple of tired cows from the old man, we drove them across the road in front of the bridge beneath the very noses of the Jerries, and then through a little hayfield in which a dozen peasants labored over their scythes. Coming to a grove of trees on the riverbank beyond sight of the bridge, we returned the cows to their owner and accomplished a precarious river crossing upon a scraggly dead tree that lay in the water, and soon we lay in a hedge that bordered the final obstacle: the far highway. The kid took a looksee and we dashed across the road just as the leading machine of a long motor-truck convoy came around a bend heading for Pont L'Évêque.

Lou and I, after an arduous half-hour trek up the mountainside, slumped to the ground beneath the tall pines. Our tireless guide, asking that we wait for him where we were, turned and ran down the slope as fast as he could go. Lou and I sat and smoked and wondered from where might all our luck be coming. That young Maquis lad had done us a good turn.

In an hour there came to our ears a little whistle, like the song of a bird. Our friend was again with us, with a basket slung over his arm. "Petite-dejeuner, messieurs!" he cried. And having not eaten since noon of the previous day and having accomplished much physical exertion in the interim, this unexpected breakfast was a welcome thing to behold. Wine and bread, a cupful of sweet butter, and a half-dozen eggs. A wonderful little feast we had there on the mountainside, and we wolfed it down. That is, we wolfed all but the eggs and they, being raw, presented a special problem. I poked a small hole in either end of an egg with a twig, put it to my hungry mouth, and built up a little manifold pressure. The white strung down my throat to form a steadily deepening puddle in the pit of my stomach and then the yolk—slightly heavier—followed along. I discovered that while sucking eggs one must think desperately of other things.

We sat in the hot morning sunshine and shared our tobacco with the youth who'd saved our day. When we'd killed off the two litres of vin rouge that he'd brought us, we felt no pain. I suggested that we put our show on the road, and we barreled up the mountainside to follow a series of country roads. Our half-drunk guide lurched along doing the thinking, and Lou and I trailed behind some twenty paces to the rear.

A lovely morning it was, and we were full of good chow and wine. Our guide never hesitated in selecting the correct fork at any of the various little junctions we came upon. With the kilometers fading away under our heels, he led until about noon, when we came to the main highway that led from Pont L'Évêque—now behind us—to Dozulé and Caen. The way was crowded with eastbound civilian refugees, all evacuating the front-line area.

Horse-drawn carts all laden with miserable remnants of household belongings; whole families trudging along wearily; folks on bicycles and kids pulling coaster wagons piled high with bundles of bedclothes; old people riding in wobbly-wheeled tumbrels drawn by sad old plow horses. And once there came past us a couple of very young boys who pushed a wheelchair in which, calmly smoking his long-stemmed pipe, sat an old greybeard.

I buttonholed one old duffer to ask if les Boches were examining papers at the crossroads. The Frenchman, gaping at my reckless use of his language, replied that they stopped everyone.

Except for an occasional Jerry meat-wagon, our trio was the only westbound traffic on the highway and I maintained that three Frenchmen heading for the front while all others were scrambling for their lives in the opposite direction was a fishy-looking setup to any Jerry soldier; so we bid the Maquis lad a fond adieu and gave him half our tobacco by way of thanks for his good work.

Lou and I walked a few kilometers to the south and then hit out across country, roughly paralleling the highway. And it was slow going. Immediately we were forced off course when we came upon a sprawling cluster of buildings at the edge of a wood. A huge Red Cross was painted on the roof of the main building and forty or fifty ambulances were queued up at the entrance, disgorging their cargoes of freshly clobbered Jerries. We made the mistake of detouring on the downwind side, and the stink was that of a stockyard on a hot afternoon. But pretty soon we were hiking through country that put me in mind of the Black Hills of Dakota: pine forest, rough hills, and many creeks, and in the attempt to hold a compass course of a wee bit south of west, my navigation became a difficult trek from checkpoint to checkpoint.

Damned dry by late afternoon, I bellied through the base of the five-hundredth hedgerow of the day and when my head emerged on the far side I lifted it up and looked around like a turtle, then motioned for Lou to come ahead. For we found ourselves to be in the backyard of a tiny farmhouse, and in the sunshine played a little boy and a little girl, and their mother and an old grandmère type sat in the shade. As we picked ourselves up out of their garden, dusted ourselves off, and taxied toward these folks with visions of a jug of cider in mind, they looked at us as though we wore horns and long tails, so we accompanied our song-and-dance of identification with many a friendly leer calculated to put these womenfolk at ease.

The old one puckered up into a gummy smile and let out a gleeful croak. The younger woman, upon learning that she'd suddenly become hostess to two good reasons for her perfunctory execution by the Boches, gave a spasmodic twitch that lifted her a good ten centimeters into the blue. She came down looking worried, but each tot—not knowing the score because of his tender age—dashed over and latched onto Lou and me, wanting to make a game.

We were hustled to a flowery corner of the yard where there was a hut to screen our dangerous presence from the adjacent gravel road, and a snack of fresh cookies and cider was brought from the house. I showed the old gal my roadmap and—after much bewildered running of wrinkled fingers over it, accompanied by a muttered string of "Hmmm's" and "Tsk-tsks"— she finally indicated a spot where she thought we now stood.

Her guess was a good hundred kilometers off, but we could see a couple of villages visible in a valley beyond the farm, and upon learning their names I quickly oriented our expedition.

Now the old soul became very cooperative, volunteering the intelligence that, Eh, là-bas, down yonder, were 10,000 Boches! Beaucoup Jerries camped in and around the villages! Mon Dieu! It was perilous for us to walk there. But Lou and I, having evolved the right answer to such pernicious talk, laughingly replied: "Dix mille Boches, deux Americains. C'est égal, Madame!"—inferring that two Yanks were an even match for 10,000 Jerries. A stark, raving lie to be sure, but always good for an extra litre of wine. And sure enough, grandma whooped and slapped her leg and ordered up another tray full of cookies, a huge jug of cool amber cider, and a bottle of vin rouge for the two Americans.

So we assuaged our hunger and then, rolling cigarettes for all, chatted a while about the forthcoming liberation; and when we made our thanks and arose to leave, the whole kit and caboodle tagged along, giving us escort across the road and through an orchard to the brow of a hill. The old lady jabbered away, pointing out countless little pinpoint locations on the horizon, saying, "Beware! Beware! Do not go there, or there! Remain distant from there, too, and there and there and there, là-bas! Eh, beaucoup Boches partout!"

Away we went, coasting downhill with long and easy strides, and pausing at the bottom we looked back to see the whole family up on the skyline waving their hankies at us. We whipped off our berets and flapped them madly in fond farewell and then headed west again, feeling refreshed and delighted at having met such a gay old dame.

We sloshed through a creek and were dry long before we'd topped the far wall of the valley, and as we slipped into another forest my skinny legs were weary and the blisters on my heels were tickling; but Lady Luck, viewing our fatigue with a kindly eye, led us to a fine trail that cut straight through the tangles of ferns and brush and led us magically through the cool, wild-smelling woods. Spared the effort of battling the undergrowth, we trudged merrily westward for hour upon hour, and then the daylight faded. The sun blazed into our faces for a few short minutes and then it became necessary to halt at intervals to pick out the two faintly luminous dots that marked the north tip of my compass needle. As the moon sneaked up over the trees we were again able to select quite distant checkpoints toward which to walk, and we kept moving. When we'd consider calling it quits for the day, we'd pick a distant hilltop and resolve to carry on that far, at least. One such goal led to another, and the kilometers disappeared behind us.

Some eighteen hours, finally, had we walked since our nap in the fireplace in the old hut near Pont L'Évêque. The impromptu breakfast courtesy of the young Maquis courier and the cookies donated by the old woman were not the sort of chow to sustain a forced march, and despite wrapping my scarf tightly about my waist there still lingered the sensation of gnawing mice within my belly. At last, shaky with hunger and quite tired-out, we spotted a small farmhouse on a far, moonlit slope. Lou wanted to dig into a moldy old haystack and sleep, but despite the hour I had a good feeling about that particular farm, and I suggested we give the house a try in an effort to panhandle a meal. So we pulled a bead on the farm and headed for it, literally on our last legs. We stumbled immediately into the perimeter area of a flak battery, made a quick and silent detour, and approached the farm from a different angle. Lou remained in the shadows of a hedge while I set forth on a solo reconnaissance, tiptoeing along a dark wall of the house.

I poked a cautious eye around the front corner to peer into the farmyard. A narrow dash of firelight escaped from a door ajar to dance dimly upon the cobblestone yard. I prowled the front wall with ears tuned to maximum sensitivity, but there was nothing to be heard but friendly farm sounds: crickets squeaking . . . a cow chomping grass . . . the rustle of leaves in the midnight breeze . . . the occasional thud of a cherry dropping to the ground. Then somewhere in the darkness of the yard, a rusty winch squealed, a chain clattered, and a bucket banged in a well. Pretty soon from out of the gloom came an ancient Frenchman, his sabots tapping on the stones.

He was very old and bent, and I went "Sssssst!" He lowered his pail of water to the ground and stood in his tracks, hand cupped to ear. I hissed again and he saw me leaning against the doorjamb of his house. When I whispered, "Bonsoir, mon vieux!" the old man approached me without fear, and when I told him that my comrade and I were fugitives and had come far without food, the old one gave me a hard, gnarled hand and I led him around the house to where Lou was hidden.

When my rough-looking fellow pedestrian stepped from the shadows into the moonlight, the old man was startled, and so excited was he that he hopped about like a bird, whispering so fast that his white beard became a blur. With shaking hands he rolled a lumpy cigarette with tobacco we offered him, and I lit him up with a sulphur match, carefully concealing the tiny blue flame. As he smoked we explained how we had come to be on his farm in the middle of the night.

The old one pushed us to the shadows and scuttled away, whispering that he'd return in ten minutes. I—trusting soul—trailed him to ascertain his immediate destination, and when he ducked into his house I rejoined Lou and we waited for perhaps a quarter-hour. The greybeard returned with a tap-tap-tap, and he whistled us out of the gloom to introduce us proudly to his equally ancient and prune-faced wife: "Les deux aviateurs Americains! Hee-hee-hee-hee!" And the sweet old lady planted on each of our cheeks a dry old kiss. She and her husband well remembered, she told us, la guerre terrible of twenty-five years past when the Americans had helped to save France: now she and her husband were happy to be able to help the sons of those other soldats Americains. And would we again drive from France the wicked Boches?

Upon our assurance that within another few months everything'd be all right, the old lady snatched a cloth from the kettle she carried. Lou's eyeballs dangled halfway down to the kettle. I took a look and saliva sprang in a fountain from the insides of my cheeks, for we'd hit the old jackpot! Before us lay a platter of hot potatoes and hunks of cold fried chicken, slabs of beefsteak, and a bowl of salad and a bottle of wine. We dug in with ill-mannered haste, pausing now and then to moan with delight upon savoring a particularly choice bit. Not until the platter gleamed in the moonlight did our host tell us of our precarious position.

"At my front gate, thirty paces from us, there stands a soldat allemande avec fusil!"—a Jerry with a rifle. And the old man whispered that all along the little road that passed in front of his farmhouse were many more German soldiers with rifles. Many soldiers who always stood guard over the forest, in which there were many great piles of bombs and cannon shells. So had Lou and I walked another thirty seconds, we'd have taxied right into a veritable buzz-saw. It was plain to see that our luck still was in very good condition.

Well, we'd wait until dawn to dope out a plan of action. Rigor mortis was about to set in after our long trek, so I asked the old man if he knew of a place where we might sleep in safety, and—obviously tickled at having fed two Americans right under the Nazi nose—he thought for a bit, then led us to a pasture in the center of which stood a tiny round hut with a conical thatched roof. Prizing open a splintery door, he told us sleep well, to not worry, and that he'd visit us in the morning. We had the place to ourselves. The little room was half full of baled hay, and we each dug out a coffin-shaped pit in which to lay our weary bones.

A not too distant rumble of cannon and the very nearby clatter of wagons and the shouts of German soldiers awakened me. Peering out across the meadow I was highly pleased to see that this was a chilly, foggy, dawn. The fog, lovely and thick and swirling, and the Wehrmacht and our two-man outfit would be mutually invisible. I studied our map and had a smoke and then the old man showed up with a bucketful of fresh milk. For that we were grateful, for we'd slept cold and the warm milk put new life into us, and we drank it to the last drop. We thanked the brave old geezer and he wished us luck, and just before sunrise we set out through the concealing ground fog, hurrying to circumnavigate the dangerous ammunition dump before the sun might dissipate our friendly camouflage.

We chopped through a few hedges: ten feet of hedge, a hundred paces across a meadow, and another hedge. Being unable due to circumstances to cuss at the top of my lungs, I whispered dreadful things at the brambles and had soon improved upon my frightful and most original vocabulary. But in an hour we poked our beret-clad heads from a bush, looked up and down the length of a dirt road, and then allowed as how we must by this time have passed the edges of the dump. Walking quite openly and blindly through the heavy fog, we jumped into the brush on the far side of the road and soon hit an abrupt slope that was surprisingly steep and rather barren of vegetation. I was a bit amazed when a dozen climbing paces brought us to the top of the little knoll, and we both were startled to discover a square iron door countersunk in the opposite slope. We had taxied on up and over an ammunition bunker. Instead of navigating cautiously around the closely guarded dump, we were inspecting it: a dandy place, I thought, for the Jerries to capture two disguised American officers.

For lack of a better idea I held to a compass course of due west, and the fog was thinning out as we came to a rundown old farmhouse. It was now a case of either penetrating a dozen hedges and skirting the place or walking through the yard to a gate that opened onto a road: so we would act as though we belonged here, we decided, and to hell with the hedges. And so we hoofed it though the yard to the gate, which I opened. We went through and I turned around to latch it behind us, and when I again turned to the road there stood Lou, motionless and with a woebegone look on his bearded face.

Following the direction of his gaze I beheld a husky Jerry sentry some fifteen feet away and close to the hedge that had concealed him from us. With his rifle tucked under one arm and helmet buckled under his chin, he stood alongside a large white signboard on which was painted in shrieking red letters: "DEFENDU! MUNITIONS! Forbidden to Trespass all Civilians!"—Keep the hell out! Stay away! Scat! And, having heard the rattle of the gate, the sentry faced us and there was but one thing to do—that being to comply with the orders written on the warning sign. Somehow displaying a reasonable facsimile of nonchalance, we crossed the road and proceeded along a logging trail for twenty counted paces. I watched each of my shoes come forward and hit the dirt, and I waited for the command to halt. Each step jarred loose from my chin one drop of sweat. Then I knelt, as though to tie a shoe, and cast a glance to the rear: the fog and a little underbrush hid us from the sentry and I took off using full military power, with Lou breathing hot down my neck all the way. When winded we sat down on the ground and exchanged simple grins. "Yuk yuk yuk!" I chuckled. "We done it agin!"

Well, hot damn! Dozulé today, it would be, and beyond there we didn't have a thought. Once there our agent, the redoubtable M. Ash, would take over with his plans and see us through to the English lines. But to attain Dozulé would require extremely cautious navigation, for the home stretch would be the most dangerous. We were now penetrating the fringes of the Jerry fighting army, and the woods were literally full of 'em. But I didn't care, for somewhere along the line Mother Nature had stepped in to help me out. Unknown senses, long dormant, had awakened: now my ears would actually twitch upon reception of some faint sound coming in on the wind—sounds ordinarily passing unnoticed. My eyes were more keenly aware of everything within range, and at this stage of the game I scrupulously obeyed the dictates of an atavistically prickling scalp. And for no good reason I was happy as a lark, loving the life I was leading, and mightily interested in the series of unique incidents I was uncovering. Comrade Lou was a good type to have around, for he was always ready to take a chance and always enjoying the skullduggery involved in our safari.

With Pont L'Évêque behind us, we steered west for Dozulé, but it was slow going: one tedious detour after another. It still was early morning and the fog had been replaced by a steady, refreshing drizzle; and under cover of the low overcast, which kept our strafing fighters away, the Jerries were on the move with truck convoys and columns of bicycle troops and tanks, utilizing every road to full advantage. But as the morning wore on, the overcast lifted and then the snarl of our single-engine fighters filled the skies. After that, there was little highway traffic to plague us.

Feeling no pain after having gotten away with our blundering tour of the ammo dump, we took a nice long swig apiece from my flask and soon were in high spirits. The countryside was deceptively charming, and as we trudged through the gullies and over the hills, I began to sing: "Hi diddle dee-dee, it's a pilot's life for me; drink all night and fly all day, kin hardly wait to spend my pay. Hi diddle dee-dee, it's a pilot's life fer meee!" I sang like a bird. And very soon I had cunningly maneuvered us into another awkward corner.

Cruising past a corral full of sleek saddle horses—which was fair warning in itself—we angled toward a farmhouse, waving gaily en route to a few peasants who toiled in a truck garden. Crawling through a wire fence, we drifted happily through an orchard and came upon a concrete highway. About to cross over, our plans were changed abruptly by the sudden appearance of a pair of bicycle troopers who were patrolling the road, pedaling to and fro in precise formation. So we paralleled the road for a few hundred paces, only to be stopped at a bridge. Atop the bridge lounged a quartet of jolly sentries, obviously bored and ready for any sort of diversion, such as making meatballs out of stray citizens. We were being herded around again, and it made me mad.

Without breaking stride, we swung into a 90-degree starboard turn, intending to detour the bridge by the simple expedient of cutting through the back yard of the farmhouse, which faced the highway at the point of the bridge. I stepped through a convenient hole in a hedgerow and placed my size-10E government-issue clodhoppers squarely into the midst of a chummy group of twenty-odd Jerries who sat around the backyard chatting, polishing brass, and oiling up their Mausers. A nasty little dog ran over and yapped around my ankles. Lou came through the hedge and joined me, and we were at a loss for words.

The Jerries paused in their puttering and stared at us. We stared at them. Onto my face I affixed a humble-apology-for-intrusion type smile. Stalling for time, I snaked out a battered butt and struck a light with a slow-burning sulphur match. No better plan than that of strategic withdrawal came to mind, so we turned our backs to the Wehrmacht and scuttled back through the hedge from whence we'd sprung.

"Don't look now," whispered Lou from the corner of his mouth, "But we got two bandits closing in at six o'clock level!"

We peeled off to stand beneath a convenient cherry tree where we commenced to fill our jacket pockets. The pair of inquisitive soldiers who had fallen in behind us now halted in indecision. Plucking cherries rapidly, in time with thudding of our hearts, we succeeded in creating an illusion of innocence and leisure; for the Germans' indecision crystallized into belief that we were harmless yokels and they turned on their heels and rejoined their comrades in the farmyard.

Drifting from tree to tree, we came upon a deep drainage ditch and lowered ourselves to the bottom. We sat down and had a little drink. We had another and settled down to plotting and planning a way out of the immediate area. Our position was not difficult to savvy: we were in a bottle, and the bridge was the cork.

So we crept along the ditch until close upon the bridge, and then we saw the hole in the cork: a two-foot culvert! The four sentries were laughing heartily and seemed to be in fine humor as we crawled silently through the little tunnel beneath them. We popped into the underbrush on the far side, and wondered what the merry hell had gotten into us to try pulling a stunt like we'd just pulled—but we were unbottled.

About noontime, after several more hours of equally cautious navigation, we gazed down the length of a long dog-leg valley at the far end of which, we figured, should lie Dozulé, our goal, perhaps ten kilometers from our high hilltop. Having selected a prominent notch in the far skyline as a checkpoint, we trotted downhill to the valley floor. Traces of fog still clung to the low places, and grey smoke spiraled thinly from village chimneys. Winding, white-graveled roads cut through the countryside, and from a distance it all looked mighty peaceful and friendly.

Leaping a white board fence, we set out eagerly to cross the wooded grounds of an elaborate estate, and a half-foot layer of dry leaves underfoot permitted us to move with all the secrecy of a herd of cattle wandering through a parched cornfield. Then emerging from a deep ravine, we found ourselves to be some twenty paces from the back door of a little brick house. Visible through a screen of shrubbery we could see in the yard a chubby, half-dressed Jerry officer. His shirttails fluttered in the morning breeze and his hat was tilted to the back of his head, and he heard us stomping through the leaves. He cocked his fat head for a moment, listening, and then started our way. Lou picked one tree and I slipped behind another, and as the Jerry approached, we kept circling around the boles of our respective trees—and this curious fellow trudged noisily between us. Then some ten paces beyond, from beneath his feet there jumped a frightened little cottontail that scurried away with a rustle of twigs and leaves marking his progress. The gullible Jerry paddlefoot saw our friend M. Lapin and jumped to conclusions. Changing course, he pulled a bead on the ravine latrine with more urgent affairs at hand than investigation of forest noises. And thought I, stifling a snicker, "Ain't nobody here but us rabbits, Doc!" So we were lucky again, but he was luckier: for we'd drawn our long knives, and had Jerry poked his head around either of our trees he would definitely have drawn back a stub. He was rather old and fat and Lou and I were thinned down and feeling mean anyway.

We got a little chuckle out of the deal. Lou, snatching off his beret and bowing low toward the brush, whispered: "I'll never eat any more rabbits, I promise!"

Early in the afternoon we mounted a high vantage point to check our position against the valley layout, and there, just a few kilometers to the north of our lofty perch, lay Dozulé! I felt extremely self-satisfied. It had been a zigzagging, backtracking, two-day trek, and I considered it to have been a peachy job of navigation with a ten-cent compass and an old French road map to have fetched up so close to our goal. There remained in my rubber pouch only enough crumbs with which to construct one puny cigarette, and by way of celebration we smoked it down to a nubbin.

Dozulé! Somewhere in that old town down there was the citizen who would expedite our sneak through the lines. That Maquis leader, René, had told us to just cruise into town and look him up, but we figured we'd case the place a bit before making such a rash move. So we angled down the mountainside for a way, and round at the edge of the forest lay a farm and a civilian stood cranking a windlass over a well. Since there was plenty of tall timber directly at our backs, I didn't give a hoot whether or not this Frenchman might be a bad one, and I waved my scarf until his attention was drawn. I called to him: "Hey! Venez-ici!" Drive over here, Jacques! We'd have a word with you!

Suspicious-like, the farmer moseyed toward the thicket in which we stood half-concealed. When he got in range I spoke up again to proclaim that we were two Americans; that the day of liberation was not far off, and that in truth he would be a wise man to keep shut the mouth today about having seen us. With threats delivered, I proceeded to pump him.

"What does one call that village là-bas?"

"C'est Dozulé, M'sieur."

"How many German soldiers down there?"

"Cinq-mille, peut-être." And he added that, over yonder—waving a hand to indicate the country through which we'd just wandered—there were beaucoup, beaucoup Boches, perhaps 20,000. And it would be, he said, impossible for us to cross that valley là-bas! Having just crossed that valley là-bas, we let his warning ride.

"There are sentries at the entrances to Dozulé?"

"Oui."

"These sentries, do they examine the papers of all who enter?"

"Certainement!"

"You will show us how to enter Dozulé without seeing the sentries?"

"Oui"—nervously.

So the reluctant farmer led us through his yard, past the pigpen and the well and the water trough, down to the gate. There was a narrow dirt path leading toward town, and the farmer told us to follow the path for two kilometers; when the path became a road, to follow the road; when the road turned to the right into town, we would continue straight ahead through the yard of a farm, and then we would be in the back streets of Dozulé.

"Merci bien," I said, "and remember well, Frenchman, you have not seen us. Compris?"

"Oui, Monsieur, oui!"

We hoofed it down the trail, hashing things over en route. If the town were as loaded with troops as the farmer had said, then to contact our man would be a risky affair. After coming this far intact and with so much dirty-work behind us, we didn't dare to be foolishly hobnobbing with a couple of thousand characters, each of whom would take great delight in pulling a trigger on us.

Our path became a little road and there was much sign of soldiery: boot prints, bicycle tire tracks, empty cigarette packages, and matches, and we acquired a few dandy butts with the finesse befitting our present station in life—two French bums. Presently we came upon the turning of the road, to where it led down a gentle hill for a bit and then turned again toward Dozulé. To our left the road paralleled a hedgerow and petered out in a few hundred paces. Immediately on our left was a farmhouse and directly ahead, as the farmer had said, was a break in the hedge, and I sortied on through for a looksee. I topped a little knoll and gazed into the farmyard. And I quietly reversed course, picked up Lou, trotted up the trail, and scuttled into a thicket. Thirty or forty soldiers and a few officers had been milling about in the yard. Trucks and staff cars were there with camouflage nets over them. And that Frenchman had told us to walk through that farmyard and so into Dozulé! Some sense of humor had that shiftless bastard!

Upon one point were Lou and I agreed: to hell with our grand entrance into Dozulé. We would instead find some reliable citizen to carry our chestnuts into town and to deliver them to M. Ash. For our courier we would find either a very youthful or a very elderly Frenchman, for they seemed to be the most trustworthy types. Young and old were patriots, while those in between—having learned the advantages but not the disadvantages of greed—were more inclined toward collaboration.

With this excellent plan in mind, we proceeded to the little farm on our side of the hedgerow and we prowled all around the place. In the yard we saw only a young woman who played with two tiny children, and a grey-haired old woman who was harnessing a pony to a two-wheeled cart. We lay on our bellies in the garden and watched the old one throw some gunnysacks into the cart and then, pulling the pony by its halter, she headed for the gate. It was evident that she was on the beam for Dozulé. What luck! I would dicker with her to take our message to M. Ash.

I jumped up and scurried around the border of the farm, arriving at the front gate just in time to make rendezvous with the woman and her cart. Unlatching the gate, I let her through, then latched the gate behind her, but without so much as a muttered "Merci," she taxied on down the road toward town.

"Un moment, Madame! One word, please."

She glared at me and jerked the pony to a standstill.

"We are two Americans, my comrade and I," I began, waggling a thumb up the trail to where Lou stood looking like a bashful hillbilly.

The old crone didn't bat an eye, and she remained silent. Showing her my dog tag and wings, I told her that it was imperative that we get a message into Dozulé. Would she deliver it for us? And still, no sign of life. Figuring that perhaps this quiet squaw had forgotten to install her teeth that morning, or that maybe she had no tongue at all, I took a little gamble on her patriotism and sprung the whole deal: would she please go to a certain address, locate "M. Ash," and ask him to meet us at five o'clock? We would be waiting for him alongside that big thicket, two hundred meters up the trail.

She just stared at the road and uttered nary a word, and with a shrug she snatched the pony into action. Down the road they went, she pulling the pony and the pony pulling the cart, and I was baffled. I gave Lou a full report and neither of us could dope out the score. Then, noticing that the young woman of the farm had her eye on us, we sauntered up the trail and went into hiding some fifty paces from the agreed-upon rendezvous point, just in case the old woman should happen to blab to the wrong people. I dozed off, to dream of a Scotch-and-soda soon to be quaffed in the choicest bar in London.

A woman's sweet voice singing a little tune aroused me. Peering from the thicket I could see the young woman of the farm as she walked past our hiding place. She was leading a very small boy by the hand, and she was singing to him. Three times she walked past our hiding place: and then we knew that she singing to us. I crept out onto the trail and she came to me.

"Vous êtes les Americans, oui?" she said. Well, our message had been delivered to M. Ash. She smiled and said that we had chosen a very dangerous place to hide, for very often would German soldiers walk along this pathway. She asked if we were hungry, and until then I'd forgotten my belly in the joy of having achieved Dozulé. But I told her that we weren't hungry. It was best that she went away, for should les Boches catch her with us they'd clobber her and maybe the kid, too. The girl agreed that it was the truth, and she left us, again singing to her child.

For a while we watched the soldiers moving about in Dozulé, for on the far side of our thicket there sloped away a wheat stubble-field that terminated at the edge of town. Just before five o'clock we heard footsteps and faint voices coming along the trail. But it wasn't our friend Ash. Instead, a trio of Jerries strolled past ten feet from where we lay. Five o'clock and no M. Ash. I was damned impatient. Six o'clock, and again a little bird sang and the lovely young woman returned, alone this time. She placed a wicker basket in a weed patch and went away.

I retrieved the basket and crawled back into our bush, and there we had a wonderful feast: two litres of cool milk, a chunk of meat as big as two fists, and a piece of black bread. It was our first chow of a long day and we were grateful to the girl for her evidence of friendship.

We watched the activity in Dozulé and sweated out old Ash. The sun went down and already in the dusky sky could be seen the red pinpoints of bursting flak, and the rumble of cannon was constant. As we were about convinced that our deal had fallen through, four men stepped from the brush and walked to the agreed rendezvous. Four Frenchmen they were, and we watched them for a moment, then came from hiding to join them.

I recognized Roger and another of the Pont L'Évêque Maquis, and I was quite astonished for they were a long ways from their stamping grounds. Numbers three and four were strangers, and one was rigged out like the old gentleman farmer himself: beret, plaid jacket, whipcord pants, and shiny puttees. Greeting Roger with a handshake, I piped up, "Monsieur Ash?"

The simple question had a reaction quite like that obtained by shoving the plunger on a charge of dynamite. Monsieur Ash it was—that fourth stranger—and he shouted in English, with great anger and violence: "You! How did you find me out? Who told you to see me?"

I told him my information had come straight from René, the leader of the Paris Maquis.

"Mon Dieu! Crazy fool! Insane man! My identity has been kept the secret for four years! Now you stupid fools come to give me away! What could you want with me?"

René, I replied, had said that we would be guided from Dozulé through the German lines.

"I refuse to help you! It's impossible and you are insane! You will never get through the German lines. You would be captured and then I would be captured. Mon Dieu!" Blowing his top in general, M. Ash worked himself into a fine rage and raved on, giving Lou hell. He gave me the same, and likewise he cussed out the Maquis man from Paris. When Ash had ceased his jabbering, to refresh his memory I again demanded that he fulfill his part of the deal. Thrashing his arms and beating his fist against his palm, he delivered his final answer—an emphatic, "NO!"

"You will return to Pont L'Évêque with Roger!" said he furiously "You will join again the Maquis there. Tonight you hide here and at dawn there will come the old man to guide you through Dozulé. You will walk down the street and leave Dozulé and you will meet Roger at the second crossroad at nine o'clock. You will walk with him back to the Maquis!"

I thought of the days of difficult maneuvering we'd accomplished in getting from there to here. I remembered the countless hedgerows through which we'd cussed our way. I thought of the way the Jerries had herded us around the countryside. And I thought that right now I'd agree to whatever M. Ash was babbling about and, when he had gone away, I'd do as I damned well pleased. So to shut him up, I told him that naturally we would return to Pont L'Évêque as he wished. You betcher boots, Ash. First thing in the morning.

And so the old bastard took off back to town, muttering to himself and beating his forehead with his fist. I was glad to be rid of him. Our obvious dejection now moved the remaining members of Ash's party to make us a gift of a pack of Jerry cigarettes. Escorted to a tumbledown shanty nearby, we were told to expect the old man to show up at sunrise.

"Á demain, Roger, á neuf heures!" said I, shaking his hand. We'd be seeing him on the morrow at nine o'clock, at the crossroad. And so long, pal, I thought. Like hell you'll see me again!

A chill wind whistled through the cabin. We looked the joint over. Dust and manure was deep on the floor. A pair of dejected, maltreated, deserted, and forlorn hobos, we huddled in a drafty corner and lit up a tasty Jerry cigarette. The abrupt refusal of promised assistance had knocked all the props from under us, for we'd plotted our course no farther than Dozulé. Gloom filled our ramshackle old homestead to flow in a black and sticky stream out over the moonlit meadow beyond. Mad and sad by turns, it was decided automatically and unanimously that we would not mess around with Roger and his Maquis. Ten minutes of deep and brooding silence. Another cigarette.

Lou broke the spell, croaking, "Go to hell if ya think I'm gonna walk one goddam inch back east after crawlin' on my hands and knees clear from Amiens!"

"Likewise," I muttered sunnily.

After a bit of such scintillating chitchat and a few more cigarettes, plus a strictly rationed jolt from my silver flask, our natural animal spirits overpowered the blue gremlins who rode our shoulders and we steadied down to another plot-and-plan session.

Backtracking was out of the question. Walking further westward was also out, for the most concentrated and murderous stretch of front line lay at Caen, a few kilometers from us. Eight hundred kilometers to the south of us lay the Pyrenees and Spain, but I wasn't about to leave a trail of shoe leather and blisters over that tried-and-true route. What the merry hell! We were damned near on top of the British army right where we sat, and it seemed quite foolish to retreat. So with three points of the compass discussed and discarded, but one was left. Hot damn! We were northbound at the crack of dawn to give the Channel Coast a whack. We'd find a small bateau, maybe a little AAF dinghy or something, and then, By God, we'd shove out to sea, perhaps to sail past the mouth of the Orne to land on the beachhead!

Perhaps during our reconnaissance of the Channel Coast Monty would launch his long-awaited drive eastward, and then we'd just hole up until the battle had drifted past us. We lit up a splinter and studied our map. Some 15 kilometers directly north of us on the beach were the adjoining towns of Houlgate and Cabourg. Once there, we'd find a way! The more we plotted, the better looked our plan, and the night was good again. The ornery M. Ash was forgotten. We had another invincible plan!

At midnight the RAF began to work over the front lines near Caen, and Lou and I sat in the shadows of our hut and watched the show. The western skies were aflame as from the horizon a splendid cascade of tracers and dazzling showers of heavy flak curved lazily skyward. The fiery streams fanned slowly back and forth as the Jerry gunners sought out their targets; and infrequently, as a ship was knocked down, a gout of orange flame would appear high in the sky to arc swiftly earthward. This reckless show continued for perhaps an hour, and as bomb-bays were emptied tremendous puffs of wind and vivid sheet lightning flashes and a deep and dangerous grumbling roar would reach out for us.

The night was damned chilly and we were sorely tempted to kindle a wee fire, but knowing that it would be tempting fate, we desisted: some two hundred paces from our cabin was a barn full of slumbering troopers. I scratched together a bed of twigs and pulled a fencepost under my head for a pillow; and the last sounds I heard were the squeak of a lonely cricket and the drone of a solitary night-fighter, and the inarticulate, profane mumblings of Lou in his beard as he, lodged in the fireplace, squirmed about in futile effort to achieve comfort where none was available.

Before sunrise, the throbbing of many aircraft engines and the heavy pounding of flak guns brought us stumbling in haste to the doorway, and from that vantage point we watched the damnedest air show ever seen by mortal eye. As far as we could figure, this was about the eighteenth of July, and a lovely day was in the making. Lacy wisps of cirrus cloud fanned delicately across the high skies, and fragments of low scud burned pink in the sunrise as in from the Channel flew an endless train of American and British bombers. There must have been 2,000 of them, and they flew an oval pattern coming in from England to follow along the River Orne; then swinging over Caen, they passed over Dozulé in their wide turn back toward England. The target area was centered on the Jerry lines at Caen—the same area that had taken such a beating only a few hours before. Hundreds of dive-bombing and strafing fighters were concentrating on the flak batteries, but they couldn't get them all, for in and around the boxes of bombers the bursts were thick as a flock of blackbirds. From our distant observation post, they looked to be as harmless, too; but both Lou and I well knew that each puff was big as a barn and dirty black and full of grief.

I'd seen heavy flak over Bremen and Berlin and Happy Valley, but that of this morning was a rare thing, and I was perfectly content to be sitting right where I was.

I guess we watched a dozen or fifteen of our big ships go down, and it was too damned bad, for this was much too nice a morning to see everything ended for anybody. One unfortunate B-24 straggled behind its squadron after the bomb run and flew a solo flight right down the length of an ugly flak alley. As it ran the gauntlet, every gun in the Dozulé area concentrated on it, with one battery taking over where the last left off; and, when the ship was overhead, four or five guns—one but a few hundred yards from our hut—opened up savagely. The doomed pilot put his ship through a series of wild convolutions in frantic evasive action but the Jerries had him cold, and shortly after scored a direct hit. Flaming bits of B-24 and its crew of ten came trickling earthward for a quarter-hour.

Boxes of our bombers, caught in the terrific flak, broke formation to scatter like ducks over a blind, and the guns focused on the singles. A half-dozen B-26s were downed, and drifting slowly overhead were a pitifully few tiny white parachutes. Flak was bursting around some of the airmen as they dangled high in the sky, helpless in their chute harness. This was a reckless affair, and our old hut bounced about with the concussions of the bombs falling upon the Jerry lines.

A whooping and hollering bombardment such as this, we reasoned, could only be the initial phase of the overdue British assault upon the German forces at Caen. If the anxiously awaited breakthrough was indeed at hand, and if the British ground forces followed up the advantage given them by this terrific carpet bombing, why then it might be only a matter of hours until the Dozulé area would be fought over. But with a degree of cynicism, we reckoned that even should the bombardment permit Monty to forge ahead, when eleven o'clock came around he'd dig in where ever he might be and stoke up the old teakettles, thusly fouling things up for another month or two. So for our expedition, it was on to the town of Houlgate on the Channel Coast.

Our guide through Dozulé showed up on schedule. To fool my belly into believing that it contained a hearty breakfast, I cinched my scarf tightly around it. And with the old geezer guiding us, we were off and away. Trudging down through the stubble-field toward town I noticed, in one corner of the field, where yesterday there had been nothing, there was now dug in a mean-looking artillery gun: a long-barreled weapon, with its crew of ten or twelve standing around picking their noses.

Folks were just beginning to mill around in the streets of Dozulé as we strolled past a row of side-street shops and thence to the main stem. The thudding of German boots was suddenly loud in our ears as a squad of Wehrmacht warriors bore down upon our position.

The old duffer who was navigating our expedition took one look at the oncoming soldiers. He took another look at Lou and me. Jerking a thumb in the direction we were to travel, he whispered, "Bonne chance!" and forthwith deserted us.

We were having one helluva time keeping track of our guides!

Getting in practice—Ted, on left, at the Army Air Corps Classification Center, Santa Ana, California 1942.

With the party car: waiting to be a pilot at the AAC Classification Center.

Graduation picture: Ted
receiving his wings at
Luke Field, Phoenix, 1942.

Ted sporting the "crusher"
look, post-graduation.

Above: 486th briefing room. *Below*: 486th squadron room, both at Bodney Airfield, England.

Aiming a Mustang's guns, Bodney Airfield.

Pilot's room, with Ted in the middle getting some sun.

March 1944: transition from Thunderbolts
to the Mustang at Bodney Airfield.

Thunderbolts taking off from Bodney Airfield.

Ted with parachute rigger and future lifesaver Sgt. Mike Sandorse at Bodney Airfield.

Ted and crew atop *The Joker*.

Group shot: C-Flight with plane *Sweetie*—Ted is 3rd from left.

Ted with friend and flight-mate Don "Mac" McKibben on Thunderbolt wing at Bodney Airfield.

Jeanne Longuet, "The Flea," of the Pont Audemer Maquis, one of Ted's key helpers.

César, chief of the Maquis of Pont Audemer: friend, boss, and helper.

Sending a toast to Tayo:
Jeanne and Cesar, 1952.

Maurice and
Helene Marais
and their daughter,
who is wearing a
christening dress
made from Ted's
parachute: his
first helpers.

Above: Suzanne and Vitrice Richard, Ted's friends and helpers in St. Nicholas de Bois in the months just before the liberation, 1944.
Below: Suzanne and Vitrice Richard in a post-war snapshot.

Various snapshots taken in 1947: the Maquis helpers from Pont Audemer visiting those in St. Nicholas du Bois, including Suzanne, Vitrice and The Flea.

Ted's honorary membership card from the Maquis Surcouf, Pont Audemer, France.

Vitrice saying a few last words at Boche gravesite, the handiwork of his "bear trap."

Chapter **6**

SQUEEZE-PLAY

◈

S ome rat-race, Dozulé! Shopkeepers sweeping their sidewalks, refugees hauling-ass out of town, and half the German army stomping
belligerently about. Lou and I, cigarettes dangling from our lips,
plodded through the lot of them, saying nothing and minding our own
damn business as becomes every true fugitive. Catching a glimpse of our
reflection in a store window, I was childishly pleased to see for myself that
my comrade and I were dead ringers for any other two French hobos. After
brushing past a number of burly Wehrmacht types I did, however, begin
to feel a bit out of place; and to avoid that very thing we left the sidewalks
and walked in the street, only to be driven back by a long string of trucks
and ambulances that came racing through Dozulé en route to Caen.

At the edge of town, wondering where to go from there, we paused
and puttered around a public well. When a couple of soldiers began to
stare at us, we ambled on down the highway that led toward Pont L'Évêque.
At a junction, a signpost pointed north, and Houlgate was fourteen kilometers that way. Proceeding along our road for another kilometer, we
jumped the ditch and crawled under a fence to head north across-country.

As we neared a range of timbered hills, four RAF Typhoon fighters
whined overhead to zoom and peel off on a hilltop target. It was a well-
executed attack, with each pilot first firing a long burst of machine-gun
fire, then triggering off his rockets that would accelerate out ahead of the
diving ship to streak with a sharp crack into the target. I'd never seen fighters using rockets before, and the process was interesting.

Wading a bit of a creek, we wandered into a tiny village and there was a small girl of tender age swinging on a gate. I smiled and asked her if there were German soldiers in her village, and she peeped, "Non, M'sieur!" and scampered into her house; whereupon we poked around town until we found the village bulletin board, from which we acquired some interesting and educational data. One poop-sheet announced that a death penalty would be exacted for any variety of sabotage. Another put out by the German Commandant of this area ordered the evacuation of all citizens by the twenty-fifth day of July, from the area between a line drawn from Dozulé to the Channel and another from Pont L'Évêque to the Channel. After that date all civilians apprehended in that area would be dealt with as partizans. An earlier order told us that right now no civilians were permitted to the east of the Dozulé-Channel line—the line along which we were now walking. Well, it was fair warning. Digging out my pencil stub, I initialed the bulletin: "TPF, 1st Lt., USAAF," to signify that I'd read and understood the orders. Lou, chuckling, followed suit and when he'd affixed his signature we laughed and laughed "Hee hee hee!" for we thought it to be a dandy joke.

We mushed on northward. The terrain in these foothills was ready and waiting for the British attack. They'd have a hard go, for the Jerries had prepared thousands of foxholes, zigzag trenches, and tank revetments to cover any and all approaches from the west and north. Deciding finally to give up battling the underbrush in favor of walking the riskier Dozulé-Houlgate highway, we intercepted the tar road that slanted up ahead of us to top a high hill. A little way ahead of us two civilians suddenly popped from the brush, and upon seeing us they just as suddenly disappeared. Then one, a bicycle expert, came barreling toward us, his legs a blur of action. As this gentleman sailed past us on the downgrade, we observed that he had all the earmarks of belonging to somebody's Maquis outfit. The second man reappeared and approached us afoot. A nice-looking lad, dressed as we were, and I took a gander at him and remarked to Lou that here came another "pilote sans avion." I knew damned well that this guy was one of us, but still I didn't quite dare to speak to him as he passed. I knelt to tie a shoelace and sneaked a look back. The stranger, too, was kneeling on the pavement peeking over his shoulder at us. After another fifty paces, I again checked back over my shoulder and the stranger, too, was checking back over his shoulder. I just about gave him a long-call, but thought better of it. And we went our way and he went his, a clipped-wing flyboy if I ever saw one.

Up over the brow of the hill we came upon a bunch of Jerries. Tattered and dusty, clutching submachine guns and Mausers, they were milling around and hollering. The air was hazy with smoke and the road was cratered and littered with mud and chunks of dirt and stone and parts of trees, and on either side of the road were scattered remnants of Jerries and 40mm flak guns. It appeared that we had stumbled into the middle of the Typhoons' target! As of one mind, we reversed our course and started back downhill with the intent of detouring the area; but as four soldiers came around a curve below us, we made another quick turnabout, again heading uphill. A squeeze-play, it was, with us in the middle. Tugging our berets to a more reckless angle, we shuffled through the scene of recent disaster, picking our way carefully around the rocket craters. Twenty or so German soldiers puttered dismally amidst the wreckage, and an officer squatting in the ditch was shrieking into a field telephone. To my ear, it rang like profanity. The Jerry caught me grinning at him and dealt me one long, hard, narrow-eyed stare in which I read sudden death. I was bitterly worried until we'd faded around a bend and out of his view. Breathing again, I noticed that Lou and his inevitable lucky charm were having a go at it.

The topic of discussion, having been diverted momentarily from aircraft and sex, now swung to a critique of each other's acting ability. Lou's bucolic, sagging-jawed, blank-eyed shuffle was so cockeyed phony, I claimed, that the next Jerry we met was very likely to holler: "Achtung, Yank!" and lob a grenade our way. Lou, stung to the core by my unkind remarks, yelped, "You got no room to squawk, fer chrissake! Ya swing yer skinny arms like a goddam Limey soldat!"

Since we had touched upon the delicate subject of capture, I remarked, "Monsieur Lynch, guess where we stand if the bastards catch us up here, and us making like civilians?"

Lou ventured that we'd either stand under a scaffold or in front of a stone wall, he wasn't sure which. He gave his lucky charm another rub or two. We both knew that capture in this neck of the woods meant that we'd be classified automatically as spies and dealt with accordingly.

More kilometers. We taxied through an artillery outfit where the master race was earning its pay, sweatily and profanely throwing great camouflage nets and boughs over their tractors and guns. We trudged past a bunch of troopers who were queued up for chow. Ladling out the slop was a four-eyed, slick-haired Jap in Jerry uniform.

More kilometers. We hit the dirt in an instinctive reaction to a deafening explosion, to lurch foolishly to our feet upon the realization that an artillery gun had cut loose from just behind the hedge paralleling the highway. All along the road now, guns began sending stuff over toward the beachhead, and the godawful racket kept me jumping like a one-legged man at a fanny-kicking contest.

When we came to a "Y" in the road, we flipped a coin and so took the left turning. It proved to be correct, because pretty soon we rounded a bend to behold a high dune beyond which lay the English Channel. A half-kilometer to the west lay Houlgate, with Cabourg a bit farther along. Well, we were here, and we'd been coming so fast we couldn't stop. A bit of reconnaissance was in order: a prowl to the top of the dune for a looksee.

These dunes would be well patrolled and apt to hold various concealed defenses, so we proceeded with maximum stealth, seeking out a fence line that ran straight up the side of the dune. A heavy growth of wiry grass afforded fair cover during our hands-and-knees climb, and when we came to the top and poked up our heads to look out over the choppy Channel, the brisk breeze whipped much sand into our jaundiced eyes, making observation very trying. A glance at the beach and we abandoned all hope of further operation in that direction, for soldiers in quantity strolled to and fro amidst a formidable collection of ingenious obstacles: mines, sinuous coils of snarled wire, fences, and a multitude of iron stakes all connected by well-worn guard posts. Our projected regatta, it seemed, had been the hastily conceived product of two desperate minds. To hell with the Channel. We withdrew from the dune as cautiously as we'd made entry.

I wasn't discouraged. I hated cold water anyway. We'd dream up another angle. But first, having walked through half the German army to get here, I thought we might as well poke around in the resort towns. We might just panhandle a square meal at somebody's back door. Maybe we could find a cozy little waterfront bistro and have a quick jolt or two. Or maybe we could find a boat. So we headed for town to see what we could see. Our expedition came to another grinding halt upon approaching an underpass that was the entrance to Houlgate; for lurking therein were two sentries who, as we watched, dutifully checked the papers of all who entered. With our minds a blank, we sat down at the edge of the road and smoked. Then with a cry of delight I said to Lou, "So here comes our lunch!"

My hungry eyes had focused upon a milk can. The can was slung on the handlebars of a bicycle and the bicycle was being propelled through the underpass by a woman. As she neared us, I intercepted her. Waving a hundred-franc note under her nose, I propositioned: "Vous avez du lait, Madame?"

I drew a blank look, and the woman watched Lou blow a few smoke rings. Then she cased me, from GI shoes to borrowed beret. I smiled sweetly, and she in return forced a sickly grin. She was pondering my unique accent.

"You are Germans, no?"

"Hmp-mm." I shook my head.

"You are not Frenchmen, yes?"

"That is the truth, Madame."

"Ha! Then you are Polish and your comrade there is a Spaniard!"

"Ha-ha-ha! No, Madame, you are mistaken, for we are two Americans. We have beaucoup thirst. Now, have you some milk for us?"

A group of soldiers passed us by on their way up the hill, and the woman waited for them to get out of earshot. "Hmmmm!" she said. And the good woman refused my money, handed us a tin cup, and told us to drink our fill. Since more soldiers were approaching, I thanked the woman and walked away, intending to seek out another route into town. I was alone, however, for I saw that Lou still was standing beside the woman. He was patting his belly, pointing to his mouth, and with a pitiful expression on his face he was hollering at our harried hostess: "Faim! J'ai faim!" And the woman motioned for me to return: we should follow her at a distance. In reply to the triumphant look cast me by Lou, I muttered that he'd better not let Franco catch him begging like that.

So keeping a wide interval, we tailed the woman on up the hill and she turned along a farm road and gave us an all-clear from the house. Playing in the yard was a score of children for it was, explained the woman, a Red Cross refugee pool. To comply with the orders of the local German

Commandant, evacuation was to be accomplished within a day or two.

Two giggling girls fried us up a batch of eggs, and as we ate we were hard put to preserve our dignity. People around here found our appearance to be highly amusing and I couldn't blame them, for we looked as though we'd hatched out from under a rock: stubbled faces streaked with soot, hands grimy and scratched, clothes matted with mud and hanging in shreds. But what the hell, I was happy. It was again a fine day, for we'd hiked our fifteen or twenty kilometers and ended up with full bellies.

Two lads led us to the barn and up a flight of rickety steps that led to the loft. They fetched us a bucket of water and a dull razor and a scrap of soap, and in a few minutes we were pretty again. I asked the boys if they could find us a petit bateau: a canoe, raft, or rowboat, anything floatable. They replied that there were no boats and even if there had been, it would be impossible to cross the beach to the Channel. I asked if it were possible for one to journey along the coastline to banks of the Orne, and they cried in unison, "C'est impossible!"—for between Cabourg and the Orne were 100,000 Boches, and in that zone no civilians were permitted to remain alive. Six kilometers of perilous swamp and several rivers with quicksand would we have to cross. And the lads advised that we latch onto the trickle of refugees and get the hell out in that manner. But that I couldn't see. We were just a few kilometers from the British lines, and I was willing to creep the distance at night if that's what it would take to swing the deal.

So with no plans whatsoever, we lay on the floor of the loft and slept, only to be rudely awakened by a mighty blast and accompanying jolt that bounced us a foot off the floor. Peering worriedly through a crack in the wall we saw, in a haze of gun smoke that hung in the faint moonlight, a crew of Jerries milling around the great-granddaddy of all cannon. So there was a coastal artillery battery some fifty paces from our barn, and from then on, every half-hour or so, the boys would crank their goddam gun up out of a hole, tilt up the barrel, and lob a charge right close over the roof of our inn, with a fine bead pulled on the Limeys. Each shot liked to've scared us out of our wits, and along with each blast there fell upon our weary heads a shower of twigs and straw from the thatched roof overhead. All this tended to make sleep a rather precarious thing at best. Some hotel. Now all along the line other cannon joined in on the fun, and the hellish racket was fortified by an occasional different-sounding blast, which we assumed to be incoming stuff. We hoped sincerely that the RAF would stay home tonight. All we needed was a stick of bombs across our neighboring gun battery.

We'd know what to do with our expedition if only we knew whether or not the British had followed up the morning's attack. Providing that the breakthrough had been a success, then our best bet would be to swipe a sackful of chow and dig in a nearby forest to sweat out the liberation: on the other hand, if the British attack had failed, then it would be necessary for us to clear out of the Channel Coast. The new stalemate at the front would no doubt be in effect for quite a while, and within this very week the zone we were now in would be off-limits for everybody but Wehrmacht types. As we sat nervously anticipating the next round out of the big gun behind us, the whole danged Channel Coast expedition seemed in retrospect like a hare-brained idea, and we both wished fervently that our efforts had been expended in the opposite direction out of Dozulé.

At midnight there appeared in our barn a young Frenchman who acted as though we were his duty and he wanted to get us done. Jumpy as a cat was he, and scared: darting his eyes continually to the shadows, he whispered repeatedly that we were encircled by many Boches. Dazed, flak-happy, melancholy, angry; I couldn't quite dope out his state of mind. After sharing a cigarette, we stepped out into the night and an overcast had blanketed the sky, with resulting inky blackness. Circling the coastal batteries, we tiptoed through a meadow where our guide, halting at the edge of a half-dozen huge bomb craters, kicked at the splinters of what had once been a house. "When the bombs fell," he whispered softly, "all my family was in this house." The RAF, he added, had done the job. Squeezing my arm until it hurt, he asked, "Why?"

There was no answer to that question except to tell him that the bombs had been intended for the guns but had fallen short. The Frenchman rubbed a sleeve across his eyes and whispered, bitterly, "Oui . . . c'est la guerre . . ."

The tragedy of this poor man's life had been wrought by Allied airmen, and now, at the very scene of the extermination of his clan, he was engaged in the completely dangerous act of taking a pair of such aviators through an area alive with German soldiers. Of such spirit I could feel only deep admiration.

Only unnatural sounds were in the wind tonight: no songs of night birds but just the stupid blasting of guns, some near and some distant. As we stood silently by the funeral craters on the hillside, we suddenly caught the snarl of a fighter engine overlaying the throb of a twin-engine ship, and directly overhead was drawn across the black skies a short and brilliant line of tracers. A brief rattling of machine guns hit our ears and an aircraft exploded and slid down the sky, silhouetted starkly against its own flames. A Junkers 88 it was, and it went in with a resounding thud but a few kilometers from us. A cheery thing to see, that, and in better humor we set out again. Creeping up the hill and through a grove of trees, we scrunched along the gravel drive of a chateau. We would, said our guide, sleep in the small building ahead of us: a garage or servants' quarters, perhaps. Pussyfooting closer to it, we blundered into several small trucks and a staff car parked in the deep shadows of a hedge. The Frenchman muttered an explosive "Merde!" and we took out of there like three scalded cats, for the Jerries had beaten us to the draw. Soon we stood before a little cottage: our guide's house, and we would stay with him tonight.

The RAF was over the front now, and the skies flickered merrily as sticks of heavy bombs rumbled in. Crisscrossing arcs of tracers lashed the low horizon and deadly Roman-candle columns of heavy flak sailed leisurely skywards: and the violent scenery over the front decided me then and there to keep the hell out of such furious doings. The constant angry flashes and the solid, incendiary mass of hot steel that flew about in that neighborhood gave me a quick insight into the weather one could expect should he venture out into no-man's land.

A gypsy girl with her castanets had nothing on that Frenchman when he played his key in the lock in the kitchen door, and when it finally swung open we stumbled into pitch blackness. Fearful of lighting even a match, our friend rummaged around and came up with three bottles of champagne, but he trembled so that Lou and I took over—Lou popping the corks and me filling our glasses by the simple blackout expedient of dangling a thumb inside the glass and pouring until the wine level approached a top knuckle. So we sat in the dark for an hour, whispering and clinking glasses, and when the bottles were dry we lurched up a ladder and into a bedroom where our friend indicated a double bed and said, "Bonsoir." We tumbled onto a feather quilt, fully dressed and ready for any emergency takeoff, but in expecting sleep to overtake us without delay we were wrong, for now the fun began.

Having given us his own bed, the Frenchman now set about fixing himself a place to sleep. With a load of blankets in his arms and a load of champagne under his belt, he journeyed from a chest of drawers in our room to a bare mattress in the room adjoining. On his first trip, he staggered a bit off course and tripped over a little tin thunder-mug, which sat expectantly in the center of our room. As it clattered across the floor, the Frenchman let out a muffled curse; then all was quiet but for a squeak, squeak, squeak as he headed across the room for another load of bedding. Whang! Another direct hit on the animated pissoir, followed by a much less muffled string of violent curses. We tried not to laugh, out of politeness, but twice again he crossed the room and twice again he stumbled over the same item, and then at last, invisible in some corner, with the final shreds of his control snapped, the Frenchman stood shrieking dreadful imprecations down upon the mischievous pot. Our hysterical guffaws added to the hullabaloo.

Awake before dawn, we lit a smoke and by match-light snooped around the attic. Amidst gloomy old family portraits was a tiny wedding statuette with its wee bride and groom standing patiently, hand in hand, beneath a tall glass dome. Spread on the floor were apples and onions and from a string of drying tobacco leaves I requisitioned a handful for future reference. Then our hung-over friend joined us, and as we left the attic he grinned sheepishly and booted the malicious little pot across the room. With an apology, he explained that it was necessary we leave without delay, for every morning German officers came to have breakfast in his kitchen. Handing us a little packet of food and litre bottle of cider, he bade us adieu.

An eerie shroud of wet and chilly fog swirled over the dark countryside, and the visibility was a scant ten paces. With an hour before sunup, we made our way to a shed where we wolfed down our little breakfast. Then with a piece of wrapping paper and a leaf of tobacco I constructed a fine cigar upon which we puffed, blowing smoke rings while formulating a rough plan of action.

First off, to hell with the English lines. In this mess, discretion seemed far the better part of valor. Wedged against the beach as we were, we were in a tight spot with damned little maneuverability permitted us. We'd had phenomenal luck in bluffing our way from Dozulé to the Channel, and to squirm our way out of the fire and back into the frying pan would require equally good luck. Backtracking ran against my grain, but there was little else to do. We'd retrace our painful steps to Dozulé, then cruise southward for a couple or three days. Then a trek to the west for a hundred or so kilometers should position us for a stab at the American lines, wherever they might be. There really being nothing much to discuss, we set foot upon a strange highway that, we calculated, would lead us to the Dozulé-Houlgate road.

A few minutes later, the bleak dawn was made warm and cheery by the appearance of two German officers who emerged from the fog ahead of us and halted to observe the strange sight of a pair of early-rising French bums who mounted the hill below them.

Each officer was armed with Luger pistol and bulging briefcase, and I put myself in their shiny boots; what the hell would two honest Frenchmen be doing on the highway at this ungodly hour of the morning? We shifted into low gear and the Jerries watched us as we took ten slow paces toward them. Then with one last sharp look, they crossed the highway and went about their business and we went about our own, sweating freely despite the chill of dawn.

And an eventful four or five kilometers later, we realized that we'd missed the Dozulé road in the fog; but since our highway was beamed roughly in the right direction, we continued along it. The sun blinked up and burned away the mists just in time to enable us to spot up ahead of us a cluster of German sentries and Vichy gendarmes who stood at a major crossroads. In the process of circumnavigating this dangerous junction, we blundered upon a bivouacked wagon train, which forced us into a detour of our original detour. Fading in haste to the brush, we dodged again to remain unseen by a squad of Jerries who puttered about in the woods stringing wire. So times was gettin' tough again, and we were getting ourselves quite well lost, what with the continual backtracking and circling and dodging around the whole countryside. Unable to orient ourselves with the map, we picked up a compass course of a shade east of south and trudged off across-country. We walked through rugged, timbered hill country, and the sun was hot in a cloudless sky. The wild perfume of the humid pine woods filled me with the joy of living. I was having a dandy time. A steady pace we held until midmorning, when we paused to quench our thirst at a charming little mountain spring. After a long, long drink of cool, clear water, a smoke.

Now we trod a little dirt road that followed along a twisting, gurgling creek at the bottom of a deep ravine. Each bend in the road was hidden from the next by the heavy forest, and I shortly rounded a sharp bend to bump squarely into an item that instantly caused my morale to take a turn for the worse: a German armored reconnaissance truck, an open-air job wherein sat eight soldiers, rifles poised militaristically upon their knees. Talking into a radio transmitter was an officer, and the whole lousy crew of this machine turned their heads to regard me.

With a frantic wriggling of fingers behind my back as a warning to Lou, I came to a shuddering halt, knowing instinctively that a bluff would not take us past this patrol unchallenged. A few highly pregnant seconds passed. A camouflaged retreat was the only way out. So meeting the hostile glares from the armored car with a disinterested glance, I whipped out the old ruse and took a nonchalant leak, then turned and walked back around the bend and out of sight. After logging a record-breaking one-kilometer sprint, Lou remarked that as long as my kidneys behaved so admirably, we'd be all right.

Away to hell and gone off-course now, we left the woods in favor of a pretty country road. From the forest we'd just left there cracked out a flurry of rifle shots: a couple of Jerries hunting rabbits, we hoped. As it seemed that the forests and roads were equally hazardous, for the sake of easier walking we kept to the roads for a while.

Pair after pair of soldiers cycled past, and as each patrol eyed us we did our level best to convince them that what they looked upon with suspicion was only a pair of legitimate citizens of Normandy: a couple of ragged yokels out for a stroll and engaged in a furious, gesturing discussion of crops and weather. Had any one of these cruising patrols overheard our arguments they would, perhaps, have been a bit bewildered. With a hand stuffed into a jacket pocket and the other describing grand circles, I would sputter to Lou: "Hey! Janvier, Fevrier, Mars, Monsieur Lynch! Avril, Mai, Juin, n'est ce pas?" When I'd pocket my waving hand, my comrade would take over for a while: "Ah oui, Monsieur Tayo! Un, deux, trios! Ou est le vin rouge? Voici le vin rouge! Ha ha ha! Cinq, six, sept. Wisht I wuz in Joisey City! Un deux trios, M'sieu!"

And unchallenged we stood again at the edge of the coastal hills to gaze down into Dozulé. Aiming now to detour the troop concentration there, we set course to the southeast and sauntered down the slope feeling pretty cocky. Nothin' to this racket! In four or five hours we'd covered any number of crooked, zigzag kilometers and slipped through the most dangerous zone. We made happy haste along a good gravel road at the foot of the range of hills, whistling and chatting and now and then flinging a rock at a rabbit or bird just to see him scamper. And we cruised blithely into the middle of a German infantry outfit that, as we neared an innocent-looking stretch of country road, popped from a deep ditch to clamber onto the highway where they milled around, forming ranks. Since they'd all had one good look at us, we cruised ahead to push our way through, walking along behind their rear rank. Upon passing them safely, however, our silent shrieks of joy dwindled to audible moans of frustration as an officer barked out a guttural command—whereupon every last one of the bastards did a snappy right-face, forward-march and fell in behind our outnumbered American spearhead. They were soon hot on our heels and closing the interval rapidly, for the deliberately lazy shuffle we were forced to assume was no match for the pounding German army stride. About to be overtaken, we proceeded with undignified haste along a convenient tree-lined side road. The clomp-clomp-clomp of boots faded in the distance.

"Christ almighty!" said Lou, giving his lucky charm a rub or two. We had a pow-wow and a smoke and came to the conclusion that our luck was wearing well. By nightfall, we calculated, we'd be out of the trap and into less warlike territory. For the remainder of the morning we trudged boldly along the least important highways, picking our merry way unchallenged through an amazing variety of Wehrmacht units that cluttered the countryside.

We called a halt outside a village, for ahead of us at the dead end of our road was a little group of gendarmes and sentries. As we watched, a girl escorting a pony cart full of milk cans left the village and came our way. I slipped her a friendly smile and a line of chatter and twenty francs and she gave us all the milk we could hold at one sitting. When I asked her if those folks ahead of us were inquisitive as to the papers of passing pedestrians, the girl assured us that such was the case.

Which way should we detour the village—east or west? A coin landing heads-down in the dirt gave us our answer, so we headed west down a muddy little trail. Foot-deep hoof prints showed where weary mules had labored to haul overloaded wagons through the soggy low places; and it hadn't been too long before our arrival, as evidenced by the blades of grass and weeds that were just now beginning to spring erect from the wagon ruts. A little pile of smoldering twigs and a profusion of cigarette butts marked a place where the Jerries had called a halt, perhaps to wait out the departure of strafing Thunderbolts. We paused there while Lou made up a bundle of his extra clothes. Despite the streams of sweat that trickled and tickled and ran into my shoes, I preferred to wear all my clothes rather than be bothered with carrying a parcel. The sun was extremely hot, but thinking of the chilly nights to come I hung onto my flying jacket, which was nicely covered by the tattered black suitcoat. At the end of the muddy trail we crossed over a concrete highway and headed along a tar toad, galloping when the way was clear and shifting down to a stroll whenever patrols cycled toward us. As one particular two-man patrol whizzed past us, I sneaked a look at the soldiers' faces and thought that I'd seen them before someplace. It would be risky to be seen by the same patrol more than once, for then we would no longer appear to be local boys but would instead seem to be a pair of young Frenchmen who were clocking off a helluva lot of kilometers in an obvious hurry. Curiosity would lead to suspicious thoughts, and those were two things we would rather keep out of the picture. So it became necessary that we leave this good tar road.

As we stood discussing the advisability of following a little lane we'd come upon, from an unlikely patch of weeds there arose the head of a German soldier. As he talked into a field telephone he kept a glassy eye focused on Lou and me, and we ceased our laughing and joking, changing the subject quickly to a recitation of disjointed bits of French. As we walked away, the Jerry faded back into his dugout and we went to seek out a less populated side road.

As a long, front-bound column of bicycle troops whirred past us, we made a second attempt to abandon this busy thoroughfare. After a few paces down our second-choice road, we saw a sentry who stood like a totem pole at the barbed-wire gate to some sort of prison or guardhouse. Retreating again to the blacktop highway, we carried on for four or five kilometers with a swinging, easy stride which gradually put behind us the mountains and brought us to more level country. On either hand was just a rolling spread of brushland and scrub pine, and there were far fewer soldiers to harass us. For a full half hour not one patrol came along, and we saw not a sign of the enemy.

We'd soon be southbound, and I hummed a gay little tune; hungry I was, but feeling no pain. For we were a hot-shot pair of agents! We'd just strolled up to look over the situation on the Channel Coast and, finding it to be an unpleasant place, we'd strolled away again. We had just jumped out of the fire, climbed out of the lion's mouth, removed our heads from the chopping block, and tested the noose for size. What the hell, if we weren't right now traveling in the right direction, we were at least covering a lot of country. At the rate we were making tracks we'd soon be safely away and poised for another whack at the lines, this time from a different angle!

And as we walked gaily along, patting each other on the head and telling each other what smart boys we were, a mounted patrol of two bicycle troopers rolled into view from over the crest of a hill ahead of us. We cut our long-legged pace back to a casual saunter, hung cigarette butts from our lips and shoved hands in pockets. With berets draped jauntily over ears, an innocent pair were we. Fifty paces between us: and we were being looked over, but that was normal. The interval narrowed and closed and, at the last moment before passing us, the leader of the patrol swerved sharply to our side of the tar road. Swinging from the saddle, he stood blocking our way.

"Aussweiss!" barked the sergeant, accosting Lou. Lou fumbled in his jacket pocket and came up with his passport and identity cards, all skillfully counterfeited by the Amiens Underground.

The sergeant: professional, shrewd-faced, tough, and definitely a suspicious bastard. His partner was a reluctant-draftee type: middle-aged, pale-eyed, dull-faced, and I recognized the pair as having looked us over earlier in the day.

"Aussweiss!" the sergeant had said to Lou. Keerist! He would next ask to see my papers. My saddened heart flopped about like a gasping bullhead in the dry bottom of a rowboat. The rusty machinery in my head picked up a few hundred rpm's and ground out an astoundingly unsatisfactory pile of reckless plans, wild ideas, subterfuges, angles, and deals; all produced at top speed and discarded as rapidly as they appeared.

The German sergeant was going over Lou's papers with thoroughness, and Lou watched the process with an air of injured innocence. The sad expression on his face and the gaping mouth would have done credit to any old village idjit. The Jerry examined the photograph on Lou's aussweiss; glanced from the picture to Lou's face and back again, and finally he nodded, returning the hot papers. He asked Lou what he had in the parcel. "Vetements civiles, Monsieur!" mumbled Lou in a humble tone, and he knelt on the pavement to unwrap his bundle. To stall off the inevitable demand for my papers, I knelt alongside him and we began fiddling with the knots. We goofed around for so long that the sergeant shouted, "Vite! Vite!" at us, and reaching down ripped the package from our palsied fingers. Breaking the twine with a savage jerk, he dumped Lou's Sunday duds carelessly upon the highway.

Snatching up a tan trench coat and waving it in our faces, the irritable sergeant shouted triumphantly, "Englander! Das ist Englander!"

That I interpreted correctly to mean he thought it to be of English origin, and I corrected him: "Non, M'sieur! C'est français: regardez la goddam label!" Dame Fortune, with remarkable foresight, had sewn into the tan coat a label that read "Deauville, France," and the sergeant, scowling because he had been in error, went over the rest of the clothes. Satisfied at last, he then turned to me. He was going to be awfully angry.

But I had taken heart. The sergeant had examined Lou's papers on every one of which was inscribed in bold, black script: "Sourd et Muet!" Deaf and dumb, that is; and Lou and the two soldiers had been carrying on a merry parley. Figuring that both the sergeant and the corporal were little slow on the uptake, I prepared to run a bluff until the last dog was hung.

The stony-eyed sergeant shoved his pointing finger into my puny chest: "Vos papiers!!"

I compounded an angelic expression and fastened it to my face. I felt around in my inside coat pocket, fumbling for nonexistent papers: and as I clawed around under my coat I wished fervently for my Colt pistol, which now hung in its shoulder holster in a far distant parachute locker in England. We were in open country, and the Jerries' rifles were still slung over their shoulders.

I pulled out an empty hand, slapped a few more pockets, and without half trying, assumed a worried look. I snapped my fingers. "Merde!" I exclaimed, "Today I have forgotten my papers! They rest in the pocket of my other coat, back at the old homestead!" Not the most original alibi, but fast if not good.

The sergeant's eyebrows jerked upwards a suspicious notch or two and he grilled me, luckily speaking a brand of French two stages less fluent than mine.

"Where is this house of yours?" "Just at the edge of Dozulé, M'sieur. I am a poor country boy and I live with my old maw and paw on this little farm. My papers, they are in the other coat. Merde!"

"Why are you so far away? Where are you going so fast?"

"I go to visit my old grandmaw, who is ailing."

"This grandmère, she lives where?"

"Sixteen kilometers thisaway, then four kilometers thataway. I will leave now to find mes papiers, eh?"

I had all the answers, and where they came from I don't know. I was straining my French to the limit, but I still had this character outnumbered. After a most sincere song-and-dance had been wrung from me, the tired old corporal peevishly suggested to the sergeant that these two Frenchmen were all right: let them alone. Quit pickin' on 'em and leave us be on our way. My spirits gave a joyous surge, for I thought that Lou's correct papers and my propwash had convinced the patrol of our innocence.

I was playing my role so wholeheartedly that I'd begun to believe all the crap I was laying out, and I felt a flash of righteous indignation when the nosy sergeant flipped his Mauser from his shoulder and nuzzled me with the muzzle of it.

"We'll see," he remarked. "Start walking." I gave him a long look and he poked me again with his rifle. I shrugged and started walking, Lou at my side. Ten paces. I looked around hoping to see the Jerries pedaling in the opposite direction; but they were trudging along behind us, pushing their bicycles. Their rifles were laid over the handlebars and pointed, one each, at Lou's back and mine, and fingers were curled around triggers. The sergeant grinned a foxy grin and I nodded and we clumped along the highway. I had a kind of lynched feeling.

The way it looked to me, Lou was in the clear: and the sergeant, with nothing better to do, was forcing my story and making me lead the way to grandmother's house. I whispered to Lou that at the first crossroads we came to we would stop, shake hands, and he should take off on his own while I led the Jerries around for a while. I figured to lead the sergeant and his partner around the backwoods country until perhaps an opportunity for escape might present itself. I started doping out a line of chatter to hand my captors when I would finally come to the end of my rope, unable to locate the house of my imaginary grandma. We marched steadily for an hour under the blazing sun, and not one crossroads did we come to.

And then the plan went all to hell when the sergeant hollered, "Halt!" and motioned us into a farmyard. A score of grey-uniformed soldiers were tinkering about the neat white house, and I protested:

"Mon sergeant! This is not the farm of my grandmère! Her place is down the road a piece!"

By way of reply he dug the muzzle of his excellent fusil into my starboard kidney, whereupon I willingly accompanied him to the rear of the farmhouse. Peering through an open doorway, I perceived a room full of radio equipment where a number of perspiring Jerry GI's pounded typewriters, turning out great quantities of poop in quadruplicate, all in the best rear-echelon fashion. The corporal guarded us almost sheepishly while the sergeant stomped into the house to return in a moment with a haughty Oberleutenant who, with an exaggerated air of boredom, flicked through Lou's papers and returned them. In miserable French, he then asked a few simple questions, to which Lou responded remarkably well for a deaf-mute. Satisfied, the lieutenant turned to me to ask why I had been walking the highway without my aussweiss. I explained to the lieutenant as I had explained to the sergeant, and as my desperation mounted my French improved proportionately. When I'd had my say, there was a moment of silence, until the lieutenant—cautious type—politely invited us into the house for an interview with the Commandant.

Twiddling our thumbs, Lou and I stood amidst the clacking German-made typewriters while the young snot went out to round up his C.O. I espied on a windowsill a half-dozen egg-sized black plastic concussion grenades; and for a moment I entertained few wild ideas, all of which I let slide. In the first place, I didn't know how to work the damned things: secondly, being no Jesse James, I would have most likely just made a mess with me as the principle ingredient: and lastly, our bluff was working.

The lieutenant returned with a bald-headed old retread in tow. A major he was, some sixty years old and heavy-jowled. A few fancy ribbons decorated his class-A uniform, and damned if the old bastard didn't have a monocle stuffed into one eye! He motioned us outside where the malevolent sergeant clicked his heels and saluted. I knew no German, but from his inflections I thought that he was going out of his way to build up a case against us.

Fumbling, the major started in on me, and his French was so atrocious that I don't think I'd have much trouble with him.

"Votre nom?" he queried.

"Jean Pierre Beaupré, mon General!" I replied in fine accents. That was the French-est sounding name I could dream up on the spur of the moment, and when I humbly boosted the major three full grades he smirked at his lieutenant as though to say: "See there! This ignorant yokel at least realizes my true value to the cause!"

"Monsieur Beaupré," said the major, childishly pleased with his promotion, "why do you walk so far and so fast?"

I did an involuntary double-take before realizing that he'd addressed me. "As a good Frenchman," I replied, "I am only doing my level best to comply with the orders from German high command, which has demanded that all civilians evacuate the Dozulé area by the twenty-fifth day of July." Explaining further, I added that I had departed from my little farm in such a hurry that I had foolishly forgotten my aussweiss. The major, seeking a flaw in my story, cagily asked me the name of the mayor of Dozulé. Figuring that this fathead didn't any more know the name of the mayor of Dozulé than I did, I told him that surely everyone knew the good citizen André Dubois!

With that pat answer, the major let me alone and I hooked my thumbs into my pockets and watched him give Lou a going-over. Examining Lou's counterfeit papers, he too found them to be in order. My sourd-et-muet comrade answered all questions courteously, and that amazing fact lay in my mind and tickled until inside I was grinning like a cat eating spit.

Turning again to me the major asked, in even worse English than had been his French; "Speak you the English, Monsieur Beaupré?"

I made a maximum effort to sound like a Frenchman talking broken

English with a French accent: "Oui, mon General! I spik ze leetle I have learn in l'école!"

Lou's extremely shaky sense of humor was touched off by that corny statement and he suffered a sudden fit of coughing, through which I could detect a strange strangling sound. He recovered hastily and we stood there with such dumb, pleading faces that the major decided that such a pair of stupid farmers could never entertain a thought hostile to the mighty War Machine. Turning to his sergeant, he made a guttural remark that had all the earmarks of being a nasty crack: we could give any town dummy in the Reich a run for his money! With a warning to me that it was dangerous to walk without papers, the old major gestured to us: "Allez! Raus mit uns!" Get out, now, and don't bother me any longer.

My heart was pounding as we walked toward the gate. Hot damn! We'd run the one and original whizzer on these characters! Heh heh heh! I was already chuckling to Lou as I reached out to lift the latch on the gate. And then the sergeant's voice lanced out: "Halt! Halt! HALT!"

I froze in my tracks and turned slowly around.

Chapter 7

"YOU ARE A SPY!"

◆

The sergeant charged toward us through the dust of the farmyard. He staggered me with a couple of punches to my chest and shoulders then, grinning like the devil himself, with one savage jerk he ripped open my suitcoat without bothering to mess around with the buttons.

So there I was, like they say, at zero altitude . . . a long way from home and low on petrol . . . a Jerry on my tail, and me with all guns jammed. I stood in the sun-baked yard of the little German headquarters, my secrets revealed in the brilliant Normandy sunlight, an AAF flying jacket zipped to my neck. From one pocket dangled my soft leather helmet to which I'd clung through thick and thin; from the other pocket a tattered bit of silk danced merrily in the breeze, and when the sergeant tugged at the end of silk, about four yards of parachute panel followed along. The sergeant whipped it recklessly about his head, screaming, "Ah-ha! Ah-ha!" until the major and the lieutenant and a dozen of Der Führer's small fry came running from the farmhouse to form a wolf-pack circle around Lou and Tayo and the nosy sergeant.

The silk scarf and flying helmet were passed around the circle for inspection, and the sergeant shouted, "Qu'est ce que c'est?"

Not quite ready to give up the ghost, I shrugged: "It is nothing! These things I have stolen from the body of the dead aviateur Americain who has crashed near my farm!"

Sarcastic looks from the audience followed this pitiful explanation, and the sergeant, probing deeper into my pockets, came up with my Zippo lighter upon which I had painstakingly engraved: "TPF-486 Fighter Squadron-USAAF."

I stood at bay with an "I've been framed" expression on my face while the sergeant patted a bulge in the front of my jacket to remove—from a skillfully constructed secret pocket in the lining—the skinning knife with worn bone handle, razor-sharp blade, and butt engraved: "Marble USA." The sergeant handed the knife to the major and the major, impaling me upon his eyeballs, shouted, "Amerikanisher!!"

Bright boy, the major. What the hell, I thought. I've had it. Forgetting my hillbilly slouch, I straightened my back and shoved my hands into the blue: "Okay, you son of a bitch! So I'm an American pilot. I surrender!"

The quick change from humble citizen to American flyboy caused quite a reaction: the Jerries jabbered and snapped and growled like a pack of hounds. The major and the lieutenant and especially the sergeant were all grinning like jackals, but I had to laugh at the major, for he was trying to act as though he'd seen through me all the while.

Speaking broken English, the major asked, "Your comrade. He is also American aviator?" I replied, "No, just a friendly Frenchman I met on the highway this morning." Grinning, the major translated for the benefit of his soldiers and everybody laughed and slapped his neighbor on the shoulder. Lou spit on the ground and put his hands up.

So the good knife—twelfth birthday gift from my dad—disappeared into the sergeant's boot, a reward for his good morning's work. Now running expert fingers over the seams of my shirt, the sergeant soon made a little rip and snaked out a hacksaw blade. A little further along he ripped again to display to public view a tiny compass. Another saw blade and a second compass, and each new find was greeted by a nodding of heads and a ripple of laughter and a scattering of applause from the encircling Jerries. That headquarters detail must have been a damned dreary affair until we showed up.

The cigarette case—a gift from César—was lifted from my hip pocket, and when it snapped open, my road map fluttered to the ground. I was glad to've refrained from marking it, for that would have been clinching evidence at anybody's spy trial. Now the sergeant hauled out the hanky into which my trinkets were sewn, and I lowered my hands and snatched it back, ripping out my army ring and stuffing it onto a finger before any of these greedy soldats could claim it as loot. I pinned on my wings and collar insignia, but they looked a bit out of place on a threadbare civilian suitcoat. When the sergeant latched onto my silver flask—six pounds, ten shillings on New Bond Street—and handed it over to the major, I stepped across the circle and retrieved it, unscrewed the cap, and gestured to the major: "Bon santé, Meat-head!" Draining the four or five little swigs of high-octane, I tossed the flask to the Commandant. He'd have gotten it anyway, and I thought maybe he'd feel better if I gave it to him: "Souvenir, mon General!"

Feeling better, I asked the sergeant a question: "Why did you halt us after your officers had freed us?" The sergeant grinned and pointed: my neck was too thin for my body. Wearing so many clothes had made me unnaturally bulky in spots. Hi ho.

Orders were shouted. Our original captors were reinforced by a third party, who menaced us with an oily burp-gun. A dig in the ribs with a gun barrel took the place of further linguistic efforts, and we headed back down the highway, bound for parts unknown. I'd been hoping that the major would keep us at his HQ, for strangely enough we'd won his friendship or a reasonable facsimile thereof. These next people might take a dim view of a pair of Yanks captured in the lines while rigged out like Frenchmen.

The blazing afternoon sun burned down upon our heads as we were forced to retrace our steps. I kept glancing longingly into the brush along the highway until the sergeant came up alongside and made talk with me: "Nix courir, aviateur, nix courir!" He smiled, friendly-like, and patted his rifle. To acknowledge receipt of his warning, I replied that his Mauser was indeed un bon fusil—a fine gun. I wasn't about to try outrunning a slug from it, either, unless a decent opportunity for a break should present itself.

So past the little guardhouse and past the road where Lou and I had questioned the girl with the milk cart; through the tiny village there and under the baleful scrutiny of the group of sentries and gendarmes we'd detoured so carefully; and in another hour we paused at a junction, feet burning, blood pounding in our heads, throats parched. The Jerries checked a map and drank from their canteens.

"Hey, goddammit! Nous avons soif aussi, soldats!" I hollered, kind of mad. We were thirsty, too. The sergeant just grinned and stowed away his canteen, but the corporal tossed us his and we drained it, and thanked him. It tasted like ersatz tea, but it was wet.

Another hour and we skirted Dozulé and trudged up the mountainside beyond. Our gravel road led us through the middle of a large ammo dump, where in the woods on either side were great stacks of shells. I made a mental note of the kilometer post there: 3.8 kilos to Dozulé. If I got to London in time, I'd steer a few bombers to a choice target.

At the crest of the high hill we called a halt at another farmhouse HQ, and the good sergeant went inside to report delivery of two prisoners. Looking browbeaten, he returned accompanied by a highly irritated paddlefoot who chewed out our three guards in great style. And Lou and I made no effort to conceal our amusement as the officer jabbed a pudgy finger into the sergeant's map: wrong place, dumbhead! The detail was snafu. As in our army, the sergeant blamed the corporal, who in turn passed the buck along to the Tommy-gunner. The latter, being at the dead end of the chain of command, stood silent under the shower of abuse. Our little group trudged back down the mountainside, clomped through Dozulé, and headed up a long grade on a main highway.

Also climbing the hill were throngs of weary refugees with their cartloads of furniture and bedding and offspring; and every Frenchman, fearful of showing any trace of recognition for his unfortunate countrymen—namely us—averted his eyes from our party. Halfway up the hill a fine herd of cattle was being cursed along the road by two dusty, red-faced troopers who were kept in a state of continual high rage by their ornery charges. The cattle strayed maliciously into the yards of the houses on the outskirts of town, and the pair of Jerries would no sooner get one old heifer squared away when two others would drift off-course. I chuckled when I watched a deadpan pair of old Frenchmen throw twigs at the cows in compliance with the apoplectic Jerries' hoarse shouts for assistance. Our guards shouted a Jerry-type razzberries, which did nothing to improve the herders' tempers.

Our fugitive status being all shot to hell, with all cause for stealth and secrecy gone, I could find nothing to worry about despite the three guns now focused on the small of my back. For a fact, it was a downright relief to be able to stroll openly for a change through the villages, past the road-

blocks and sentries and Vichy gendarmes. With capture, fear of capture
had disappeared. I figured this recent turn of affairs to be just a delay along
the trail; and with plans for maneuvering through the lines now temporarily shelved, the sole thought beating through my brain was that of
escape. Methods and risks involved in regaining my freelance status would
be determined upon ascertaining the extent of my welcome into the Wehrmacht. Should my captors broadmindedly receive me as a legitimate prisoner of war, then I'd bide my time and escape at a moment involving the
least risk and maximum chances for success. On the other hand, should
the Jerries seek to install me in a wooden kimono, then regardless of the
odds any old escape attempt would suffice. A reckless try would be far better than none at all.

Our dreary procession halted at a farmyard pump and we all had a
drink, the Jerries requesting slave labor on the pump handle. As we were
about to move on, the corporal grumbled something at me and into my
willing hands he shoved my flying helmet.

After having searched me, the Jerries had dumped my escape material
and pocket trinkets into my helmet, making a handy bundle that the corporal had been packing now for many a kilometer under the hot sun. After
casting many a wistful glance his way, I'd given up hopes of ever getting
my hands on some of the more useful items he carried. Perhaps the power
of suggestion had at last seeped through the corporal's thick skull, for now
the jughead ordered me to carry the helmet full of junk. Amazed at my
luck, I complied.

With our trio of guards keeping their five paces to the rear, I held the
helmet in front of me and casually slipped a couple of probing fingers into
the jumble of trinkets. Locating one small compass, I popped it into my
mouth. After another kilometer I had the hacksaw blade. Ripping the rubber casing away and throwing the bits into the ditches, I plastered the bare
blade against my sweating belly and went back into the helmet for more.
Balling up a few franc notes, I tucked them into the lining of my coat and,
fearing to stretch my luck too far, I ceased operations. Chuckling happily,
I again swung the helmet in full view of the guards. The turn of unbelievable luck, donated by the brainless corporal, had given me a shot in the
arm. I was delighted to've recovered some of my escape stuff and grateful
for the corporal's assistance. I tried sticking the compass up my nose, but

it felt strange there and bulged too obviously so I chewed it up, spit out the brass case and the tiny shards of glass, and tucked the little magnetic needle beneath my lip.

At dusk we marched into a farmyard—an isolated place just off a narrow dirt road on the side of a wooded hill. In a barbed-wire pen at the rear of the place were some fifteen British soldiers, half of them wounded, who were guarded by a trio of Jerries armed with wicked-looking machine pistols. "What d'ya say, Tommy!" hollered Lou, and the Limeys hollered right back, "Cheerio, Yank!" A German officer barked at us: "You are prisoners and will not talk to the other prisoners!" So we sat on the top rail of a fence and awaited developments. I was glad to have arrived someplace. We'd been on the road for better than fifteen hours and we were bushed. We felt even more so after calculating that we'd covered between sixty and seventy kilometers since before dawn. Wasted effort!

A small French boy came from the farmhouse and our guards told him to fetch them some cider. When the kid came out with a pitcher and glasses, we signaled him over and gulped down a few quick ones before the sergeant could do anything. Laughing at the hurt look on his face, we told him that it was excellent cider and offered him a drink. He snatched the pitcher from our hands, and as he and the corporal were guzzling I slipped the boy ten francs and gave him the word. He scurried to the house, returning with two tall glasses of cider, which we drained before the furious sergeant could interfere. Dodging a slap, clutching his francs, and grinning impishly, our little friend dashed across the yard.

I wondered when the fireworks would begin, for the helmet full of loot had been taken into the house for examination and inventory, and when the shortages were discovered there was going to be a helluva squawk. But a lantern was placed in a little lean-to and a Jerry seated himself at a wooden table and he pointed at me: "You. Come here."

I sat on a chopping block—of all the damned places—across the table from a German lieutenant and I put myself on guard, for he spoke a better brand of English than I. He slid a card and a pen across the table and told me to fill it out. I entered my name, rank, and serial number in the spaces provided, then slid the card back to him.

"Mmm. Fahrenwald, eh? A good German name! You fight on the wrong side!"

I told him that he'd think he was on the wrong side if he could watch some of his cities disappearing the way I had.

He let that crack pass, then handed the card back to me demanding that I fill out the remaining blanks: squadron number, group number, name of commanding officer, type aircraft flown, and so on down a long sucker-list. I handed him the card and said that I refused to give that information

The lieutenant beat his fist on the table: "You will fill out every blank. You will do as I tell you. You are a prisoner!" I pounded my fist on the table: "You know as well as I do that under the Rules of War a soldier is required to give only his name, rank, and number."

"Ah ha!" replied the lieutenant, "but you are not entitled to those considerations, my friend. For you are not a soldier!"

I knew what he was driving at, but I asked him anyway: "Look, Jack. If I ain't a soldier, what the hell am I?"

"A spy," he retorted sharply. He fished out a cigarette, lit up, and leaned back, letting that last remark sink in. I grinned and asked him for a cigarette, but the discourteous bastard stuffed the pack back into his pocket. Then he started in on me.

"Why do you spy in our front lines, Oberleutenant?"

"I wasn't spyin'. Just walking through."

"What are doing in France?"

"I bailed out."

"Where?"

"In France."

"Exactly where in France?"

"In France."

"Ha! You were parachuted for espionage!"

"Well, hell if I was! I just bailed out, that's all."

"Our flak perhaps, or a Messerschmitt?"

"Just a little engine trouble."

"You are a bomber pilot?"

"Hell no! Fighter!"—he'd gained a bit of information but I had to correct him on that score, for he'd cast a grave reflection on my character.

"A fighter pilot. Hmmm. How many engines—single or twin?"

"Enough."

"If you are a pilot, where is your uniform?"

"Threw it away. Buried it."

"Why?"

"It's obvious. You try the American lines in your uniform!"

"Where did you bury it?"

"In France."

"I find that hard to believe. Who gave you those clothes?"

"I stole them. In France. Off'n a clothesline! And a long ways from here, Jack."

"You lie. Every word is a lie. You were supplied with civilian disguise by your American Intelligence before you were dropped into France. We capture all who spy on our lines. You are aware of the penalty."

"You talk like an old woman."

"Ha! If you are not a spy, show me your identification!"

And he looked at my dog tags and asked for other identification papers. I advised him that American combat pilots had orders to fly with dog tags only.

"Too bad, Lieutenant," said the Jerry. Anybody can acquire a dog tag. The fact that you were in our front lines without uniform or identification leads us to one conclusion. You are a spy. You will be shot."

"Well, that's a helluva way to look at it," I said. "You know goddam well that plenty of your pilots in American PW camps have escaped and been recaptured in disguise. We don't shoot 'em. Why be for shootin' me?"

"If you're not a spy, Oberleutnant, then perhaps you can tell me the names of those Frenchmen who have helped you?"

"You've got my name, rank, and number. That's all I can tell you."

After receiving the same reply to further and more technical questions, the Jerry gave up trying to scare me. He offered me a smoke, lit it for me, and then took off on a different angle.

"I admire your courage, Lieutenant, in trying to penetrate our impregnable front!"

When I told him that flattery would get him noplace, he lost his temper and slapped his hand on the tabletop. "You are stupid. Your leaders are stupid. The German Army will soon throw the English and your American army back into the sea!"

I grinned at him and he sent me away. I sat on the fence and watched

Lou get the treatment, and every other word I caught was, "SPY!" Lou just stood there denying all charges, and sometimes with a French accent: he'd been talking French to strangers for so long that it was habit now. The inquisitor used Lou's counterfeit papers as a lever in an effort to extract from him information concerning the Resistance, but all he got was another name, rank, and number. When Lou rejoined me, his future looked dark and brief, for his phony papers were tangible evidence against him. I hoped the Jerry officer's tactics were standard operating procedure for bluffing military information out of prisoners.

As we sat atop the rail fence, the interrogator approached us and asked, friendly-like, if he might look at my fine ring. I wiggled my fist under his nose and he read off the inscription: Pilot-Officer, USAAF. Then he asked me to take it off so that he could better admire it. Recognizing a souvenir hunter, I tugged at my finger for a moment, then remarked that the ring seemed to be stuck right where it was.

The Jerry flushed and stomped away, then wheeled around and shouted back at me: "Why are you Americans fighting against us in France? You have no right to be here!"

I hollered back at him: "You're no Frenchman yourself, Fritz!" and I let it go at that.

We sat beneath an apple tree. A guard tossed us a half-loaf of stale black bread and a pot of axle grease that he said was ersatz jam. I know it was axle grease, but it filled the gap behind the belt. When a flight of P-47s roared low out of the sunset, Lou ran from under the tree to watch them pass, and he just damned near got himself clobbered. In one voice the guards shouted for him to get out of sight, and one pulled down on him with his rifle. Lou caught on quick and hid under the branches, and it was just as well. Had one of the trigger-happy jockeys peered from his cockpit and seen activity in the farmyard, he'd have peeled down to deliver a royal job of strafing.

Now it appeared that the inventory of our belongings had been completed, for the Jerry lieutenant came charging from the house to accost me: "Where is the little compass, the file, the money?"

"Beats the hell outta me, Lieutenant!" I shrugged: "Your soldiers must have swiped the stuff. Last I saw, they had it all!"

Corralling our guards, the lieutenant accused them angrily. When they indignantly denied all charges, I stood up and was searched again but nothing was found, since I'd given the file to Lou and kept the compass under my lip. Everybody was mad. I'd done it and was glad.

So I sat in the deepening darkness, my back against the apple tree, memorizing the lay of the land and making mental notes of the routes: and pretty soon I had a dandy maneuver plotted out in paces, so that I could run a definite course in the blackout without stumbling or blundering. A few seconds head start was all I'd need, so I watched and waited for the guards to relax their extreme vigilance.

When our night fighters droned overhead, all on the ground became strictly blacked out. A steady rumble came from the front, and intermittent sprays of tracers laced through the skies and the flak twinkled like crazy. Then at midnight, a great canvas-covered truck came groaning up the steep road to back clumsily into the driveway of the farm—beating in one corner of the house and smashing a section of the neat fence in the process. All prisoners were rousted out and queued up at the back of the truck, and the Jerries began to count us aboard. I slipped to the rear of the line in hopes of being unguarded for a moment, but starlight gleamed on too many efficient weapons and I climbed aboard with the others. Two guards sat at the tailgate covering us with Lugers, and we rattled away through the night.

We low-geared up and down the rut roads and clouds of fine dust billowed in over us. Where we were bound, nobody knew or much cared. After an hour or so the truck paused at a gateway where the driver exchanged gruff words with a sentry. We rolled up to a cluster of low buildings and were ordered out. Cinders crunched underfoot. We were counted into a cell and the door was chained behind us. Feeling about in the blackness, I found the only furniture to be the floor, so I flopped flat out in a corner and slept, done in. It had been quite a day.

The clank of a padlock and chain, the bang of a door, and the thud of a rifle butt against the sole of my shoe brought me back into the world at dawn, and it definitely was *not* a case of being awakened and not knowing for a moment just where one might be. We were searched again and the soldier running the show was the meanest looking cuss I'd ever laid eyes on: about five-eight, he was lean and hard with eyes of pale blue ice in a cast-iron face. With one gander at him, I recognized the soldier type that barely exists between atrocities. And when this gentleman focused his gaze upon Lou and me—the two "spies"—his eyes glittered and his voice rasped: "Nix soldats! Espions! Kaput!" I took a rather dim view of his attitude, but remained silent for a change. When the soldier frisking me latched onto the parachute panel I had wrapped around my waist, I retrieved it, explaining that it was a binding for my aching back. I spent a worried moment when asked to remove my shoes, for there was a four-inch saw blade tucked under the heel of one: but it was overlooked, fortunately.

By the dim dawn light I looked the joint over, and the place appeared to've been a brick factory before the Jerries had turned it into a prison. And it made a pretty fair jailhouse, too. We were lodged in a twelve-by-twenty room with iron roof, tile walls, and brick floor and much barbed wire was strung lavishly across the glassless windows. A length of log chain and an enormous padlock made the door quite secure. A heap of moldy straw lay in one corner, and in another was a battered bucket that emitted a blend of choice aromas.

Outside to the south, a graveled path, a high wire fence, and the blank wall of another building. To the west, thirty feet of cindered yard that sloped down to a scummy, greenish, stagnant pool. Beyond the pool, a hill and a hedge and open country, and I caressed with my eyes the distant wooded hills. In vain we waited for breakfast, to dine at last upon individual mental portions of bacon, eggs, and coffee—after which I tightened my belt another notch. Our comrades were an agreeable lot of English soldiers, some captured just the day before and all in various states of disrepair. The prize of the lot was a husky young paratrooper from Scotland, Peacock by name. A lively gent full of jokes and songs, he was mad to the core for having wasted his years of commando training; and in his educationally profane brogue, Private Peacock gave us his sad cry. Dropped at midnight of D-Day, he'd been; but the bloody aviators had chucked him into the swamps on the wrong side of the Orne. Five friggin' weeks had he spent livin' like a friggin' mole in amongst the forward Jerry outposts, existing on rations salvaged from crashed gliders and upon raw meat salvaged from the dazed cattle that wandered around no-man's land. He'd finally squirmed to within fifty yards of the English outposts, had been fired upon by both German and English, and had then been captured. When I told Peacock that I was quite put out with General Montgomery's leisurely liberation schedule, he informed us that if we thought we'd been cursing Monty's bones; we should have been tuned in on the exiled paratroopers as they lay out in no-man's land for a month and a half!

I learned that three British assaults had been launched in an effort to break the German lines at Caen. Each had been notable for its lack of success. Following the terrific aerial bombardment that Lou and I had watched from the hut above Dozulé, English armored columns had actually penetrated to within six kilometers of where we sat, but they'd paused indecisively, to be cut off and chopped up. Our guess at that time had been pretty good, for we'd figured it rightly; only now I could see why the attack might have failed. I'd seen at firsthand how well the Jerries had exploited the excellent defensive features of the coastal terrain.

Since Lou and I thought solely of escape, I was a bit surprised to find that we were alone in that attitude. Too risky, said the other prisoners. Several expressed the thought that we had holes in our heads, for the bloody war was over. Well, I figured that it was every man to his own opinion. The war would be with us for a long time to come, and I craved to be out.

Whetting my desire for freedom was the critical tobacco situation. It was extremely sad, but nobody had any cigarettes at all. When I hollered "Tobac?" at a guard, he just spat through the wire and walked away. That settled that. We went through our clothes, scraping seams and shaking crumbs until we'd accumulated a tiny cone of tobacco and lint, enough to roll up a few smokes. So we sat in a circle and told lies and passed around a lumpy cigarette and everything was rosy.

At sundown our door was unlocked and a couple of Jerries carried in a kettle of watery potato-peel soup. We ate it. After dark, as the others slept, Lou and I stood quietly at the window noting the methods of our guards. That bastard sergeant came along, and seeing us he raised his fist and his voice: we should lie on the floor and stay away from the windows at night. So we did, and so ended our first day in prison. The hours had dragged. The day had been a month. And swearing to hell I wouldn't be caged for very long, I went to sleep amidst a swirl of dirty deals which rat-raced around in my head.

Breakfast at six: a cup of bitter ersatz coffee. After a few hundred laps around the room, I dug out my pencil stub and set out to beautify the wall of our cell. In a couple of hours I had before my delighted eyes a magnificent panorama of a terrific dogfight between the AAF and the Luftwaffe. Mustangs and Jugs whizzed about, clobbering hell out of a bunch of 190s and 109s; and if I do say it myself, it was a masterpiece. Two guards who'd been watching me through the window now unlocked the door and came in for a better look. One laughed: "Trés bon," he said, "But not . . . ahh . . ." and he waved his hand for expression. He put a finger on the insignia of a flaming Focke-Wulf and said, "Ha ha! Amerikaner!" and I grinned and said, "Ha ha! Luftwaffe!"—and he held out his hand for my pencil and walked out with it. All of which killed the afternoon very nicely.

Came suppertime and chunks of rock-like bread and a pot of nauseous jam were passed through the window to us, along with the comment that we'd have to make it last until the following night. But a minute and a half later there remained only crumbs, and the silence was shattered by sarcastic belches and hums of mock satisfaction. And that was that. After dark our door banged open and a half-dozen new prisoners stumbled in.

Among the new guests were two British fighter pilots, a Scot, and an Aussie, and both had breakfasted amongst friends and both were now bleeding in places and were very dejected citizens. But I was really glad to see them, for besides having a half-pack of cigarettes apiece, each was a fellow stick-and-rudder boy. They divvied up their tobacco with us and, after having smoked dung and straw for so long, my first drag on a Player caused the room to whirl and I was forced to sit down.

This Aussie was quite a jockey, with a dozen victories under his belt. This day, however, while hot on the tail of his thirteenth victim, a pair of hot-rock 109s had ganged up on his Spitfire and had shot it all to hell up over the front, and he'd bailed out into the unkind clutches of the tough Jerry infantrymen. The other flier, to my delight, I found to be a fellow Mustang pilot. Flight Leftenant Jock Warnock was his name and he hailed from Glasgow, and he was but twenty-one years old, calm and philosophical, and he spoke with a fine, rich brogue. Jock too had been up over the German front, and he related the facts of his downfall. Circling around like a big-assed bird he'd been, and directing by radio the English artillery fire, when a pair of sly Messerschmitts had pounced in out of the sun, crawled up his tail, and clobbered him but good. He'd parachuted into a thicket where he'd lain, crippled and silent, until a prowling Jerry had stuck him in the leg with a probing bayonet. So here he was.

As each of these pilots had bailed out of his swift little fighter, he'd been swept back into the horizontal stabilizer of his ship, with the result that the Aussie's leg was broken and splinted roughly, while Warnock's was split open along the calf from ankle to knee and bound around with paper bandages through which his blood seeped slowly. But each pilot made jokes over their troubles, for each knew truthfully that he was just damned good and lucky that he wasn't a charred four-pound roast smoldering at the bottom of a scrap-lined hole in the ground. That's an instantaneous transformation at 500 mph.

Each to his own—ground-grabbers in one bunch and airmen in another—we sat on the floor and swapped dirty jokes and war stories and smoked and howled at the guards whenever they'd peer in at us. It was a dandy night, but a square meal and a fifth of rye would have made a considerable contribution to the party. Lou and I envied the British pilots their trim woolen battle dress, both for the warmth against the chilly darkness and for the exact category in which it placed them. As for Lou and me, for quite a while now spiteful faces had been appearing intermittently at our window to shout at us savagely: "Nix soldat! Espion! Kaput!" I wished to hell that somebody would make up his mind about us one way or the other.

And the following morning the malignant sergeant showed up conducting a trio of dapper officers on a tour of inspection. The detail came to a halt outside our window to gaze in upon the two disguised aviators, whereupon the sergeant—christened by Lou "The Bastard of Bonnesbocque"—pleaded bitterly with his officers, biting off his words and spitting them in our direction. The argument was in German and I didn't know that ugly language, but it wasn't too hard to follow: "Lookit the spies, Herr Hauptmann! Dirty Amerikaner spies! Pretty soon I shoot them, eh? Maybe today I shoot the spies, please?"

I watched the little conference with interest. The ranking officer, cranking a monocle into his face, stepped to the barbed wire to focus a bleak eyeball upon Lou and me. I grinned and said, "Bonjour!" and I thought I saw a trace of amusement where before there'd been only orneriness. This character backed off, barked a string of orders to the sergeant, and then the officers piled into a jeep and took off.

The Bastard entered our cell, pointed to Lou and me and Jock, jerked his head, and we trailed him out into the light of day. Wordlessly he ushered us into an adjoining cell, slammed the door savagely, and hung a gigantic padlock in the latch. Hot damn!

Had just Lou and I been cut out of the herd, I'd have settled down to some dead-earnest worrying. But Jock, the only other officer/prisoner, had been included in the transfer and I figured that the Jerry officers had ordered the sergeant to segregate his prisoners: officers in one cell, enlisted men in another. And the Bastard was plenty mad about it all, for soon he appeared at our window to snarl, "Pah! Officiers Americains, nix gut! Come to France to fight and throw away their uniforms!"

I figured I was safe now, so I swapped insult for insult and gave the Bastard a nasty grin: "Heh heh! You are almost a civilian yourself with the battle away off yonder. You're in grave danger!" The son of a bitch had a Polish campaign ribbon stuck on his chest and I knew he'd done his share of slaughter, but I felt like needling him.

Pale with fury and obviously deep in murderous thought, the sergeant paced slowly away. Our BOQ was a pleasant suite of two small rooms with floors of red tile and walls plastered in a charming shade of powder blue. One room, six by eight, had a window to the west and a heavy door to the north. The other, eight by ten, had a long window that afforded a fine view of the main gate and the building at the north edge of the compound. A table we had now, and two chairs, and instead of the cheerless, battered, bucket-type latrine we now had exclusive rights to a cheerless, battered, kettle-type affair. On the floor of the larger room was a thin, square, verminous straw mat. Even in prison, it seemed, did rank have its privileges!

At midday our forlorn trio stood staring gloomily out over the prison yard, and I was lost in a hazy recollection that, back in the dim past, this part of the day had been known as "lunchtime"—whatever that meant. To disturb our reveries, along came the Bastard twirling a bunch of keys at the end of a chain.

We directed a couple of insolent belches in his direction and fixed our eyes upon him. He stopped and stared back, and squaring off he leveled a finger at us and made with the old refrain: "Espions! Kaput!" I growled out that he could stick that up his nose, and Lou snarlingly offered even less delicate advice, and we stared at the Bastard until the corners of his mouth jerked viciously downward. A hard man, that sergeant. I've never laid eyes on a guy who wanted so badly to knock somebody off as did the Bastard who craved to liquidate us.

To be caged was a sad thing. Now Lou paced the floor in tighter and tighter concentric circles until I feared he might soon, with a shrill cry, disappear up his own chimney. As usual, he was polishing the merry hell out of the little fetish he clutched in hands clasped at his back. Pretty soon I fell in behind him to better observe the manipulation of this charm, which appeared to be a string of wampum or of seeds or the like. I noted that my worthy comrade made medicine quite systematically, tweaking his talisman bit by bit and notch by notch: rubbing one little nubbin while muttering an incantation, then fumbling to the next to mutter another. Endlessly around the string his fingers traveled, and there was no appreciable variance to the monotonous abracadabra. I suspected my partner of having substituted this device for his share of the brainwork in our battle of wits with the Wehrmacht. And I was irritated.

"Hey Lou!" I asked. "You've been banking on that modified rabbit's-foot to get us through some of the tight spots, eh?"

He admitted that he'd been relying upon it pretty heavily all along the line. I suggested tactfully that maybe if he'd try rubbing all the bones at once, and hollering instead of mumbling, perhaps he could arrange to have us sprung. But he said with some reluctance that he didn't think that'd work. I let the subject drop before I blew a gasket.

I set about examining our new cell inch by inch, and when I came to a small stovepipe hole in the partition between the two rooms I thrust an exploratory arm up into the opening. My fingers touched something, and I fished it out and looked and chuckled. I was amazed. For I'd found tucked away in the chimney hole—placed there either as a result of Lou's witchery or the desperation of some previous prisoner—a long thin bar of steel that had a knife-like flat part forged on either end!

I was amazed, you see, because set into the rear wall of our larger cell was a knobless locked door; and consumed by curiosity as to what might lie behind that door, I'd scratched and pried and given it up as a bad job. But now, chuckling with glee, I posted Lou and Jock at the windows, straightened out one end of the tool, and set about probing the keyhole of the mysterious door. In a few minutes I'd managed to pick the lock. I redesigned the tool to form a device to operate the spring catch, and I probed some more, and before long the door swung open and I poked a cautious head through the crack and took a looksee. I held my breath, quietly closed the door, crawled over to a chair and sat there. My two spotters gazed at me doubtfully, for I shook with uncontrollable mirth and was unable to talk. Wiping the tears from my eyes I lurched over to Lou, clutched his shoulder and choked out the hysterical news:"It's a hee hee hee! Ho ho ho! It's a ha ha ha! It's a goddam TOOLSHED!"

For a truly delightful scene had met my eyes in that little room behind the knobless door. The Jerries, upon appropriation of the little brick factory, had evidently cleaned out the rooms and had dumped tools, books, files, and assorted junk into that one storeroom. They'd locked the door, removed the knob, and—for want of intelligence—had assumed that since there was no knob, nobody would open the door! Sacré bleu! We were practically back in Piccadilly!

Jock and Lou kept close watch at the windows while I operated with maximum stealth on hands and knees prowling the dusty dark storeroom, fetching out on each trip whatever I thought might come in handy sometime: a screwdriver, a bundle of brand-new hacksaw blades, a ball-peen hammer, a pick-mattock, a dandy tire iron, an eighteen-inch crowbar, a trowel! Each item I stashed lovingly away, with the smaller tools going up into the chimney hole or into the straw mat, and the pick, shovel, hammer, and crowbar sliding into position beneath the tabletop. For use whenever escape work might be impossible, I brought out a ream of paper and a handful of pencils, and as the scanty hiding places in our cell became loaded with equipment, the absurdity of the affair grew upon us. My dry chuckles and Lou's sharp laughter floated out across the prison yard until I feared that our guards might wonder if their prize prisoners were sounding a bit too cheerful. In the course of an hour, our morale had zoomed from the deck right on up to thirty thousand feet and our barren cell had been transformed into a veritable machine shop. We had a surplus of gadgets worth fifty bucks per ounce in Alcatraz! Hot damn! I relocked the door and rubbed a little spit and dust into the jimmy marks around the lock.

Tinkering around experimentally, I bored a hole through eight inches of tile wall for use as a speaking tube between our cell and that of Peacock and the soldiers, and the first message to come through was one of profanity from the paratrooper. It seemed that as I'd been grinding the hole through the wall, a guard had been searching Peacock's cell, and the latter, to cover our scratchings, had been forced into constant song for a full half-hour. Now, in exchange for late war news from newly arrived prisoners, I passed through the hole a pencil and a few saw blades. And upon learning that the front lines were quite static, we spent a jolly afternoon working on the barbed wire over the windows, whistling to drown out the rasp of the saw teeth. Before long we had a half-dozen strands of wire cut nearly through, and we filled the slots with bits of bread.

Famished by suppertime, we dined royally upon brackish water and bits of foul bread, which we mixed together to create a tasty paste. This bread was by far the worst yet—very sad stuff which, if poured upon the floor, would disintegrate into a pile of green powder. It made me mad, and I cut through a few more wires before calling it quits for the day.

And the guns rumbled and planes moaned around overhead, while the boots of our guards crunched slowly back and forth outside our cell. Crickets peeped as squadrons of voracious mosquitoes droned up from the stagnant pond to feed upon the prisoners, and I was lucky to have the parachute panel to wrap around my face. With hands stuffed into pockets and beret pulled low over my forehead, I was able to sleep relatively unmolested by the varied species of life that thrived in our straw mat and filled the air about us.

In the middle of the night there came a short burst of submachine-gun fire, and in the morning a dead mongrel dog lay out on the cinders. A most effective warning to us, for the night had been completely dark when one of the guards had squirted his burp-gun toward a strange sound.

Our old pal the English-speaking interrogator and a medic came to the prison, and while Jock's leg was being dressed Lou and I bitched about the room service, demanding more food, drinking water, a razor, and water to wash in. Since it was plain to see that our sad cries failed to cause the lieutenant's heart to bleed, I tauntingly inquired of him as to who was winning the war. He went away mad. Soon, however, a guard unlocked our cell to permit me to fetch from the swamp a pail of water, and before long we were all sweet and clean.

Not aiming to let this doghouse life run me down, I established a rigid routine of exercises calculated to maintain the excellent physical condition I'd been in when captured. Now, calisthenics for anybody but a jailbird are a crock of sour owl droppings, but I had to keep in shape somehow, and every morning I'd draw an interested audience of guards who would watch me dancing uninhibitedly about the cell, skinning-the-cat from the doorway, squatting, stooping, and running nowhere fast. Their expressions told me that they thought I was a leetle off my rocker, but I was feeling fine. The lack of food didn't even bother me, for I'd never eaten much anyway.

We sawed wire at every opportunity, singing and whistling frantically to cover the furious scratchings of our saws, with the result that our dingy cell sounded like a non-union carpenters' shop full of happy, eager workers. The Jerries really believed that we'd all made the turn and I could scarcely blame them: for booming forth from our cell for hours on end came our three voices singing three different songs, which were all mixed up and punctuated by fits of wild laughter whenever the comedy of the situation would overtake us. When a curious or confused sentry would walk over to look for himself, he'd see three grinning citizens industriously cleaning their fingernails with splinters, or playing with the ants that lived in a corner.

When the guards got too curious, we passed the hours with pencil and paper, having made a checkerboard and a deck of cards that enabled us to lose millions of theoretical pounds to one another at various games of chance. The ream of paper acquired from the tool shed came in handy, for it consisted of tally sheets from a big gambling house on the Channel Coast. Engraved at the top of the sheets was the name "Casino de Cabourg," and in vertical columns were spaces for tallying gains and losses at Vingt-et-un, Chemin de Fer, roulette, and other equally interesting hobbies.

Keeping track of the guard mount, we soon learned that there were ten guards in all plus their ringleader, The Bastard. What a bunch of characters! There was Egg-Head: soft, fat, fortyish, bald like an egg and equally stupid. Sharpy was tall, lean, sloppy, and distrusting of Lou's and my motives, for he kept his beady black eyes on us, forcing us continually to break off work. Grumpy was a fat old buck-private of extremely sour disposition; temperamental, he was, and always quarreling peevishly with the other guards. Snoopy could generally be found sneaking along the wall toward our cell, highly suspicious of our singing and whistling. He smelled a large-sized rat somewhere but couldn't quite put his finger on it. A preening, weak-faced type was Liver-Lips who, we calculated, was queer as an eight-dollar bill. Hitler-Youth was a six-foot-six, flashing-toothed, blond young warrior who looked as though he'd been machined to perfection rather than having been dropped by some old squaw in Berlin.

But the prize of the entire detachment was The Rooster: a runty, funny-looking, big-nosed, sad-sack gremlin, he acted so much like a rooster that I think there must have been a flurry in the dust at his conception. His head was too small for his helmet, his uniform was too large for his frame, and his boots were sloppy on his feet, but he paced his beat with much dignity. Whenever he'd catch himself smiling back at our derisive hoots, he would change his smile into a self-conscious scowl and change his strut into a stiff-legged semi-goosestep. Every fifth step he would toss back his head with a nervous tic, to look exactly like a banty rooster readying itself for a resounding crowing. We actually held our breath sometimes, waiting for the eruption, and poor Lou with his touchy funny-bone would watch the Rooster for a few minutes then sink to the floor howling with laughter and clawing his ribs.

These guards, however, were good soldiers: blindly obedient, duty-struck, pig-headed, and obsequious before the slightest symbol of authority, they saluted one another until I thought there would be arms broken in the process. The run of the nine guards at least smiled once in a while and acted like people, but not so the Bastard. A robot, he, with a one-track mind, his single obsession being a hearty bang-bang to anybody not on his team. One could have swung an axe at that character with a dented blade as the sole result, for the only human feeling in his makeup was hate. From dawn til dark each day, Lou and I razzed the lot of them indiscriminately, once running a check to determine which guards understood English. Our method was simplicity itself, for as each sentry passed our window we called him every unprintable name in our very complete vocabularies; the theory being that if they savvied our lingo at all, they'd show a definite reaction. Liver-Lips—among others who became quite hot under the collar—replied to our insults with remarks shouted angrily in German. We chalked him up as being unsafe to talk in front of. An amusing and educational experiment.

After the fourth day, our chow showed a slight improvement when Italian labor troops took over the task of feeding the prisoners. Morning and evening they provided the comic relief for our show. Wearing green

Wehrmacht uniforms topped by gaily feathered Alpine caps, they all wore fine beards: fork-tailed, curly, and magnificent beards. Treated by the Jerries with contempt and not even trusted with weapons, theirs was a worthless role and they were aware of it. But now we knew when to expect our supper, for of an evening, away off in the distance, we'd hear a meaty voice singing fancy long-hair stuff and we'd grin at one another and listen: I could imagine the unhappy Eyetie walking along the dirt road leading the pony cart with a tub of chow aboard. With heart and soul back in Italy, he'd sing at the top of his lungs, stopping when particularly inspired to wave his arms about as he pumped out the solo part with maximum feeling. Snapping back to humiliating reality, with a shake of his bearded head he'd continue along to the prison gate. When the cart would stop at our window we'd holler Dago cuss words at the driver and his helper, but they seldom dared look at us in fear of incurring the Jerries' wrath. Sometimes, though, after looking around carefully they'd duck their heads down to cast a foolish smile at us. Maybe they appreciated our laughter, for we began to get a few hunks of meat in our potato soup: horse meat, dog meat, cat meat, mule meat, lungs, guts, and so on—all the finer cuts. Some of the meat was curious stuff, tough and gristly with little white tits sticking up all over; but it was meat and we gobbled it hungrily.

After a week in Bonnesbocque Jailhouse, a new batch of prisoners came in, all British enlisted men and mostly wounded. Peacock gave me the latest Invasion news via our speaking tube, and I was inspired to action.

I sketched on the smooth blue wall a large and intricate map of the Invasion front, every contour of which I knew by heart. I drew in the south coast of England, and in the rollicking waves between the two countries fishes leaped hither and yon while a few merry pilots floated gaily about in their rubber dinghies. Since I had plenty of time on my hands, the map was done in the best of cartographic style, with a fine compass rose in one corner and Old Man Weather nearby, puffing out a stream of cirrus clouds. At Cherbourg I planted an American flag, and the Union Jack fluttered above The Master's deep dugout near Caen. Assorted tanks and guns and fighter aircraft were all busily blasting hell out of a flock of little Jerries, and down near the location of our prison I drew a large and animated swastika with a little shoe on each leg, and the thing was rolling fast past a signpost that pointed "To Paris."

As the finishing touch, I put in a herd of wee helmeted Jerries all high-tailing for points eastward amidst a swarm of flying bullets. In all, I spent five or six grinning hours on the map. It was a professional job and I was proud of it. Lou and Jock, however, were slightly perturbed, for they claimed that the Bastard would blow his top when he saw it.

That night, as usual, the Italians came vocalizing along the trail with our skimpy evening ration of ersatz coffee and potato soup, but an additional treat was in store for us! Egg-Head brought in a six-inch length of bologna sausage and, by gestures, told us that it was all ours. The meat looked peachy and Egg-Head's generosity was overwhelming. We eagerly borrowed his knife and divided our feast into thirds, whereupon our mouths stopped watering. For upon closer examination, we realized that we would have to work for our supper. The meat was fifty percent dead and fifty percent alive and kicking with a thriving tribe of fat white maggots. Grinning at our consternation, Egg-Head locked the door behind him as he left us. A delightful half hour was spent in picking maggots from the meat; and when that feat was more or less accomplished we spread the remnants of bologna over a few salvaged chunks of bread and ate all with gusto, telling each other philosophically that the maggots missed would add that much meat to the diet. I smacked my chops and smoked an imaginary cigarette and wandered over to the window. Egg-Head, in a lean-to some twenty feet from our cell, was cooking himself some supper over an open fire. Beefsteak and potatoes sputtered juicily in a frying pan, and it smelled very good, and I got mad. Indelicately snuffling up an oyster, with a mighty and highly accurate puff I lobbed the charge through the wire, high into the air, across the yard, and into the very center of Egg-Head's culinary activities. Lou hollered across the yard: "Bombs away, Egg-Head!" Egg-Head shook his fist and dumped the contents of the frying pan onto the ground, shouting at us in German. I cussed him out in American and we all felt better about the maggots.

For the past three or four evenings Lou had been lecturing to Jock upon the advantages of Joisey City, while I had needled Lou with baseless comments about that city being the most corrupt establishment west of Berlin. Lou had covered his subject well, expounding profoundly upon the climate, industries, parks, babes, movies, government, transportation system, waterfront, Lou's relatives—including a defunct uncle who had driven a trolley car over the Palisades into the Hudson back in Ought-nine and so on and on and on, with me picking his story to bits as he unraveled it.

But tonight Lou sat stroking his Weary-Willie beard and Jock sat stroking his flaming Scottish beard, and I sat playing mumblety-peg with the knife that Egg-Head had forgotten to reclaim. Jock at last gave with his sad cry, which involved his great romance with a beautiful girl test-pilot back in England, and a tender tale it was. Jock was worried now, for fear she thought him dead and might possibly assuage her great grief by flinging her lovely body into the arms of some other flying type. Lou and I helpfully said that such was no doubt the case by now; and so to bed we went, with a bit of drizzle blowing through the barbed wire in upon us.

Bright and early in the morning the Bastard unbolted our door and stomped in. Someone had tipped him off that there was dirty work afoot, for he inspected our cell quite carefully. Examining the barbed wire, he gave several strands an experimental tug and, oddly enough they held together. He ran his hand up into the stovepipe hole and felt around. Had the son of a bitch put his hand another inch higher, he'd have been badly cut and bruised by the great weight of tools that would have tumbled upon his head. He felt everywhere in the straw mat except where the numerous items were concealed and then, with his back to us, he saw the mural on the wall.

His shoulders stiffened noticeably. The back of his neck took up a glow. His hands clenched as he stared for a full minute at the map. He did an about-face, and his face was bleakly devoid of any semblance of humor. Shouting at us in German and receiving no answer, since none of us knew his goddam language, he shouted again, pointing at us and then at the wall. A pair of his yardbirds came into the cell to see what might be the difficulty. Grumpy looked at the map, a hurt expression crossing his face, and Snoopy, looking like a cat eating spit, was happy that we were on the receiving end of the Bastard's temper. The latter was working himself into a fine frenzy.

"Who done it?" he shouted, in bad French.

"C'est á moi," I confessed.

"Stand up when you speak to me!" he shouted. I complied, there being little else to do under the circumstances. The Bastard pointed to the flags that waved merrily from the beachhead.

"What are these?" he barked.

"Las drapeaux alliées."

With a mighty blow to the wall he indicated the swarm of little gremlins that overran the German lines: "What are these?"

"Beaucoup soldats alliées!"

He jabbed a forefinger into the running swastika. "What is this?" he screamed.

It was perfectly obvious. But he was asking the questions so I explained: naturellement, it represented the Wehrmacht.

Peering closely at the map, the Bastard noted the little shoes on the swastika. Driving his finger into the wall, he demanded that I tell him what they were.

"Petits sabots, sergeant," I explained, thinking to myself that if he couldn't recognize them as such, either he or I had better give up.

"Quel significance?" he shouted, as if he didn't know.

"Les Boches, they run for Paris," I replied. It was a grave faux pas on my part, for one does not call a Boche that to his face. There was quite a reaction: his eyes narrowed and glittered like those of a bird. The veins of his temples throbbed noticeably.

Jerking out his Luger, with the muzzle of it he poked me over into a corner of the cell, and I thought that perhaps my goose was cooked. "Je suis Oberleutenant: vous êtes un sergeant!" I reminded the Bastard, thinking that perhaps a mention of rank would register in his German mind. I saw in his eyes a change of mind . . . a little indecision. He raised the pistol as though to swat me across the face with it: and then the Bastard got a grip on his childish rage, becoming suddenly very military. Returning the gun to his belt he backed away and, still white-hot and standing at rigid attention, he yowled at me a mixture of French and German to the effect that three high officers of le Gestapo would he bring to see my map and to question me. Having finished that outburst, he had cooled down somewhat and almost had regained control of himself: but then, looking over my shoulder, he did a regular old double-take and screamed out at me once again: "Did you write that?"

Looking around, I saw that he had noticed a small but elaborately lettered sign that had been drawn on the wall.

It read succinctly, "Down Mit Der Nazzys!"

I denied all knowledge of it, erasing the smile from my face before it appeared, for I realized that the sergeant had taken the message to heart. He found, upon inquiry, that neither Lou nor Jock had written the sign. Backing off a pace, The Bastard leveled a finger at me, of all people, and in English he shouted: "YOU LIE!"

And with that wild claim hanging in the air, the Bastard took off like a horse-opera villain.

We flopped onto our mat and I remarked to the boys: "Some joke, eh?"

Jock said, "Aye, lad."

And Lou waggled a finger at me and muttered, "You lie!" whereupon he went into a frenzy of wild laughter.

I pondered the Bastard's reactions: such an insanely stupid type was definitely a hazard to my longevity. I was, however, delighted to have been the instigator of such furor, and I was greatly pleased to have been able to get under the sergeant's thick skin. His dignity was spread all over the countryside.

In a couple of hours, people entered our cell without first knocking: three black-uniformed SS officers accompanied by The Bastard, Snoopy, and Hitler-Youth. There was a lot of rank around and everybody started in saluting: the Bastard clicked his boot heels and saluted the officers. They returned the salute. All the guards saluted. The officers returned the honor. The SS officers turned to Lou and Jock and me and stuck out their arms in a Hitler-highball: we gave them back two American and one quivering RAF-type salutes.

The SS people looked first at the map while the sergeant, with angry commentary, indicated all the finer points. No reaction. One of the officers said, in passable English: "It is very good!" There was a little twinkle in his eye. The committee filed up to read the tiny sign: "Down Mit Der Nazzys!" Again, no reaction: and the Bastard was frantic because nobody was mad but him. He piped up that we had all denied having written the sign. The officer who'd admired my mural asked me if I'd printed the little slogan. I denied all.

"Do you give your word of honor as an American officer that you have not written this?"

Figuring that this honor-among-thieves business was a lot of sheep-dip, and in order to lower the Bastard's stock a little more, I replied, "Yessir!" and that closed the trial.

People again began saluting with a reckless flurry of arms, and our cell was very small for that sort of thing. Caught in the crossfire, I returned the SS officers' outthrust-arm salute with another just like it. But it wasn't a traitorous thing: I was just confused for the moment. So ended my first public art exhibit. Keeerist, what a sensation!

The trio of SS wheels stood out in the cinder yard and, to our delight, they chewed out the sergeant—evidently for having made a fool of himself. Peacock, who savvied a bit of German, reported through the speaking tube that the Bastard had been told that, despite the fact that Lou and I were in civilian clothes, we were still Americaner officers and would be treated according to Hoyle. The SS might have gone around stomping on robins and sparrows, but they at least appreciated a good sketch when they saw one.

The Bastard re-entered our cell after the officers had left the prison. Perhaps having been told that there was, after all, an element of humor in the matter, he stood before the map and glared at it. He snarled something at the wall. Snatching up his key ring, with two violent passes he scarred a big X across the scene. Turning to Lou and me he hollered, disappointedly: "Pah! Just like two officers Americains! Draw on the walls and then tell lies!" With a mean look and one last "Kaput!" he trudged away, wounded deeply. In a little while a soldier came along with a toolbox and installed a new and heavier padlock on our front door.

Lou examined the scratches on the wall: "Christ! They're an inch deep!" The Bastard paced back and forth in the prison yard, thinking. Then he came to our window to hold out a hand, saying, "Stylo! Stylo!"

Hell, I had pencils to burn, so I gave him a couple and he went away, happy in the thought that he had stymied further artistic efforts on my part.

We sat and dreamed up new and different ways to irritate the prison detachment. With Peacock's able assistance, we got up an inter-cell, mellow barbershop quartet and rendered "Der Führer's Face" (until ordered to stop) and other of the old songs. And pretty soon I had another run-in with the Bastard: as I was tripping blithely down to the slough to empty the honey bucket, the sergeant ran to the top of the hill where he stood pointing his pistol at me and hollering, "Halt! Halt!" Dropping the bucket, I put up my hands and all the boys could see that I wasn't trying to run for it. Mad as all hell, I yowled up at the sergeant: "Yah! Ya simple son of a bitch!"

Liver-Lips, standing by, evidently translated, for the Bastard grinned and walked away. I reckoned that he was just trying to get a rise out of me— which he did.

The entire evening was spent in an effort to lure to our windowsill one of the flock of skinny chickens that always moseyed around the prison yard. We'd been using these chickens all along to test our moldy bread for us: if they ate the stuff, so would we, and when they'd spit it out and walk away, we'd follow suit. But tonight we plotted hungrily: we'd catch one, jack it up, and build a fire under it. Finding a chunk of bread to their taste, we tossed out a trail of crumbs and pretty soon one old hen stood directly below us, but the smart little rascal refused to hop to within range of our eager fingers. At last the Bastard wised up to our game and shooed away the flock. He made Lou go out and pick up all the crumbs.

At dawn Lou let out a rather horrified whisper and called me to the window, and I saw that the prison complement had formed in a circle on the cinder yard. In the center of the circle with bowed head stood a creature dressed only in tattered trousers: a man with shaven skull and starved and bony face, with glaring eyes burning from deep-sunken sockets. His age might have been twenty or it might have been fifty, for it was difficult to penetrate his dreadful disguise. "Ivan!" shouted Egg-Head, and the living ghost shambled over to him. Whirling him about, Egg-Head booted him across the circle and another soldier booted him back again. To and fro flew Ivan until he fell in a limp heap. With a kick and a jerk, a guard pulled him to a vertical position, and all the boys were laughing and howling and hollering, "Ivan! Ivan! Ivan!" They were having a helluva good time. The Bastard came along then, and it was the first time I'd seen him really smile. Picking up a shovel, he handed it to Ivan and indicated a pile of cinders, then pointed to some mushy spots in the cinder yard. Ivan shuffled slowly to the cinder pile. Scrabbling a cupful of cinders onto the shovel, he carried the tiny load laboriously across the yard and poured it into a low place. This ordeal went on for some time, and poor Ivan was mighty weak and tortured and most likely insane; but several times I saw him lift his eyes to his guards, and the look in them made me shiver, for it was a look of pure murder. When the Jerries had finally tired of their sport they booted Ivan into a windowless shed and locked the door. He was, we guessed, a captive from the Russian front kept around this little prison to do the dirty work and to provide amusement for the small detachment here. We hoped that his tormentors might one day receive what was promised them in Ivan's eyes.

All that afternoon, our cell again took on the aspect of a small machine shop. Having done all we could do to the barbed wire, we started in on the door. Removing the screws from the hinges, I enlarged the holes and slipped the screws back in place. Digging through the doorjamb, I weakened the hasp that secured the padlock and camouflaged the work with chunks of moldy bread: one good shove now and the door would fall out. Up near the ceiling was a tiny window through which one might barely squirm, so we removed the molding that held the frame in place. It too would fall inward under slight pressure now. All our digging and gouging and cutting took a great deal of time, for we were constantly interrupted by the increasingly curious guards; but at last I was satisfied that we could do no more undermining of our cell without having the roof fall in upon our weary heads. For despite the fact that the cell appeared to be just as strong as when we'd entered it, the termites were now forced to hold hands to keep the place together.

The Italians failed to show at all, and Lou and I put our hungry heads together to come up with a plan of action: we would blow this firetrap the following night. Jock, with his crippled leg, would have to stay behind.

During the evening, a pair of young Frenchmen shackled together were brought in. Both were about eighteen and both were badly bruised and bleeding from a very recent beating. One was scared and the other defiant as they were thrown into a garage across the prison yard from our cell. Of the Maquis, we guessed they were, and that being the case they were slated for immediate execution. A carriage pulled up to the gate shortly after the boys were imprisoned, and an old man and woman and a girl pleaded tearfully with the Bastard for information about their son and sweetheart; but they might as well have been wailing to a stone wall for all the good it did them. The Bastard shouted that he had never heard of, much less had he seen the Frenchmen they were crying about. And angrily he ordered them away.

By damn! It was our last night in Bonnesbocque. We spent a couple of hours working out the final details of our escape, then with everything settled we drifted into sleep . . .

Violent curses and a terrific amount of excited shouting rang through the prison early in the morning, and we soon learned that one of the young Frenchman, sometime during the night, had burrowed under the garage door, flipped the wall, and made his getaway! Two officers now had the Bastard backed against a wall and they were reaming him out in a very systematic manner. They ran through the list of foul names and insults and then started over again, and that made us happy. Then a searching party was organized and a half-dozen furious Jerries galloped off in all directions, but we knew they'd never find the kid. Doubtless, he knew the back trails like a sly old fox in his own stamping grounds. But the guard was redoubled and our escape plot was all fouled up. Now, to make use of our rickety cell, we'd be forced to sweat it out and hope for some sort of diversion that would suck the guards away: an air raid or heavy storm would turn the trick.

So we settled down to home life again: political arguments, tall tales, more lectures on the beauties of Joisey City, louse hunts, chicken-baiting, and other such domestic chores. Raiding the storeroom again, I found a few choice dime novels that I translated painfully for the lads. I also found a double handful of tiny wire brads that I sewed into a canvas sock, thusly fabricating a dandy home-size blackjack. But our day was soon livened up a bit.

Fighters snarled overhead in mid-afternoon and we dashed to the west window just as a shiny new Messerschmitt 109 howled across the prison yard, diving just a few hundred feet off the deck. Dead astern were a pair of Spitfires and their guns were blazing as they poured long and solid bursts into the doomed Jerry: ricochets screamed around the prison yard and we dove to the floor, and immediately after the three ships had roared out of sight beyond the buildings there came to our ears a terrific, explosive thud. The pair of Spits chandelled up to the left and right and their pilots accomplished smooth victory rolls. The faces of our guards were quite impassive as from the next cell came the joyous whoops of Peacock and the boys. Lou and Jock and I remained silent, knowing quite well how the Jerry throttle-jockey had felt about the whole thing. The affair did tend to liven things up a bit, and pretty soon we had some more.

At sundown, through the blood-colored clouds some thousand AAF bombers with fighter escort came wheeling in from England to turn westward over our prison and make a circle tour of the front lines. As they bombed the daylights out of things up that way, the ground beneath us trembled and the air beat with steady concussions. Our ships caught a lot of flak and several were hard hit and headed for home, smoking and losing altitude, and we watched the black puffs close in on a straggler B-24. The flak concentrated on it and pretty quick, whang! a direct hit. A flash, a cloud of smoke, and the big ship just disappeared but for a little shower of flaming wreckage. The Rooster walked over to our window and inquired, "Combien hommes kaput?" and when I said, "Ten men dead," he just shook his head sorrowfully and walked away.

And so—according to Lou's line of X's on the wall—went by ten days in Bonnesbocque Jailhouse. Minute by minute, hour by hour: to be in a cage is a sorry thing. The gunfire at the front had moved no closer to us, for Monty the inscrutable was still perfecting his Invasion plan. We were beginning to think that Jerry had thrown away the key to our cell, but that evening as I stood by the window gazing up into the skies a little dark-haired guard sauntered over to me. After looking around carefully, he lit up a smoke and passed it through the wire to me. "Merci bien!" I said, highly surprised; and after Lou and Jock and I had burned it down, I went back to the window where the guard still lingered, now singing softly and in a strange tongue.

Taking my cue, I remarked, "You do not sing in German . . ."

"Non," said he, low-voiced, "c'est Polonais!" So Polish he was, and drafted into the Wehrmacht. "Where are the front lines? The American Army, it has been driven back into the sea?"

"La guerre fini, à bientôt! Les Boches kaput!" I told him. The Allies were soon to exterminate the Jerries, and he would be a wise man to desert his sinking Wehrmacht while the chance still was available: "Tell the other soldiers, and take off!" I advised.

Slipping me another cigarette and a match, the little Polish guard whispered that all the prisoners were to be moved out at midnight: to where, he didn't know!

I spread the good word. Any change of scenery was going to be a welcomed thing, but I envied the batch of prisoners who might next occupy our cell, for Lou and I had done one hell of a job of redecorating during our ten-day stay. Divvying up the tools, we filled our shoes with saw blades and strapped the crowbar and tire iron to our legs; then, stuffing the black-jack into a pocket, I sat in a corner and sweated out the midnight ride.

Right on schedule a truck rolled into the yard followed by an American jeep, and the prisoners were hustled out onto the moonlit prison yard. The Rooster was there too, strutting pompously around the two vehicles, and when we directed a final, mocking shout in his direction, he threw back his head and damned if he didn't let out a sort of strangled, "Uuuurrrrrk!"

"Tayo! I kin leave Bonnesbocque prison happy now!" cried Lou, his face a masterpiece of bewildered disbelief, "'cause that son of a bitch just crowed!"

And he laughed so hard he could hardly make it into the truck!

Chapter 8

A MODEL CONVICT

◆

We were unguarded in the back of the truck, and I was amazed at our luck. Eight or ten heavy planks, however, were spiked across the open end, and—as the sides and roof were of heavy sheet-metal—we were quite well walled in. But as I fingered my crowbar, I figured that I wouldn't be long with this outfit!

As the truck rolled from the prison yard and through the gate, I peered through a crack in the plank barricade and soon learned why we'd been left without a guard: for the jeep, with a quartet of Tommy-gunners aboard, throttled up to a position some thirty yards dead-astern of our truck, and it matched our every change of speed. In short order, I had a couple of boards pried loose at one end, trying to arrange things so that I could squeeze past and bail out should the jeep lag behind for a moment. As Lou and I operated like a couple of beavers, the cargo of Limeys set up a terrific whining: "For Chrissake, Yanks! Sit down! Those blokes catch you at that and they'll shoot their bloody rifles through the bloody truck and we've all had it!" We made appropriate replies and kept right on squeaking nails loose. They might have been content with their lot in life, but damned if I was.

We kept our eyes glued to the slit and watched and awaited our chance. The moon was bright as we wheeled along the asphalt highway through Dozulé and then along toward Caen, and I hoped the night-fighters would mind their own damned business, for we were quite close to the front now. Pretty soon we angled southwards along a dark tree-lined road, and right about then our truck ran off the road into the ditch where it turned slowly over on its side like a tired old horse lying down for the last time.

A Tiger tank, it seemed, had come charging toward us traveling in the opposite direction, and our narrow road could accommodate but one: tank or truck, and the tank hadn't varied its clanking course one whit. So all of us slaves in the back of the truck now sat on the roof, yapping like a pack of coyotes. Any delay between prisons was better than no delay, and I was also happy in the thought that the Jerries were fouled up. All the guards and the drivers of the two vehicles lined up on the down-side of the truck and, with a mighty chorus of grunts, tried to boost us upright. We all sat on the down-side to make it heavier for them, and we stayed in the ditch yowling and howling with glee. A flashlight beamed into the truck accompanied by the muzzle of a Mauser, and some Jerry with a sense of humor yelped out in English: "QUIET! You are PRISONERS and are not supposed to be happy!"

In a half hour, a sleepy Frenchman showed up with his team and we were soon once again on our merry way to someplace. Jouncing over hastily patched roads in a terrifically bombed-out city, I caught a glimpse of a signboard: Falaise it was, and the town was demolished. Across a mile of city there was only rubble with an occasional chimney to break the level ground—a mournful sight by the light of the moon.

Pausing at a roadblock outside of Falaise, we rolled steadily southward until dawn, passing many long columns of bicycle troopers who pedaled wearily toward Caen. Several times our escorting jeep fell back a bit and I made ready to jump, but each time it throttled ahead, looming up through the dusty moonlight to foil me.

Just at sunup we approached an ancient castle with high stone walls surmounted by great iron spears. Through the massive gates we rumbled and into the cobblestoned courtyard, where from high barred windows hundreds of prisoners shouted down at us as we stumbled from the truck to be counted into cells of stone block set with ponderous oaken doors. I flopped onto the filthy floor and caught a few winks.

Rousted out, we were handed tin plates and the lot of us queued up on a gigantic kettle of foul soup. With a bowl of that in my belly, I prowled the courtyard looking over the lay of the land, and I got another bright idea. The prisoners' latrine lay at the bottom of a gentle slope beyond the prison yard. Behind it an open plowed field stretched for a couple hundred yards to the edge of a deep forest. With permission of a guard, I'd walk to the outhouse, crawl out the back way, scoot across the field and so into the woods! Mulling over the simple plan for a few minutes, I approached a guard to pop the question. A sudden flurry of shots cracked out. We all watched a guy make a zigzag dash across the plowed strip as bullets kicked dust all around him until he plunged safely into the tall timber. That ended that, and we were immediately thrown back into our dark cells. Pretty soon along the old grapevine came the report that the P-47 pilot had made good his daring getaway. I consoled myself with the thought that anyway it had been a fellow fighter pilot who'd foiled my plan. Great minds run in the same channels!

The prisoners were reshuffled. The British infantrymen from Bonnesbocque were hustled into the cell block and Lou and Jock and I were joined by a bunch of enlisted RAF fliers. Twenty-five prisoners were racked up into each of two open trucks, and riding packed in and standing up we pulled out again heading southward along a tar highway. A Tommy-gunner rode the front fender of our truck, and on a bench at the tailgate three more scowling Jerries fingered the triggers of their Mausers. As the day was bright and the skies were blue, the fighter pilots in the bunch kept wary eyes peeled skywards. A truckload of men on a main road in enemy country was fair game for any prowling fighter shopping around for a target of opportunity. A Mustang could rip into us and be gone before anybody would know what had hit, and in a second or two our joyful little outfit would become a smoldering truckload of steaks and chops—and that would never do. One of the prisoners in the forward part of the truck had a long stick with a little white cloth affixed to the end. His duty was to ward off strafing aircraft, but a hot-rock driving a 60-mph Cub would never have recognized that dinky rag as a white flag, much less would a flak-happy citizen coming in at 400 realize that he shouldn't shoot. This tourist stuff was unhealthy.

Being one of two "civilians" aboard, I felt a bit out of place in this crowd of soldiers and guards, so I wangled a way to the edge of the truck and watched the scenery whiz past. The ditches were absolutely filled with a litter of wrecked German vehicles, and it pleased my professional eye to note that all had been beautifully strafed. Those that hadn't burned to a skeleton or blown up were blasted all to hell by 50-caliber stuff, and here and there the highway was pitted deeply where the armor-piercing slugs had ricocheted. I was relieved when we rolled along between a long double row of tall trees and into a city. A signpost said "Sees" and there was a helluva big twin-spired cathedral there, also a long line of meat-wagons headed for Caen. Then out of Sees and another long stretch of open road, and we hauled into the outskirts of Alençon—better than a hundred kilometers south of Caen. We bumped slowly along over a cratered road alongside the marshalling yard, and here everything was finished. A tremendous tangle of inverted locomotives and crazily perched boxcars was tied together by a snarl of twisted rails that sprouted in all directions. A good job of bombing, but wandering about the streets were a good many women who were dressed all in black.

The narrow streets of Alençon were full of soldiers and folks marketing. Once in a while a civilian, after a careful look about him, would flash us a furtive V-for-Victory signal. Now we jolted along very slowly as our driver honked furiously at a pony cart that clip-clopped leisurely along ahead of us. I inched a leg upwards and rolled it over the side of the truck, figuring to just slip down to the crowded sidewalk. Hell, I looked just like any other bum on the street—even seedier—and I'd fit right in. Tensing myself for the final thrust that would turn the trick, I made a quick check of the situation and my heart liked to've jumped clear out onto the cobblestones. The truck was nearing a little balcony that overhung the street: three German officers, wine glasses in hand, were leaning over to watch the conquered blokes pass beneath them. I swung my leg back into the truck, and by the time my knees quit trembling we were out of Alençon and traveling west along another road.

A few minutes later we drove past a quartet of sentries at a barbed-wire gate and jerked to a halt alongside an open-air bullpen where about a thousand jailbirds lounged about. After we were counted out of the trucks and turned out to graze in a roped-off pasture, a sour-faced Jerry tossed us each a chunk of hardtack and made it clear that we now had our day's rations.

I moseyed around the bullpen until I saw an English private who fondled a small sack of tobacco, and after a bit of probing he confessed that he was fresh out of papers. Well, it just so happened that I had a pack of

Riz-la papers and I had a little word with the soldier: I'd swap him a dozen papers for just one charge of his tobacco.

"It's a deal, Yank!" said the trooper, but when I set about constructing the fattest cigarette ever rolled, the Limey's eyes bugged out and he regarded me sadly, to say "Bloody Yanks!" I said, "Thanks, chum," and lit up for the first good smoke in a long time.

In a corner of the area was a soapbox orator holding forth for all who'd listen. Drifting over, I tuned in for a spell. In excellent English, this professor-type, Meerschaum-pipe-smoking character was dishing out a lot of hogwash along the lines of Joe Goebbels. Not holding with being on speaking terms with the likes of this spellbinder, I found Lou and we sat on the grass to await developments.

When somebody shouted, "Achtung!" we queued up at a table behind which sat a trio of German officers. Lou and I disposed of our crowbar and tire iron by shoving them into the sod, and into the fist-sized piece of bread I stuffed a half-dozen short lengths of saw-blade. My tiny compass needle again went back under my lip.

At the table I hoisted my hands while a pair of Jerries frisked me thoroughly. The first officer asked my name, rank, and number, and because I had no uniform he scowled and growled and threatened me for a while before passing me along to his partners. The next hot-shot barked at me: "You remain here three days. You and the other aviators go then to Dulag Luft in Germany. If you violate any rule of this camp, you will be punished severely. If you attempt to escape, you will be shot."

"Roger," I said.

My rather arrogant opponent continued: "Oberleutnant Fahrenwald, you will give me your word of honor, as an officer and gentleman of the American Army, that you have no escape materials concealed on your person; that you have no saw-blade, file, compass, map, or weapon. If you refuse to give your word you will be stripped and searched and punished if anything is found. I trust you to be honorable. Do you give me your word?"

"Yessir!"—and the thought trickled through my mind that there would have arisen a unique situation had the compass needle, as I'd spoken those fateful words, flipped from under my lip and tinkled across the table. From where I stood I could plainly see a sixteenth-inch of hacksaw blade protruding from the crust of bread, which rested directly beneath the Nazi nose. I hastily averted my eyes from that damning evidence and signed a little card, thereby promising to be a model convict. Lou and I were assigned quarters in the officers' barracks. With a sloppy salute, I was done with registration at the Hotel Alençon.

If these people ever got me into Germany, my escape chances would be slim indeed. So with no waste of time, I set out on a solo reconnaissance of the prison compound to see what I could see. The camp was a square, three hundred yards on a side, and surrounded by a ten-foot woven wire fence surmounted by a dozen strands of barbed wire. Beyond the fence was a ten-foot lane and then another fence. Patrolling the lane were numerous guards, each equipped for any number of methods of manslaughter. A sandbagged machine-gun nest at each corner covered each lane from two directions. On the west side of the compound were a dozen long windowless barns. A fence divided off part of the opposite side of the camp, and in that area were a few hundred Frenchmen rounded up, perhaps for export to Germany as slaves. As I watched them, a black sedan pulled up at the prison headquarters and a pair of black-clad Gestapo agents hauled from the car a handcuffed young Frenchmen. They booted him in with the other prisoners.

Barbed wire, guards, great quantities of prisoners: everything a good prison needed. Nothing fancy, but all efficient. My time was short and I needed some information, and in a hurry. And a little caution would be necessary, for there were English-speaking Jerries in Allied uniforms circulating amongst the prisoners to betray just such people as I. I sailed through a couple of barracks, and was not welcome after mentioning escape to numerous little groups of disgusted soldiers. I was nuts. Did I want to get shot? I didn't argue with any of them. I was in a hurry. And in a couple of hours of snooping and gentle questioning I dug out a few pertinent facts: two prisoners had escaped from a hospital detail in Alençon. One had disappeared from a working party in the Alençon railroad yards during the confusion of an air raid. But there hadn't been a work detail for some weeks now: thirty-five airmen had been selected for a detail and had been marched down the highway toward Alençon, having been told that anyone breaking ranks would be shot. Two P-47s had strafed them, killing a score of the lads. Since then, nobody cared to work for the Jerries.

I cruised into one barracks to find a feller named Underwood who had been, of all things, a hairdresser at a WAC training base in the States. When the war had gotten rough, he'd been jerked from his harem and made over into a paratrooper. What a blow that must have been! Underwood produced a pair of shears and I swapped him a piece of hacksaw blade for a haircut, the first in six months. This guy chopped away for an hour or more, and when his noble job was done my beret felt twice as large as it had before. Besides being a dandy barber, he was an eager type and said that if I was going to make a break he wanted to tag along. He'd worked for the Jerries in the hospital at Alençon and he knew the lay of the land. He sketched up a chart of the place, marking in the positions of the guards there and plotting out various avenues of escape. Hot damn! In the short afternoon I'd been here, I'd found out enough to realize that a break from the camp itself would be difficult. A work detail to get me outside the barbed wire sounded like the solution. It would take a bit of doing, though.

When a bugle sounded that evening, we formed up on the parade ground for the evening count: about two thousand men in every Allied uniform under the sun. Forty or fifty officer-prisoners formed at the end of a rectangle with the enlisted soldiers in ranks on either side, and then the Jerry staff marched to the center as their sergeants walked slowly along in front of us making the count. The Jerries had us formed up in five-man-deep files to simplify their task, but it seemed that every prisoner was in on a mischievous conspiracy to foul up the tally. We were counted twice, and on the second count the men in the rear ranks shifted from slot to slot, squatting down or bobbing their heads over so as to be counted with the next file. The second check invariably failed to tally with the first, and the third with the second. This first evening the bewildered Jerry sergeant counted the officers four times, getting a different total each trip. The sergeant shouted and an angry Jerry captain stormed over and counted us twice. He lost a few prisoners in the process and, figuring he couldn't be wrong, he instituted a search of our barracks: nobody there. Giving up in disgust, he took an average and dismissed the formation.

At suppertime I found out why the prisoners in this camp at Alençon were starving to death, and not too slowly. I'd already seen quite a few people try a couple of times before they could even stand up, and I'd seen a once-husky paratrooper weave and fall as he made his weary way toward the single water tap that supplied the entire camp.

We queued up at the cook shack. I got my hands on a plateful of soup, which was the first and last course to the dinner. It was, I believe, split pea soup; very watery and loaded with hundreds of small white maggots.

An English major, intelligence officer of a heavy bombardment outfit, spoke out in fury: "The filthy bahstids! Throwin' maggots in our bloody broth! I'll starve before I'll eat the bloody stuff!" And with that, he chucked his supper through the wire.

"Well, you'll starve if you don't eat it, too," I said. It was all in his head anyway. The maggots were dead, weren't they? What the hell: meat to the diet. I latched onto a bunch of airmen who squatted on the grass next to the fence and we polished off our soup in short order, with great smacks of delight for the benefit of those more squeamish. I dabbled up the last of the stuff with a hunk of hardtack and had a colorful sunset for dessert. Striking a light to the butt of the fat cigarette I'd swindled out of the trooper, I felt dandy. As I smoked I gazed through the wire.

To the north and west beyond the fences stretched a field of wheat, golden tops rippling in the breeze. Beyond the peaceful field, green-patched farmland led up to the fringe of a heavy forest that surged up and away into distant, gloomy mountains. As I stood in the redness of the setting sun and looked at those old hills, I could smell the pine woods and hear the rabbits scuttling one way as I scuttled another.

We sat on the grass and swapped lies and argued aircraft. A few ships droned overhead, while ten million persistent mosquitoes whined through the camp to plague us. A beautiful summer's night. At dusk there rumbled into the compound a half-dozen ambulances followed by four or five huge trucks, and a swarm of Jerries hustled about loading aboard ponderous cartons and boxes. Large Red Cross flags were spread over the cargoes and tied in position. The convoy moved out and took the highway toward Alençon. "Ammo going to the front," explained the British major. He told us that our Air Force people in England were aware of the ruse. Orders were about to go out to Fighter Command to the effect that all Red Cross-marked vehicles were to be considered as targets. The Jerries had made no bones about what they were doing, probably having done it so much that they now considered it legitimate.

We were soon locked into our dismal sheds for the night. Close-packed rows of flimsy double-deck bunks stood on the muddy floor. There was a bit of foul straw for bedding, and a few of the luckier lads had somewhere acquired burlap sacks for blankets. I turned in wearing every scrap of clothing I could muster, including my shoes, for fear that someone might requisition them during the wee hours. The night was cold and the bugs in this hotel had jaws like tin shears, and I had trouble trying to sleep. I lay for hours pondering the mass of information I'd gleaned in the course of my frantic tour of the prison this afternoon. I'd kept my mouth shut about my plans, for I was a lone hand now. He travels fastest who travels alone.

In a corner bunk lay a B-24 pilot I'd known back in '42 in flying school in Arizona. He'd had a busy day, having eaten a happy breakfast back in England this very morning. Now he lay in prison on a filthy old sack, with no skin on his face or hands. His ship had been exploded by flak and he'd been taken as soon as he'd touched the ground. The Jerries hadn't done anything for him, but a Yank medic here in the camp had found some sort of salve to rub over the unfortunate pilot's burns. Another lad who had zigged when he should have zagged, and he groaned all night.

Roll call at 4:30 in the morning. At seven, barley coffee and a tiny bit of bread, and then the sun blazed up and we could quit shivering. I ended up with the best breakfast in the whole crowd, for I spent a chuckling half hour trapping bumblebees and squeezing honey out of their little butts: and at last I had about fifty drops spread onto my bit of bread. It was very tasty, and amusing too. Scrounging around, I bummed a smoke and then I felt like a million francs!

I set out on another tour of the enlisted men's barracks, acquiring information, spreading dissatisfaction and unrest as I traveled, and hollering at frequent intervals, "Lemme outta this firetrap!" And when word came along the grapevine that all airmen were due to be deported to Germany either this night or the next, I flipped on the high blower, redoubled my efforts, and really started operating.

I tracked down the ranking Allied officer for a pow-wow, and he turned out to be an English major. This paddlefoot had been in command of the prisoners for half a year, but he looked plump and contented. When I'd introduced myself, he said, "Have a cigarette, Leftenant?"

"Don't mind if I do," I said. The bastard had a whole goddam drawer full of American cigarettes. I could see that he was doing allright for himself, so I took a handful and told him that I was about to blow this bastille.

I wanted any information and assistance he could give me. I told him my plan: to acquire a uniform to cover up my civilian clothes; to swap places with some willing GI, possibly sending him to Dulag Luft in Germany in my place should the airmen be moved out tonight; then, to be included on the first work detail the Jerries might order out. Just get me on the detail and I'd take care of the rest.

While he agreed readily to my plan, the major suggested another: he knew a guard, he said, who'd let me slip through the wire, fire a couple of shots over my head, and let me go, all for a nominal fee. If the deal is so good, I wondered, why is this major here? It stunk. I thanked him and declined the offer. No doubt the guard would ventilate me until I was stone cold dead and then, after all these years, receive his sergeant's stripes.

With the pudgy, conniving major on my team, I charged back to the barracks area where I swapped a civilian shirt for a wonderful pair of woolen sox. One Yank donated a pair of tattered combat-infantry pants and another offered a safety pin upon which I could balance my compass needle. Another gave me a combat jacket and a length of rope for use as a belt. After judicious inquiry, I located a private who'd had a snootful of fighting the war: a friendly little guy by name of Joe Vitolo. Now Joe, by luck and coincidence, had made himself an extra set of dog tags out of plexiglas, and he gave them to me. I dickered around and arranged to have him take my place, and I gave him one of my dog tags to cinch the deal, so now we were interchangeably private and lieutenant. Things were going my way, and by noon I was outfitted for the expedition. Hiding my extra duds in my bunk, I joined Lou and tried to relax while sweating out a message from the major. I was as ready as I'd ever be.

That afternoon we heard the sound of fighter engines revving up nearby. The prison was situated midway between two Jerry airdromes, one a FW-190 base and the other Me-109s. Both fields were perfectly camouflaged, with underground hangars. And the fliers amongst the prisoners perked up when a pair of Focke-Wulf fighters barreled low over the camp, just picking up their wheels as they cruised overhead. To my critical ear their engines sounded dangerously ragged, an indication of the low-grade, rotgut, ersatz fuel they were burning. Another pair crossed over, and another, until a twelve-ship squadron was airborne. What a pitiful sight it was, too!

The Jerries, trying their damnedest to duplicate American fighter tactics, were taking off in two-ship elements and then trying to join up into flights of four. These daring aeronauts couldn't even keep two ships together on takeoff, but after three complete circuits of their field they had a two-ship element intact. The second element attempted to join up. They overshot and wallered around the sky a half-mile ahead of their leader. They undershot and lost a half mile. At last, these Fokke Wulf drivers got all squared away and they buzzed the prison about fifty feet off the deck. We thumbed our noses at the stragglers and they waved at us. It made me lonesome for my old outfit: we'd get fifty-five Mustangs airborne and heading out on-course in perfect, tight formation in three minutes flat. The Jerries' sorry exhibition reminded me of a Sunday afternoon at a civilian airport: nobody knowing much about flying, but all trying hard. The air show broke the monotony, anyway.

Dinner was served at seven: soup. But tonight, by gee, there was meat in it! My plateful held two small chunks of gristly stuff that might easily have been the lungs out of some old Jerry army mule that had died of wounds suffered in the last bombardment of Alençon. I rewound the scarf more tightly around my belly and the hunger pangs diminished. A wonderful invention, that scarf, but it would never take the place of filet mignon smothered with fried onions and mushroom sauce.

After the confusion of the evening count had subsided, our mysterious news service informed us that the train the airmen were scheduled to catch for Germany had been strafed: our departure would be delayed until the following night. I went to sleep and was engulfed in a nightmare: I'd bailed out into the ocean off a reef in the South Pacific. As I swam for shore, a triangular fin swished toward me and I thrashed around and hollered and fought and the shark ripped a chunk out of my leg. Four passes the shark made at me, and four times he bit the hell out of me. And bleeding like a fountain, I crawled at last onto the reef. Came the dawn, however, and I was relieved to find that I was still in prison: but on my leg were four livid welts. Every time that goddam bug had paused to chomp on me, my dream shark had done likewise.

When the news came, it came fast: the Limey major contacted me. "Get ready, Yank! The Jerries have ordered out a fifty-man working party. Last chance! Make it good! Cheerio, ol' boy!"

Hot damn! I slipped into the barracks and pulled the scraps of uniforms over my civilian duds. I threw my beret and a chunk of hoarded bread in a pocket and I was all set. I hated to leave without saying goodbye to Lou, but two people was one too many for this deal.

Slinking into the middle of the formation of forty-nine other prisoners who'd been drafted for the job, we marched through the heavily guarded main gate to the highway, just slicker'n hell. A Jerry captain read us the riot act: "If any prisoner breaks ranks, takes one step, just one step away from the formation, the guards will shoot to kill. If your strafing planes attack, it is too bad."

We made a fast hike for a kilometer or so. With three pairs of pants, two shirts, and a field jacket for insulation, I would have felt more at home in the Frozen Northland than I did under the blazing sun of Normandy, and I was glad when we came to a couple of trucks. Split into two groups, we were loaded aboard and a stick with a little anti-strafing rag affixed was given to one man in each truck. Each truck had pilot and co-pilot and two Tommy-gunners perched on the front fenders, and in our truck four guards with Mausers sat on a bench at the tailgate: unsociable types who just sat and scowled at one another and at us.

So we rattled away through Alençon and northward on the tar highway, and after some twenty kilometers our convoy halted. The navigator looked at his map. We backed up and proceeded along a winding country road, and great swirls of dust boiled up and covered us completely. And then we were lost in a tiny, nameless hamlet: a quaint little place with a mill and a brook that gurgled merrily over a waterwheel.

The Jerries pored stupidly over a military map. After long minutes of head scratching and grumbling, they shouted at two old ladies who sunned themselves in a flower garden. There now ensued a hilarious conference as to our exact whereabouts—conducted in a tangle of French and German— and one old lady finally smiled in triumph and pointed to the north. With frenzied gestures, the other old lady contradicted, pointing south. All the Jerries shouted angrily at the old ladies and at one another. The prisoners joined in the uproar. A tall paratrooper with a knowledge of German and a sense of humor to boot suggested to the Jerries that perhaps he could be of some help. He borrowed the map from the driver and we clustered around it, offering inane directions until the Jerries wised up and snatched

their map away. As one of the old ladies hovered nearby, clucking sympa-
thetically, I asked her in French if she could, peut-être, spare a pitcher of
cider to quench the thirst of the American soldiers. Making a quick trip to
her house, she returned with a tall tin pitcher and trayful of glasses, and
we all had a cool drink.

A little later on, as we rounded a curve on a gravel road, there was a
friendly old farmhouse where the whole family stood in the yard. We waved
and they waved their hats and hankies. One of our guards snatched up his
Mauser and fired a whole clip toward the French people: no one was hurt
as far as we could see, but the yellow-bellied stunt made us all plenty mad.
We didn't, however, wave to any more Frenchmen.

At noon we bumped slowly along a dirt road then followed a hedgerow
until we came upon a railroad spur. Neatly camouflaged by twin rows
of tall trees were a dozen boxcars, and alongside them were a dozen army
trucks and a few staff cars. With a quick look around I was made happy,
for such terrain should offer good cover for my getaway: patches of woods,
tiny meadows, and grain fields, all divided by hedgerows.

We were split into work parties of six men each, and to each group
was assigned one guard armed with sub-machine gun. My paratrooper
friend and I managed to get into the same bunch, and without parlay or
delay we were set to work unloading the boxcars. Some of the boys jumped
into the cars and hauled the stuff to the doorways as the others, including
me—for I needed all the maneuverability I could get—shouldered the
items and packed them over to the trucks.

There were thousands of 200-pound bags of flour, bags of rations about
half as heavy, and salt in great square sacks weighing in the neighborhood
of 400 pounds. We worked under close surveillance and strictly according
to Jerry methods: one man to a sack of flour or rations, and three men to
the salt bags. I thought the first bag of flour would drive me into the
ground clear up to my armpits, or at least make me permanently
bowlegged; for my weight was down to around 110 at this stage of the
game, and the very word "work" had always made me shudder. But not
wishing to become conspicuous by too-obviously goofing off, I lurched
to and fro between boxcar and truck; and after a while it boiled down to
being a case of mind over matter. I got along. My three suits of clothes
gave me the appearance of being a husky type, so I was forced to sustain

the illusion by laboring that much harder. I was trapped.

When the truck groaned under a towering load of flour bags, my five comrades and I plus our guard climbed atop the pile and we took off for town. After a dozen kilometers of back roads, we hit the highway to Sees and halted just a half-block from the twin-spired cathedral there. Over the doorway of a brick building was the ominous insignia of the SS.

Hoisting a bag of flour to my thin shoulder, I trudged inside and took a good look around. On a gymnasium floor was a mighty stack of bags of flour, to which we were to make a generous addition. On a wall was a bulletin board with colorful propaganda posters and a fanciful morale cartoon that showed the mailed fist of the mighty Wehrmacht in the act of shoving the Invasion Forces back into the English Channel. Across the walls were autographed photographs of Hitler and his mangy crew. SS men worked in several offices, and it was not a very heartening place for me and my plans. Across the way from the SS building was a pleasant, shady park, and a few crippled-up old Frenchmen gathered there to watch les prisonniers Americains labor under the hot sun.

We worked as slowly as possible, which was not very slowly, for our guard and the SS men from the storehouse would howl and shove us around whenever our slowdown policy became too noticeable. I wondered once what might happen should I just wander down the street, keeping the parked truck between the guards and me at the rear of the truck. I ran a check. After sauntering ten paces away, I turned around to find a dozen pairs of beady eyes focused on me. So I flapped my arms as if limbering up, stretched and yawned, and cruised back to hoist another bag to my shoulder. When we'd emptied the first load, the paratrooper who spoke German asked our guard for drinking water. The guard grinned and shook his head.

En route back to the spur line, I made mental notes of the places along the way that offered the best chances for a successful bailout: weed-filled ditches, thickets, patches of woods that here and there bordered the country roads. A guard who permitted the escape of a prisoner was sentenced immediately to front-line duty, and our boy knew when he had a good thing. His finger was constantly curled around the trigger of his burp-gun and the safety was always in the "off" position.

As we loaded the truck for the second time, I shouldered one bag of flour too many, for as I hefted one from the boxcar door it caught me a bit off balance and I lurched away on a downhill grade and through the underbrush for a ways before stumbling and falling, to lay in a puddle of sweat. Blood pounded through my temples and a thousand fiendish little red blobs drifted dreamily before my eyes. In short, I was bushed. So I did things the old army way for a while, seemingly working at a great rate while actually accomplishing nothing, and in a little while a second wind came my way. I went back to doing my share of the dirty work with my mind in fine pitch all the while, turning out scheme after desperate scheme and weighing each against the odds.

Back at the SS storehouse I managed to duck out of sight for a moment, planning to shed my uniform, don my beret, and just walk away looking like a passing Frenchman. A guard caught me as I was beginning to unbutton my battle jacket and I went back to work in a hurry. The paratrooper hollered angrily at the SS men that we'd quit unloading their goddam flour if we didn't get water to drink: a nudge in his ribs with the muzzle of a rifle coaxed him out of that idea. On the return trip, empty, my five fellow laborers formed a nonchalant screen between me and our guard, who stood with his back to the cab of the truck. We were rolling about 30 mph, and I flung a leg over the side of the truck. As I was timing a peel-off into the weedy ditch, a little staff car rounded a curve behind us, closed in, and tailed our truck back to the spur.

During the unloading of the next truckload I found a heavy box-end wrench, which I filched from the SS building. I suggested to the paratrooper that we clobber our guard on the way back to the siding and then leave, but after a bit of thoughtful discussion we decided the idea to be unwise: if we escaped under those circumstances and were recaptured, the Jerries no doubt would put the permanent fix on us. And that would not do. The boxcars were emptied of flour and our trips to town were done with. We'd made five in all, which meant that each of us had loaded and unloaded one large truckload, singlehandedly, and that very thought made me madder'n hell. We'd had a "breakfast" of warm water and moldy bread at six a.m., and without further rations of water—but for the glass of cider donated by the old French lady—we'd put in a hard, hot day of work. Even had we been able, we couldn't have spit straight for the slow-burning rage in us.

A convoy of empty trucks rolled in and parked alongside the line of boxcars, and we began to load them up with sacks of rations and salt. Escape chances had narrowed down now, and I plotted faster.

Aiming to arrange our supper one way or another, I rammed a bag of rations into a nail protruding from the boxcar doorway and pulled. A pile of hardtack spilled to the ground and a Jerry non-com ran over and pounded my head for a while, shouting, "Saboteur!" or "Kaput!" with every other word. He cussed my hide for a few minutes, but by the time he'd finished working me over the pile of hardtack had disappeared into the prisoners' pockets. The paratrooper, quite by accident, smashed a half-gallon tin of ersatz jam and it made a dandy spread. While the Jerries stood around and scowled, we ate the whole damned tub of jam. But the character who'd clipped me was now out for my blood.

His name was Oscar, and it seemed to fit. Short and pudgy, pig-eyed and foul of breath was he, with the mentality of a small-town cop. He grabbed my shoulder and shoved me off-balance a couple of times as I dragged various bags toward the boxcar door, and then blustered about when I cussed at him. I'm lazy by nature, but today I was willing to swap even with the Jerries: one day's work for my freedom. But when this pig Oscar started pushing me around, it took my last bit of willpower to keep shut the mouth. I looked at him a couple of times, however, and that didn't seem to improve international relations to any real extent: we automatically hated each other's guts and made no bones about it. But Oscar had the power and he used it. He indicated a huge sack of salt that lay in a corner of the boxcar, and four of us went after it. Pulling the others away, he booted me toward it: I was to haul it around solo. With a wink to the paratrooper, I latched onto an ear of the sack and launched a maximum effort, which was as phony as a rasslin' match: "Ugh! OOOOmpf! Ugh!"—and the sack budged not one millimeter. I puffed and tugged while my pal Oscar showered blubbery blows upon my back until finally, happy to see that I had failed, he shoved me aside and took over. With a contemptuous snorting and much show of power, he inched the salt bag to the doorway singlehandedly. I watched closely, hoping that he might rupture himself. And all the boys stood around with hands on hips, whistling in mock awe at the feat of strength. As Oscar, facing outwards in arrogant triumph, stood in the boxcar doorway my subtle paratrooper friend brushed past his big ass and gave a nudge and Oscar made a spectacular emergency bailout, landing sprawled on the ground. It was quite a drop, too, for a big tub of dung like him and, deadpan, the paratrooper apologized: it had been purely an unfortunate accident, and he was sorry. And we kept on working.

A thousand birds were singing their last songs of the day and we were glad, for the evening coolness would be like a long drink of water. The sun, plunging below the western horizon, pushed a tremendous full moon upwards out of the woods to the east; and after a while the deep purple skies were full of sparkling stars. A perfect night it was for pouring a string of lies into a dainty ear, but one helluva night to attempt escape from a pack of eagle-eyed, trigger-happy thugs. Meadows and hedges, thickets and roads, fences and sentries' positions: I'd memorized them all by now. My time was running out. I twice tried stowing away beneath a loaded truck as it pulled out for the front lines, but each time the situation was a little wrong, and pretty soon I was glad I hadn't succeeded. For I watched a heavily laden truck low-gear across the meadow, and each time its wheels would drop into a hole it would hit bottom with a ponderous thud. I was far too thin and run-down to be playing shock absorber.

About eleven p.m. half the gang of prisoners were taken away and locked into one of the boxcars for the night, and we worked to unload the last half of the final carload of rations. A staff car now wheeled into the moonlit scene and, amidst a volley of heel-clicking and a confusion of fancy salutes, four German officers dismounted and began a tour of inspection accompanied by assorted non-coms, including Oscar. Each officer was equipped with a poker face and a ramrod up his back, and quite obviously they were the local representatives of J. Christ. Upon observing something not quite to their taste, they threw all nearby guards and sentries in quivering braces and chewed them out thoroughly—the verbal insults being accompanied in several instances by the delightful poppety-pop-pop of faces being slapped.

When the last sackful of rations had been thrown into the last truck, we stood about waiting, and I alone out of the whole crew was not happy about it: we'd soon join our comrades in the boxcar. It was a bit past midnight when an American jeep snorted into the pasture with a milk can full of cold tea for the prisoners. Queuing up, we guzzled our fill from a long-handled ladle. One of the Jerry officers, pleased at the job of work his slaves had done, tossed us a pack of cigarettes along with a warning to conceal the match light from the night fighters that droned overhead: cupping the flames carefully, we lit up. The smoke felt good. We sat around and chatted as the officers set out to inspect the sentry posts. Our sharp-eyed guard had been relieved and now my bloated enemy Oscar stood over us, fingering the controls of his burp-gun.

The moon was round and silver overhead. Across the countryside the visibility was a mellow quarter-mile. I'd come to the end of my rope, for now only seconds remained. Of its own accord, my scalp gave a slow crawl. My backbone sort of shrunk and quivered. With no definite plan of action in mind, I stood up and sauntered away from the little bunch of guards and prisoners. I walked around to the front of the truck we'd just loaded to where the can of tea nestled in the grass. I tinkered around with the ladle.

Ahead of me with his back turned stood a sentry with rifle slung over shoulder. I cast a glance to the rear: no one had trailed me. In a split second, I realized that this was a last chance and a long chance. And to hell with the odds—I took it.

Chapter 9

FREE AGENT

◆

Pussyfooting past the nose of the truck, I scuttled under the closest boxcar, eased over the cool iron rail, crept across a splintery tie, darted through a deadly patch of moonlight, and slipped soundlessly down the far embankment. A sentry stood there a few paces away, but he heard nothing. One can move quietly when his life depends upon moving quietly. Taking my cue from his position, I bellied along the thin black shadow cast by the moon at the bottom of a barbed-wire fence that paralleled the spur line, and from the corner of my eye I could see beneath a boxcar the legs of the prisoners and guards who milled around behind the loaded truck. I doubled back past them until I calculated that I was midway between them and the boxcar in which the first bunch of prisoners now slept. All was quiet. Up ahead, leaning against the side of that boxcar, were two guards talking in undertones. A bit beyond them, a dense hedgerow crossed the spur line at right angles. I couldn't crawl up and down the sentry line all night, and now I was blocked on three sides by sentries: many to the left, one dead-astern, and two dead-ahead.

To my right lay an open, flat meadow lit up like a shooting gallery by the spitefully brilliant full moon, and three sentries that I was aware of had a clear field of vision across the meadow. But I didn't have much time left, and to try anything was better than doing nothing, so I rolled under the fence. The meadow grass was a half-foot deep, soft and green and clean and drenched with heavy dew.

I took off flat-out and about six inches underground, striking a diagonal course that would intercept the hedgerow some hundred feet from its junction with the railroad tracks. Now, leprechauns and a like variety of critters may be old hands at swimming in dew, but this was my debut and I used the old Australian crawl minus the leg action; just reaching out one arm at a time, grabbing a fistful of grass at each stroke, and snaking myself forward. The grass was cool against my cheek, and wet and slippery, and the wetter I became the faster could I slither and I clocked off a fantastic speed with no effort at all—the black hedgerow drawing me toward it as though it were a mighty magnet and I a tiny needle. And under the merciless moon every millimeter of the way found a twitching or proportionately increasing intensity building up in my spine, in full anticipation of one quick and final burst from a sentry's machine pistol.

The closer came the hedge, the brighter seemed the moon, and then one outstretched hand touched a tightly-strung wire fence at the far border of the meadow. The bottom wire was but a few inches above the ground, and I either went through it or under it: I know I didn't go over it. Then plunging an arm deep into the base of the hedgerow, I jerked my thin wet carcass into the beautiful tangle of interlaced brambles and vines, and I took the first breath I'd dared to chance since leaving the bunch behind the truck . . . and I'd made my cover by a bare half-second, for the fun began the very moment that my heels disappeared into the hedge.

There sprang up the dangdest hullabaloo ever to fill a moonlit night, and at that stage of the game I shoved throttle clear through the firewall and buzzed through the base of my hedgerow (ordinarily an impassable barrier) like a jet-propelled black snake going down a corn row. Unmindful of gouging thorns and slashing brambles, I squirmed amongst the roots down along the length of the hedge for a few hundred yards; and then breaking out into the shady side where the moon cast a broad, deep shadow, I crouched down for a quick listen. Of all the ungodly rackets I'd heard to date, that which now arose behind me was by far the finest. Keeerist, what a furor! Whooping and hollering and a thudding of boots and the twang of the wire fence: guttural cries of anguish, shouts of rage; short and nasty bursts of the burp-guns punctuated by an occasional rifle shot. Now, more than likely the Jerries had found my snaky trail across the dewy meadow, for bumblebees started flying: slugs snapping and tearing through the brush close-by with a rattle of twigs to mark their passage.

Slugs spanged and ricocheted recklessly and I didn't stay around there much longer.

Breathing hard, I faded into a deep shadow for a moment, snatched my beret from a pocket, and tugged it far down over my forehead. I tore off the khaki combat jacket and pants and stuffed them into a thicket, then turned up the collar of my black suitcoat and wound around my face my black woolen scarf, leaving just a narrow slit through which to see, and now—black from head to foot—I was part of the night. I ran hard for a quarter-hour, silently as a cat on a fur rug, invisible in the shadows of hedges and trees and thickets, and when I'd have to lope through an occasional brief patch of moonlight I'd shove my hands up under my armpits to prevent any possible shine being seen. I settled into a fast dog-trot for a while, always angling away from the spur line, but it was difficult to put much crow-flight distance between me and the Jerries for, of necessity, my course was twisting and turning and sometimes doubling back in order to cling to the shady borders of the irregular fields. The Jerries were in hot pursuit and still were doing a little shooting, but the bastards didn't have a ghost of a chance, for they were shooting at shadows.

I tumbled down behind an ancient tree and chuckled and listened and chuckled some more. The German officers were still shouting—hoarsely by now—at the guards, and I chuckled faster in hopes that they might be taking turns at clubbing Oscar's rat face to an unrecognizable pulp. That thought, plus the satisfaction of having skeedaddled during an inspection of the guard by a quartet of tough Jerry officers, put the final polish to the unholy glee bubbling within me! Right now, the blade of the shiny guillotine was falling upon the plump neck of that slob, Oscar. Heh heh heh! That bastard was off to the front lines, where I hoped he would soon meet an excruciating, lingering death. I was just saddened by the thought that I couldn't be around to help him over the hump. All day long I'd pondered how I'd loved to've rammed my old Mustang up his blubbery arse, and now somebody else would soon have the chance. Heh heh heh! To repress such a moment of high triumph was difficult, and I rubbed my hands on the rough bark of the old tree and choked back a long, loud, and exultant howl at the moon. Nobody was ever happier than I was right then. I was about to explode with sheer happiness. I was a free agent, solo in a countryside so purely pretty that it like to've made me weep. And I didn't aim to be taken again.

With a sniff of the fresh night wind and a rub of my hands, I took a quick gander at the North Star and lit out, steering southwest. When I came to the road we'd trucked over during the day, a jeep came snarling along leaving in its trail moonbeams of swirling dust. So I snuck into a thicket. A pair of gravel-crunching guards trotted past, one on each side of the road, their Mausers at the ready. I ducked across the road, squirmed through a hedge, and made tracks, comfortably engulfed in the blackest shadows I could find. And soon the uproar was quite faint behind me.

But then I caught a listen that chilled my blood: the baying of a couple of hound dogs, it was, and their eager yowls were coming in against the breeze from the general direction of the area I'd just vacated . . . It might not have been what I thought it was, but I didn't waste time investigating. Using maximum rpm and war-emergency power, I took off crosswind and flew low for a long time and when I came to a little creek I went down through the shallow water like a torpedo boat, falling headlong now and then and coming up running each time. When a full-sized wake extended for several kilometers behind me, I throttled back and cupped an ear: all quiet. I plugged along, again on course.

By way of celebrating my victory, I rolled a smoke with a bit of tobacco requisitioned from a Jerry ration bag. I lay on the cool wet grass and grinned at the moon and smoked my damp cigarette right down to the last shred of tobacco. I couldn't stop chuckling.

Guns mumbled steadily in the north and west: an occasional flash of sheet lightning brightened the distant horizons. My territory was full of troops and mechanized units, and it seemed to be a busy night for the Wehrmacht: every highway looked like Route 66 with columns of tanks and trucks and endless processions of soldiers whizzing silently along on bicycles. Every road meant a careful wait until it was possible to slip through a gap in the traffic. From a hilltop I watched a bivouacked tank outfit break camp: noisy engines revving up as eight or ten massive tanks clanked slowly across a moonlit meadow to clatter down a dusty road. All about I could hear the creak and jingle of harness and wagons and the shouts of the skinners, and the groans of laboring truck engines.

Now a thin overcast had formed and my guiding stars were invisible. Polaris was hidden, and my compass needle was useless in the dark, for the luminous reference dots had dissolved in my mouth. But the moon was still faintly visible and that I would use, calculating in the southerly swing of its passage through the night skies. I walked on.

Strained through the thickening overcast, the moon became a dim blur and I had difficulty in keeping track of it. And now a heavy ground fog formed, cutting visibility down to a scant ten paces. My whole world was a milky, slow-flowing, suffocating mass of cold mist, wherein not a trace could be seen of the moon nor much of anything else.

I knew I was mounting a steep hill because I slipped backwards a couple of times, and I knew I'd blundered into a freshly prepared defensive position when I fell into a trench. I climbed out and fell into another. The whole hilltop was a maze of zigzag trenches, foxholes, tank revetments, and sandbagged pillboxes. I crawled on hands and knees now, feeling my way ahead and then I found a stick that I tapped along in front of me. Clear of that area, in desperation I fished out my compass needle, balanced it carefully on the point of a pin, and struck one of my precious matches. I picked up my course again, and within a few paces my checkpoint was lost in the swirling fog. I couldn't even guess as to just where in the hell North might have been.

So I could lay down in my tracks and wait for daybreak or I could carry on, flying blind with no instruments. The night was cold; my clothes and shoes were saturated from the wet grass and the dripping underbrush and from fording numerous creeks. I took a dim view of trying to sleep under a thicket. Anyway, I wanted to keep moving: I knew the woods and I knew all about walking in circles. But tonight, I kind of figured, my instincts were supernatural. If a goddam pigeon could get away with it, I sure as hell could make a try, anyway.

Onward over hill and dale, scrambling and skidding and now and then grabbing great chunks out of the fog in an effort to keep my balance, all the while concentrating on trying to feel southwest and to keep my paces of equal length. I savored the complete pleasure of every minute, too, for I was free as the frogs that croaked down in the hollows, while back at the miserable spur line forty-nine prisoners were jammed into a couple of boxcars; all hungry, thirsty, unhappy, uncomfortable, undignified, and subject to the whims of a lousy lot of Jerry slobs. (Minus one now, for pal Oscar was probably riding the point of a bayonet en route to the front.)

I walked on for hours, with never a dull moment. Dodging farms and chateaux and thrashing my way through countless hedges, I got jammed in the middle of one for a full quarter-hour—got lost in the goddam thing and finally emerged in a wet meadow with clothes and hide in shreds, and with temper in sorry need of a major overhaul. And it was overhauled, shortly after the incident in the hedge, when I cruised blindly over the brink of a five-foot vertical bank to land with a resounding splash in the creek below. But the wetting was turned to my advantage, for the bits of Jerry hardtack in my pockets were softened to some degree, and as I chomped on them I thought of home, for the stuff reminded me of the hound dogs I'd had before the war: the Jerry rations tasted exactly like the stuff I used to feed my dogs. (I would eat a dog biscuit now and then.)

I stumbled into the edge of a tiny village and tiptoed a stealthy retreat when I saw the fog-bound forms of soldiers sleeping beside their bicycles. While sneaking across a little wooden bridge, I perceived a sentry box and a little three-legged stool that stood before it. Nobody was around, so I tilted the sentry box over the rail and into the creek below, and it was sure that the morning guard detail would appreciate the truly delightful calling card I left for them on their little chair. Heh heh heh! For the rest of the night I was in good humor and I sang endlessly under my breath all the dirty old flying songs I could think of.

At last . . . the chilly, dim dawn, and I could make out trees ahead of me. At sunup the fog thinned out a bit and I saw, a few kilometers ahead of me, the twin spires of a cathedral. There seemed to be something a little familiar about those spires, and I ran to a hilltop for a better look. Even when I realized the facts of the matter, I didn't want to recognize them: for the spires were atop the cathedral in the heart of Sees. A half-block this side of the cathedral was SS headquarters. A short ways north of my present position was the spur line, complete with boxcars, Jerries, and forty-nine prisoners of war.

I'd left the spur line six or seven hours earlier, running southwest as fast as I could go: during the night I'd traveled a long, sweeping curve, turning always to my left, so now I was heading just about northeast. Had not the sun come up to burn away the soup when it had, I would have just about made rendezvous back at the old stand, where I knew I'd have been welcomed with open arms. Firearms, that is.

"You are one smart son of a bitch, Tayo," I told myself: and with a groan and a sigh and a shrug I chalked it all up to experience, forgot the thirty-thousand paces I'd just accomplished, turned around, and picked up a compass course to cut back across the semicircle I'd just walked. Many kilometers were gone all to pot, and taking advantage of what little fog remained I cruised fast, trying to rid myself of the exasperating sight of those twin spires.

The brighter became the day, the more slowly was I forced to travel. "A coyote," I pondered, "can run through the middle of ten thousand hunters and never be seen by one." So I adopted duplicate tactics: keeping the hell off the skyline and hugging fences and hedges and creek bottoms for protective camouflage. When the sun blazed hotly I dried out at last, and for the first time I felt tired. Rearing back, I took a mighty running jump far into the edge of a field of ripened wheat, leaving no trace of ever having entered the field: once in, I was visible only to the birds and they didn't mind, so I slept in peace for a while.

Harvesting a handful of grain, I chomped it down to a sweet cud, washing it down with a long drink from a cool brook. Tracks and other substantial evidence of many cattle were on the bank and bottom of the creek, and the water was really quite foul, but I had a thirst and figured with a chuckle that surely the Air Corps had run into my arms enough needles to take care of a little thing like that. Now, having rested and had a breakfast, I was off to the races; still mad at myself and walking faster to make up for lost time. Homing pigeon, hell!

The endless dodging and detouring really didn't matter. I wasn't going anywhere in particular and I didn't have to get there at any particular time; I was just beamed in the general direction of the Bay of Biscay in hopes of arriving in a general area where I calculated American strategy would cause our troops to be, sometime. I was happy, for the chill of the long night was out of me. The day was warm and bright, and the shadows of drifting clouds offered momentary coolness as I walked. The sight and sound of our fighters was always around me, and when a flight of roving Thunderbolts changed prop pitch and went into a circle I ran to the top of a knoll for a looksee.

They peeled off into nice straight dives for a bit of strafing: first a train of gun smoke behind each ship and then the chatter of 50s. Whatever their target was, it burned sending a pillar of smoke slanting skyward. I rolled a skimpy cigarette and gave bitter thought to the wonders of flight: those jockeys would cover, in the next five minutes, the ground that would take me one damned hard day of gravel-kicking to accomplish . . . but then again, look at the fun they were missing . . .

The hardtack long gone, for lunch I took another turn of my trusty belly-band. With the farmland behind me, I had come into pretty wild backwoods country, but despite the seeming desolation every trail showed the tracks of many boots having hobnails arranged symmetrically—which meant Jerries, since the undisciplined hands of the old French farmers always planted their shoes with hobnails in a most haphazard fashion.

In the afternoon I galloped down a long, sloping meadow and trudged up a much longer hill, skirting a forest that extended as far as my eye could reach; and I came upon a little corner of northern Minnesota, a tiny village of log houses set back into the fringe of the woods, and as I broke out into the clearing I could see a little sawmill and much sign of small-scale logging operations. Following a rut road along the edge of the forest for a kilometer or so, I came upon a scene of once-mighty industry: an abandoned turpentine still or the like, with many strange riveted iron pots strewn amongst the slash pine. Cords of wood were stacked here and there and wagon tracks crisscrossed the area, but I was the only one around. I climbed into one of the pots and went to sleep.

Opening an eye hours later, for a moment I couldn't quite figure out what was what: a round, rusty, iron cauldron with me inside, and the lid was a disk of blue sky. With a happy smile, I remembered I was free! I thought back over the odd bedrooms I'd slept in lately: bomb craters, shell holes, featherbeds, stables, master suites of grand chateaux, haystacks, straw stacks, thickets, fireplaces, caves, prison cells, wheat fields, and now a turpentine pot. What next?

There was a fine spider web strung across the chord of the kettle, and I spotted the owner and operator crouching evilly on the perimeter of his trap, waiting for business. Just for the hell of it, I rounded up a husky black beetle and dropped it into the very center of the web. When the villainous spider got the message, he streaked across the tough strands he'd spun and gave battle. It was a good show, for the spider—accustomed to winning out—was foiled this trip. My beetle, defying the spider's poisonous jaws with his armored back, just snipped his way across the web, kicked a hole in it, and dropped free. I tried the beetle again . . . same results. Capturing a pompous little cricket, I dumped him onto the web where he sat kicking stupidly in all directions. The spider pounced and stuck the little feller a few times and wrapped him in silk in a split second, twirling the cricket in his legs while spinning a shroud to completely conceal the victim. The spider laid his bundle away for future digestion. All this I pondered.

With some amusement I recalled the tale of another fugitive who had, once upon a time, watched a spider in operation: a feller by the name of Bruce who, amazed at his particular spider's persistence in accomplishing a difficult bit of engineering, had come out of his wretched hideout with renewed courage to then free his Scotland from English rule. With this legend in mind, I looked back to my little group of performers to think that it was a damned shame I had no way of dispatching the whole tiny theater and its players to the headquarters of the hibernating General Montgomery. With malicious glee, I mused over the tags I'd attach. The web would be the German front lines and the spider could play the Wehrmacht. A big beetle might play the American Army and to the cricket, heh-heh, I'd affix a label, "The Master." For additional enlightenment, I thought it would be quite a joke to include a boxful of beetles, each with the word "tank" printed on its armored back, with instructions to dump them all onto the web at one time and to observe their methods. Who knows? Had I only been able to've introduced Monty to my indomitable beetle, perhaps one day I might have been hailed as the savior of the Channel Coast of France!

Tired of puttering around, I poked my head out of the top of my iron shell like an old turtle casting a roving eye out over his pond. The sun was low and I bailed out and made for the woods. My rough logging trail petered out about sundown, and I tried a gravel road for a while, but Jerry traffic soon forced me back into the woods. Their tanks and trucks gave plenty of warning, but the silently whirring bicycle troops nearly caught me off guard a time or two. But now the old moon slid up into the sky and the night was perfect, and I felt as though I could walk a million kilometers through such country without ever tiring of the scenery.

A lovely sky with all the stars one could ask for, and the trees rattled a bit in the gentle breeze and sighed and whispered at me. The forest floor was soft and quiet for walking; dead old logs lay sunken and moldering in the ground, and rotted stuff and deep beds of pine needles filled the cool air with spice. Once in a while I'd startle some little wild critter and he'd rustle off away from me, and then I remembered the vision I'd had that evening while straining my scenery through the barbed wire of Alençon Prison. It had come true to the smallest detail!

I rested atop a mossy windfall and watched the elusive images of beefsteaks as they floated in orderly procession before my eyes. I sat on my old log sniffing the night wind and pondering the vastness of my strange world. There didn't seem to be a soul on Earth but me, and if there was anyone else anywhere they didn't know where I was. Nobody knew where I was. I didn't even know, or care much. All I knew was where I was going and where I'd been, roughly. I liked the scenery, though, and figured I wouldn't have swapped my night in the black forest of Normandy for all of the booming honky-tonks back in the States. So after a while I got up, mumbling in my beard, for I'd lost the North Star and had to spend ten stumbling minutes jockeying around trying to relocate it through the waving tops of the towering pines.

Before dawn I came upon a creek, just a trickly little thing that twisted and shone brightly under the moon, and I laid on my belly, burying my face in the icy waters to suck it up—a tired old horse guzzling from a trough. And if it was polluted, it was polluted; but to me it tasted like fifty-year-old bourbon whiskey. Hungry or not, the night was damned fine and I hated to see the sun come up.

After dawn I walked a mud road just below the skyline of a long ridge, and ahead I watched a farmer drive a team and rake into a clearing where he began to windrow his hay. Not quite liking his looks, I kept moving and he never saw me. I watched a lot of people who never saw me, and the thought struck me that perhaps many unseen eyes had observed me without my knowing it. Not too many, maybe: for by now, when I felt in the mood, I could become quite invisible in broad daylight. So I went my way.

Small mountains and big hills, rough country and an occasional farm, and for each kilometer made good on-course, there were three more of dodging and circling. Around each farmhouse, soldiers and camouflaged vehicles precluded any chances I had of panhandling a meal: green apples and wheat, plus an occasional wild strawberry didn't go far toward filling the cavern behind my belt buckle. A cold drizzle fell all that afternoon and evening, and about midnight, leery of duplicating the first night's back-tracking, I holed up in a little rank-smelling cave in a woods.

The demons screeching for chow in my belly got me out and on the trail at dawn, and from a hilltop I examined the terrain before me: nearby meadows and a chateau to detour; a half dozen farms with their tightly-hedged fields; a pair of highways; and beyond on the horizon, a great black forest. I plotted a course for a jutting salient of the distant wood, figuring that five careful hours should see me safely into the tall timber. All morning I struggled through an endless succession of snarled fences and brambled hedges, using every precaution I could think of and more that popped up instinctively. More green apples and a gulp from a brook, a final sneak along a fence line, and I sailed into the welcome shelter of the pines.

In an hour I broke out into an arm of farmland that projected into the forest. There were many tiny farms, each hidden from the next by the rolling terrain, and I decided to have a fling at rustling up some food. A ration-less forced march can become rather tedious after training on a diet of Jerry prison fare.

Spotting a little inn on a country road, and with a shot of Calvados in mind, I threw caution to the breezes and struck out across a meadow. When but a few hundred paces away, four black-uniformed Jerries emerged from the doorway of the inn. I called a halt. One of them shouted at me and I jettisoned all ideas of refreshment, turning to zigzag into a convenient ravine along which I traveled fast; not particularly caring whether or not the Jerries took out after me, knowing that in this kind of country they couldn't get their hands on me.

In a few kilometers I came upon a likely looking farmhouse that nes-tled in a curve of the hilly gravel road. I bellied under a fence and through the backyard garden to a place where I could look ten feet down into the farmyard. Faint voices floated from the kitchen, and the smell of cooking food made my mouth water in anticipation of the roasted rabbit I was about to receive. But—innocent as the layout appeared—there also appeared that curious and uneasy prickling of my scalp, so I lay in con-cealment for perhaps a half-hour. I'd almost decided to jump down into the yard and knock at the door, but to be on the safe side I sweated a little longer, watching and listening with great patience. Then from the kitchen, the chatter of a chair sliding on a board floor, a husky laugh, and a loud, "Ja! Ja!" My visions of wine and rabbit faded rapidly, as did I. Another farmhouse I cased, and another. Soldiers were billeted everywhere, so I dug out my compass and plunged again into the forest, nibbling on a bunch of underdone onions I'd snatched from a garden.

The forest was incredibly thick: pines straight and tall, tangled under-brush, and countless windfalls over which to crawl, and I had to check my course constantly for it was impossible to pick out a checkpoint very far ahead. The going was rough and I herring-boned up the steep slopes and slid down the hills where footing was precarious on the slick pine needles. Mid-afternoon now, and sensations of weakness were coming with increas-ing frequency, and I cussed and whistled and sang and got goddam good and hungry. Coming to a delightful little mountain creek, I took off my shoes and peeled away what remained of my stockings and let the cold water caress my blistered feet. I buried my head in a pool and drank, and then lay on my belly and rested. When lifting my eyes, I beheld a patch of blueberries that could have been spotted only from my worm's-eye view! Big as grapes, they were, and covered with a powder-blue dust, and they were the finest blueberries in the world.

As I climbed each hill, I thought that surely I'd see the edge of the for-est. But at the top, only another hill and an endless procession of hills. For hours without end there was forest and more forest until I thought I'd croak. At last I came across an asphalt highway and, glad for the level foot-ing, I walked the shoulder of the road. Immediately a little low-slung Jerry staff car came buzzing along to catch me by surprise, and I was forced to make an emergency jump from the road. Off the road, at that particular place, involved dive bombing—with my body—a bush some fifteen feet below the roadway. I picked my bones up out of the thicket at the bottom of the embankment. If the Jerries in that little car had been suddenly trans-formed into what I hollered after them, the least they'd have done would have been to stop their car to lift a leg at the nearest tree.

Paralleling the road, I came to a Y junction where I read the signpost. I'd never heard of any of the villages listed thereon. Kicking in the door of an abandoned log cabin there, I shopped around for some chow: just empty tin cans and a filthy litter of rubbish, and all I got out of the deal was a few choice butts—Jerry issue—that I spilt open and rerolled into one fairly decent cigarette. I dug out one last match and hit the tall timber again, puffing contentedly on my lumpy stogie.

The Jerries in this neck of the woods had done a recent and thorough job of readying things for a battle. Every little road and logging trail was cleverly blocked by trees, which had been felled in such a manner as to funnel tanks or any other vehicles into numerous natural lanes, and sighting down each lane was a massive log pillbox. Expert woodsmen had done a good job: countless pines a foot or two in diameter lay in their precise positions. But it was clear that the Jerries expected attack only from the northwest, which meant to me that they feared American attack, as these defensive positions would be useless in the event of attack from any other point of the compass.

Precisely at the time when I felt in need of a rest and a smoke, I stumbled upon an important-looking cable composed of five varicolored wires. I presumed they connected various flakbatteries and control stations and headquarters outfits, so I settled down to business. Putting a rock beneath the cable, I pounded away with a boulder until the strands parted, and after a bit of puttering and tinkering I had the insulation stripped back. I rejoined the wires, connecting the blue to the red, the red to the yellow, the yellow to the green, the green to the brown, and the brown to the blue. A neat splice it was, too. After kicking some leaves over the makeshift repair job, I trudged away feeling—for no good reason—mighty pleased. I'd much rather see direct results of my mischief, but I had to content myself with thoughts of the Jerries' confusion upon their next transmission of urgent orders over these wires.

After another battle with the underbrush, I came upon a new military road that sliced through the woods, beamed east and west. I headed west down the middle of the road, clocking off the kilometers with ease, pausing only to rip down a directional signpost here and a coded arrow there. Knowing the average I.Q. of Jerry truck drivers to be negative, they would, I figured, be hopelessly lost once they hit this now-unmarked stretch of lonesome road.

When the sun was low on the horizon ahead of me, I was tempted to call it quits for the day. But the interminable forest that had held me for so long had in my mind become a bitter and personal enemy: it seemed now to take an unholy delight in refusing to yield to my eyes the sight of civilization, and I resolved profanely to conquer this gloomy patch of pines.

Legs working automatically, I counted paces from one to a thousand, whereupon a withering stream of invective would be directed toward the grinning forest. Then another thousand. A parched throat and terrific hunger had me lightheaded now; and then it was pure orneriness that kept one foot swinging out ahead of the other. Over and over again came the whispered thought that somewhere ahead of me, if I'd only keep traveling, was a friend waiting: a friend with wine and bread and rabbit and sweet butter and milk, all I could eat. Ahead of me floated elaborate mental pictures of the feast that would be mine if I'd just walk. So I kept going, like a thin and tired greyhound chasing the ever-elusive mechanical bunny around and around the endless track. I cussed the woods and the occasional trucks that drove me momentarily into the thickets. I cussed puddles in the road as I sloshed through them. I cussed the slightly larger chunks of gravel, which forced me to lift a shoe an extra fraction of an inch.

At long last, through a fringe of trees I caught a glimpse of farmland off the port wing and I soon gazed down into a peaceful valley. I pulled a bead on the closest farmhouse, determined to eat by hook or crook. Creeping down a weedy fence line to within a few yards of the house, I saw German staff cars with camouflage netting flung over them. A quartet of Jerry officers lounged on the grass smoking their after-dinner cigars. I retreated, clinging to the edge of the forest and keeping to the long sunset shadows until I found an orchard. I gobbled a couple of green apples and wet my lips in a creek, afraid to drink the roiled water.

Just a nubbin of sun showed over the horizon as I approached a second farmhouse: guttural shouts and laughter, as though the bastards didn't know their days were numbered.

Dusk now, and I was just about kaput. Coming upon a little dirt road, I squeezed through the hedge that fenced it and followed along inside on the meadow. Ahead the road petered out in a gloomy neck of the forest, and in the fast-fading light I could make out the cobblestone wall and iron-barred windows of a desolate farmhouse. I crept through a little garden toward the cluster of ramshackle outbuildings and crawled into a tiny weathered woodshed that stood near the house.

Gluing an eye to a crack in the rear wall of the shed, I saw a half-open kitchen door from which a sliver of firelight escaped to flicker upon the cobblestones of the yard. Soft voices came from the house. In a moment a very small boy skipped from the doorway and came to within a few feet of me. Humming a tune, the little feller picked up a crooked twig and commenced to poke at a bug.

Stepping silently from cover, I made a little sound like a squirrel and the boy jumped to his feet to search me out with startled eyes. When he saw me he froze.

I flashed my fangs in a friendly smile and put a finger to my lips: "Shhhh . . . . Venez-ici! Venez-ici!" But the lad would come no closer, and I couldn't exactly blame him since I looked like the one and original bogeyman. Again warning him to silence, I whispered, "Ton père! Ton père! Fetch yore daddy outside, son!" And the kid scuttled to the doorway and disappeared.

Swiftly I tiptoed to a new hiding place. It was full darkness now, and I wanted to be able to see whoever might come from the doorway before he could see me. German or French collaborator, they were of equal danger. I was set for a hasty retreat should things go haywire.

A stocky young Frenchman strode belligerently from the house and proceeded directly to the woodshed. He found no one there. I stepped into the open and hissed, and he swung like a cat and advanced; and a little revolver leveled at my belly prompted me to put up my hands and state my claims.

Chapter 10

A DANGEROUS GUEST

◆

"**B**onsoir, mon ami. Aviateur Americain. Beaucoup faim, beaucoup soif!" Hungry and thirsty, thirsty and hungry.

The Frenchman's reply was to nuzzle my ribs with his gun.
Pushing me back into the dim light cast from the doorway, he analyzed
my tattered outfit. He felt the leather of my army shoes and patted around
to see if he could find a gun. Then he whispered softly: "Votre plaque d'i-
dentité, Monsieur."

With care I lowered one hand and dug out dog tag and wings and
insignia, all of which he examined closely—all the while keeping his little
pistol focused on my belly-button.

He shoved his gun into a hip pocket, shook hands with me, and jerked
his head toward the doorway. And I stepped over the low sill into paradise.

A fire-lit kitchen. From chains over a smoldering fire hung a blackened
kettle, and the cracked plaster walls of the room were soot-stained from a
century of cooking fires. Three persons sat around a rough plank table.
Tearing my eyes from a half-bottle of wine and a half-loaf of black bread
that lay near the single feeble candle, I greeted these folks with a smiling,
"Bonsoir Madam, Messieurs!"

My gun-toting friend announced curtly: "Un aviateur Americain." A
black-haired, soft-eyed girl of my age, and built like the proverbial brick
chateau, took over the meeting:

My name? Tayo. Well, hers was Suzanne.

I was a pilot, non?

Oui, I replied: pilot sans avion!

Ha ha ha! Suzanne laughed dutifully, for I had made a little joke. In France the Jerry robot bombs were called "Avion sans pilot," and I was just the opposite: pilot without airplane.

What age had I? Suzanne too was twenty-four. With a glance to my ring, she asked if I were married, and she seemed to be pleased when I denied all charges, explaining that mine was an Air Corps ring, thank God. And Suzanne introduced me to the others.

A hollow-cheeked, shaggy-headed, fever-eyed character of some thirty or forty years: his name was Vitrice, and as she said his name Suzanne slapped him gently.

Then his brother Robert who had come outside to fetch me. Turning to his small son, Robert told him to stand guard at the gate to the road; to cry out should les Boches approach. With an excited bob of his head, the five-year-old scampered from the house.

The last was a greybeard of perhaps sixty-five or seventy years: ruddy face and a booze-nose, straw-colored moustachios, and with a broad-brimmed hat on his head. To him I wasn't introduced. Instead, Robert palmed his little revolver and walked directly over to the old geezer. He began to spit words into the old man's face in a low, fast voice, and I couldn't follow the monologue. Robert punctuated his message with ominous jabs of his gun barrel into the greybeard's chest, and the old man's face was ruddy no more, but chalk white. Robert wound up by jerking the old duffer to his feet and, with one savage shove, thrusting him out into the night. I was curious, but since nobody volunteered an explanation, I asked no questions.

Suzanne, in the meanwhile, had given me her place at the table and stirred up the fire. Now she hopped around the little room, leaving in her wake the clatter of dishes and pans, and the smell of food made me feel shaky.

"How he trembles!" cried Suzanne. "How pinched his cheeks!"

Vitrice filled a glass with cider, which I downed with a gulp. Only after draining eight or ten tall glassfuls could I put down the jug, for it is impossible to be polite about such a thirst as I'd acquired. Then, handing over his hunting knife, Vitrice pushed the loaf of black bread across the table, and I tucked it under an arm and carved off a thin slice and began to eat it dry. Grateful for just a little, I also wanted to sort of feel out the extent of my welcome. Vitrice reached over and, taking the bread from me, spread it with a thick layer of sweet butter and with a laugh slapped it on the table before me.

When I'd finished that he had another ready, and Suzanne placed before me a bowl of steaming soup. And when the soup had followed the bread and butter, a platter of delicious roasted rabbit was mine. Each time I'd get to feeling guilty about having eaten so much and would say I'd had enough, she would smile, Suzanne, and put more food on my plate, and Vitrice kept my glass filled with exquisitely cool cider.

When finally my belly was full and my thirst a bad memory and I felt alive again, I found it difficult to keep a steady voice as I sought words with which to express my deep gratitude; Robert handed me a little square packet of tobacco and I rolled a smoke, lighting it with the candle flame, and blew a happy smoke ring.

And with the help of Suzanne, who understood my stumbling French remarkably well, I told my friends of the long trek through their country; of my abortive attempt to penetrate the lines near Dozulé a hundred kilometers or more to the North. I told of my capture and escape and of the nights and days that had taken me from the other side of Sees to this farmhouse. Either my stories were comical or my accents too much for a Frenchman to take, for Vitrice ha-ha'd continually. I plowed up his native tongue and when I'd pause to reshuffle my vocabulary into another sentence, Suzanne would jabber fast, enlarging upon what she'd picked up from my lingo. Robert expressed surprise and disbelief when he understood me to say that I'd just hiked through the local woods: "Six thousand soldiers and a Panzer division maneuver in that forest! You walked there?"

I shrugged and said I'd had good luck, peut-être. Hell, I hadn't seen anybody but the guys in that lousy staff car. At my request, Robert sketched a rough map of the Allied front as he knew it, and I could hardly believe my luck: the Yanks had taken all of Cherbourg Peninsula to then break through the Jerry lines at St. Lo up in the Bocage country. Bocage means hedgerow, and I wondered how in hell they'd done it. And the Yanks were still going strong, spearheading down along the west coast and now nearing the harbor city of Avranches. Well, my plans were set: three or four days walking westward should take me to the sea somewhere around St. Malo.

Once there, I'd lie low and await results. It occurred to me that this Robert was pretty well informed, and when I said as much he admitted to possession of a little radio that had been dropped to him from an English bomber. This, plus a few of his slightly bitter remarks concerning the Allies, added up to enough to arouse my curiosity. After a little offhand pumping, I'd soon laid bare his sad cry.

He had been, he growled, chief of the local Maquis group. After much complicated planning with London headquarters, there'd been arranged a supply drop to equip his little outfit with guns and explosives for sabotage. On the night of the drop, Robert had led his merry men to the prescribed area in the forest. At the proper time they had ignited the prearranged pattern of signal fires, and the planes had come over. They had come over, allright, but too high; and the wind had seized the little parachutes, drifting them all over hell and gone. Alerted by all this commotion, the Jerries had attacked in force, and after a wild midnight skirmish in the middle of the forest, the Maquis had come out holding the dirty end of the stick. Most of the partizans had been captured: some had been executed, and some imprisoned at Alençon. The Jerries had ended up with most of the stuff the bombers had dropped. The whole affair had been snafu, and Robert was mad at everybody.

Always the diplomat, I said that it had not been his fault that his Maquis had been wiped out, but the fault of the aviators for scattering the bundles throughout the forest. I added that I, however, was a "pilot chasseur"—fighter pilot—and we never threw things around like that.

Robert pounded the table with his fist, and the flame of the candle gave a twitch: "Merde! Those damned pilots of bombers! Pas bon!"

It was near midnight when Robert slipped out of the house for a looksee. He reported back that many tanks and trucks moved along the local roads and that many soldiers marched in the forest near the farmhouse. That was no news to me, and I took it as a gentle hint.

Scribbling my name and address on a scrap of paper, I gave it to Suzanne and asked her to write to my home after the liberation. Gulping down one last glass of cider, I shrugged into my forlorn suitcoat and tugged my beret to a sloppy angle over one ear.

I was as ready as I'd ever be. "Bon nuit, et merci encore . . . il faut partir!" Good night and thanks again . . . one must leave.

Robert shook hands and wished me luck. He parked his petit-gars—his small boy—upon the handlebars of an old bicycle and pedaled off through the gloom.

Now three of us stood in their farmyard whispering final adieus. Suzanne peered worriedly toward the inky forest: "But where do you go, Tayo?"

"West to Saint Malo to look for the Americans."

"But in the forest, les Boches! They'll get you!"

"Could be, but you know if les Boches find me here, we three are dead!"

"Oui . . . c'est perilleux!"

I shopped around the skies, seeking the North Star. All of a sudden Suzanne whispered again: "But Tayo, vous êtes beaucoup fatigué!—you've had it. Rest here this night and sleep well. We hide you and tomorrow after breakfast you can leave!"

Vitrice took on a hunted look when he heard that, but he said nothing—perhaps drawing upon previous experience. I objected, but not too strenuously, for the thought of sleep and of having guaranteed food in the morning was enough to undermine my determination to keep moving. Suzanne had made up her mind, and it was agreed.

The candle was snuffed in the kitchen. All was dark. Moving about the farm area were Jerries, their voices clearly audible. We tiptoed to the ramshackle barn, where Suzanne rummaged around and came up with a square of canvas. Vitrice grabbed up a great armful of straw, then led out through an orchard, and beyond the orchard we stumbled into an apparently solid hedgerow; but on hands and knees Vitrice led us through a tiny hole that penetrated to the center of the hedge. There, running lengthwise, was a dark tunnel along which we followed crouching low until coming to a place where overhead the stars were faintly visible. Vitrice spread the straw on the ground and laid the canvas over all. A perfect hideout.

As though just now struck by the extreme risk involved in his impromptu undertaking, Vitrice sputtered nervously: "If they find you here, you are tout á seul—all alone and on your own! He cupped an ear, raised a finger: "Écouté! Les Boches partout!" Listen! Germans all around!

He was so right. The crack of a twig nearby . . . guttural voices.

Suzanne whispered that early in the morning there would be heard the song of a bird—like so—and it would not be a bird, but only herself with food for me.

It didn't make much difference, really, but I kind of wondered where I was, so I asked: "Ou suis-je?"

"One calls this St. Nicolas des Bois . . ."

And then I was alone. I didn't even bother to lay out a route of quick exit, but just lay on my back and looked into the dim starlight that filtered through the screen of leaves above me. Then I had a little thought that maybe I was lucky.

It'd been a long solo flight through enemy territory, flying blind and bucking a headwind of hunger all the way. Then with the old fuel gauge riding on zero and my engine sputtering, I'd cut the switch, trusted to luck, and dead-sticked into a three-point landing on a long concrete runway called St. Nicolas des Bois!

The night wind rattled the leaves around me, and off in the orchard I could hear cherries thud to the ground now and then. A tank engine revved up off in the distance. I was happy, for look! Friends, food, wine, tobacco, a place to lay my weary head: all magically mine! Hell's Bells! Had I made the turn? Was I now plumbing the depths of a handy hallucination? Had I eaten one of those tantalizing mirages I'd been pursuing these days and nights? I patted my belly: warm and rounded out. Hot damn! I still was in this world! And of all places to strike upon, St. Nicolas des Bois . . . the patron saint of the forests! Talk about wading chin-deep in a vat of bubbling swill and coming out gold-plated!

I slept. A few trills and a tweet brought me quickly awake. The morning sun blazed overhead and in a moment along down the tunnel came a wicker basket followed closely by the dark-eyed, smiling Suzanne. Bread and butter, a slab of jambon—smoked ham—and a jug of cider, and as I feasted the gal hummed a happy tune. When I'd finished, she fished from her apron pocket two lumpy cigarettes. We lit up and had a chat.

Said she, conversationally: "All the morning in my kitchen there have been German soldiers."

I suggested that perhaps one couldn't blame soldiers for coming always to pass the time of day with such a beautiful girl. The expression of this thought resulted in a slap, but gentle.

"Cochons! Brigands! Sauvages!" cried Suzanne. Each day they come to my kitchen to demand butter, eggs, and cider, and this morning they have stolen one of my rabbits! Pigs! Thieves! Savages!"

I was intrigued by one incident of the previous evening: "The old man, hier soir, he was not a friend?"

She said that the old geezer bamboozled by Robert was a notorious local collaborator. She winked. "But he has fear, that old one. He will keep shut the mouth!" Robert, it seemed, had told the old bastard that should he let out a peep about me to anyone, that he—Robert—would assassinate him. "If anything should happen to me, old man," had said Robert, "you're a dead pigeon, for then Vitrice will take care of you. Should anything happen to either or both of us, my friends will liquidate you, your family, and all your relatives!"

No wonder the old feller had paled, with these threats emphasized by Robert's thumping pistol.

I learned, too, that Vitrice had been taken by the Jerries early in the war and had languished for three years in a German concentration camp. When his health had been sufficiently shattered, he'd been permitted to return to Saint Nicolas des Bois. Upon his arrival back at the old homestead, he'd discovered that his ever-loving wife had run off with an Italian soldier. Suzanne had felt so sorry for Vitrice that she'd taken him under her wing and since then they'd lived together happily.

Suzanne related to me the latest rumors of the war as told to her by the village cure, who served as a main cable in the local grapevine circuit. Strange to me were the names of the towns where American spearheads were now engaging the enemy, but I did learn that since escaping, I'd steered much too much southerly—indeed, I'd not passed too far from Alençon Prison, from whence I'd sprung myself. So I asked Suzanne to give a message to Robert: I wanted a good map of the coastal country, for that would be a requisite for the precise navigation necessary during my proposed westward trek out of here.

After Suzanne left the skies clouded up, and before long a little rain began to fall. I crouched all afternoon in my leafy lair, hoping for a map from Robert, plotting, planning, thinking, dozing, and prowling around the tunnel. No Robert and no map. At sundown Vitrice brought me a little chow and a cigarette, and since it was still raining I figured I'd spend the night under my canvas, and despite the cold all-night drizzle I slept soundly and dreamlessly.

At dawn a twig snapped and I was twenty feet away and traveling fast before I awakened to realize that it was only Vitrice and Robert come to fetch me. We left the tunnel and Robert went on ahead.

When he signaled an all-clear from the house, Vitrice and I sneaked up through the orchard and into the kitchen, and there on the table was a detailed map, a scrap of tracing paper, and some tacks, and I went to work tracing roads and villages and forests as fast as I possibly could. Haste was indicated, for my friends were nervous. Filling the uneasy air was the constant din of Jerry action: tanks and trucks roaring along nearby roads, shouts of soldiers. Robert explained that the Germans were pouring troops into a sector some sixty kilometers to the west to counterattack the Americans at Mortain. It was the sixth of August.

Vitrice and Robert took off on some mission of mischief, and Suzanne and I were alone in the house. I pored over my map for an hour, trying to dope out a logical destination. Should the Jerry counterattack succeed, then the Americans would likely swing farther south and then drive toward Paris, thereby pocketing me in a high-explosive trap along with half the Wehrmacht. I was deep in plots and plans when my reveries were shattered by the click of boots on the cobblestones of the yard, and I scampered into a back room, sat in a corner, and pulled over my head great quantities of laundry. And there I lay buried for a long time while boots clumped through the house and harsh voices filtered through to me. When all became quiet Suzanne rounded me up, and she laughed: "When the Boches come again, you are my deaf-and-dumb cousin from Paris. But hide your blond hair with your hat!"

Sure enough, about noon as we sat eating bread and milk in the kitchen, again there sounded the thud of boots. I hung my beret over an ear and started choking down more food faster, as briefed. A trio of very tough Jerries stomped in and stood looking around.

"Beurre!" grunted one of the soldiers.

Suzanne shook her head and said that the soldiers had taken all her butter.

"Oeuf!" growled the spokesman, shooting her a mean look.

Suzanne replied that she had no eggs for the soldiers either. And all the while, the leader of this ornery trio was crowding Suzanne toward the wall, and when she could retreat no further she stood, hands on hips, and glared into the trooper's savage eyes. He shouted at her in German and jabbed her in the belly with the muzzle of his Mauser. But Suzanne held her ground and rattled off a strip of furious French. The Jerry backed off a ways and said something to his partners. Then jerking a thumb to where I sat, deadpan, he asked Suzanne if I were her husband. "Non!" she said. I was her brother. And she touched her lips and ears. The trooper laughed and spit on the floor and the three soldiers left the house.

My heart was jumping around a bit, but Suzanne was so cockeyed mad that she just shook her fist at the soldiers' backs and muttered, "Cochons!" and she went about cleaning the floor. Then out of spite she fried up a batch of eggs and slapped a crock of butter onto the table in front of me. We finished our déjeuner in style.

The day was hot and clear and the humid wind from the forest made me reel like a Mustang all revved up but with chocks under the wheels. I was caught up on sleep and chow, and I took a dim view of squatting passively inside a thicket while awaiting liberation. I craved action in the worst sort of way, and I wanted to find somebody who spoke my own language. So I told Suzanne that I figured to hit the trail come sundown. I had a map now and that was all I'd lacked, and I studied it for a while then greased my tired shoes with a chunk of fat and set about checking over my equipment for the big push.

I'd lost my tiny, all-important compass needle. It was not to be found in the seams of my suitcoat, and I recruited Suzanne to aid in the search. We sifted through the pile of straw in the hedgerow, but that was like seeking the needle in the proverb. It wasn't there. Well, goddammit, I figured, to hell with it! I'd make me a compass. I'd magnetize a needle and hang it from a thread or float it on some water if and when I needed a direction.

A search of the tool shed brought out no old electrical device that might have had a magnet as part of its construction, so as a last resort I tried to magnetize a short iron bar—with which to then magnetize a needle. I tilted the damned bar to the north and swatted the end with a hammer. But I guess that Frenchmen do not rearrange molecules, because my profane hammerings were a beautiful failure. Suzanne thought I was balmy.

Came sundown and Vitrice returned, and I drew a picture of a compass and asked him to try to round one up for me. He tried, but in an hour he returned empty-handed. Robert had no compass. Nobody had one.

Clouds swept low over the forest and by evening a drizzle fell from leaden skies. The night was black and starless. Navigation, as I'd learned the hard way, would be impossible.

Taking note of my sagging morale, Vitrice hauled out a jug of rotgut Calvados and we sat around the flickering candle and had a drink or two or three. Pretty soon my host slapped my knee and called me his ol' pal. Tonight, quoth he, I need not sleep in the wet hedgerow but in the hayloft instead. And the loft was right in the farmhouse.

Adjoining, on the ground floor of this self-contained farm, lay a wood-shed, kitchen, bedroom, cow-shed, and pigpen—and rare odors from the latter would permeate the atmosphere whenever the wind was right. Above this suite of living quarters was a long hayloft that ran the length of the house, and which could be reached only by means of a ladder from without. And it was in this loft that I was installed for the night.

Bidding me an alcoholic bonsoir, Vitrice then hid the splintery, broken-runged ladder. I dug down into the soft, warm hay. A cricket gave forth with feeble chirps from a black corner of the loft. An intermittent sizzling of cold drizzle was whipped against the plank door by the gusty night wind. Branches of trees at the edge of the forest raked and scratched against the roof above me. I was grateful for the shelter.

After dawn I watched through a narrow crack in the hayloft door as muddy German soldiers drifted in and out of the farmhouse in pairs and threes and fours, refueling their canteens with Vitrice's good cider. My friends greeted their unwelcome guests with restrained hostility, doing silently as they were asked to do. And they showed no trace of the nervousness that must have been induced by their knowledge that five feet above their heads lay their death warrant in the form of a fugitive American pilot. They were brave, Vitrice and Suzanne.

This was the seventh of August and the dawn of my third day at this little farm. At breakfast Vitrice reported that the American spearhead toward Mortain had been halted by a fierce German counterattack, but that other American units were somewhere around St. Malo. Rumor also had it that the English had at long last run out of tea and were showing signs of life, fighting their way southward out of Caen.

After plotting these rumors on my map, it seemed clear to me that a gigantic pincer movement was under way, with the Americans screaming around and up from below while the English whispered southward toward Falaise. At the rate things were going, it looked as though St. Nicolas des Bois might eventually be somewhere near the center of the trap. But I didn't know how soon the trap would be sprung. Despite my lack of compass I wanted to move out, and I'd have to hope for clear night skies. Movement by day through these reinforced Jerry lines would be most tricky.

I feared for the safety of my good French friends here. At this stage of the game, with liberation almost in sight, it would be a dirty shame if they didn't live to see it. My presence on the farm was their hazard, and after breakfast I said as much. I'd leave tonight to find my comrades, and then my friends would have no more worries.

But Suzanne said, "Ha! We have no fear of les Boches! Do not leave, for you are like a brother to us. Always you laugh and make jokes, and besides that, if you stay perhaps you will teach this little pig Vitrice some manners. You smell like the goat, but you do not belch after supper!"

Well, how could one resist such hospitality? High hopes faint on a warm hearthstone. "He travels the fastest who travels alone": my old motto weakened and fell to the floor with a ponderous thud. So I replied that I'd be happy to be their dangerous guest for another few days. We'd wait and see how far the Americans might advance. Perhaps in a day or two, liberation!

Vitrice said, "Ah-ha! Now I have you to work in my field!" And he went out to look over his ripening grain.

Suzanne fetched a bucket of water from the well. She handed me a little piece of soap and a rag and a brush. She pinched her nose expressively. I was forced to strip and bathe, and it wasn't my idea but Suzanne's. I was even getting to like the billy-goat smell that hovered over me. For almost a month—since leaving le Maquis César—I hadn't had my clothes off, and now it was a rough go. As I labored, Suzanne tried to wash out my undershirt and shorts, but she returned in an hour, admitting defeat. Her miserable ersatz soap was no match for the yellowish layer of sweat, blood, grease, and mud that caked my dainties. I dried them out and put 'em back on, anyway; and we spent a merry while running blazing splinters along the seams of my old coat and pants to burn out the lice and assorted wildlife that had made a home there. A truly remarkable quantity of bugs popped and fell lifeless to the floor, but we couldn't get 'em all. Suzanne gave me a fresh shirt and a clean pair of pants and a blue velvet jacket of Vitrice's. Then with an ancient straight-edge razor I shaved, to eliminate a three-week collection of reddish whiskers. When I'd finished my face was smooth, clean, and rather bloody but I felt peachy, and when I peered cautiously into the cracked mirror I scarcely recognized myself. Great changes had been wrought during my stay with Suzanne and Vitrice!

Suzanne and I were having an after-lunch cigarette in the shade by the doorway when a little auto whizzed up to the gate. Two Jerry officers and a non-com strode into the yard and Suzanne poked me and whispered a frightened, "Allez! Allez!"—Take off! As the Jerries neared us, I picked up a wagon wheel that rested against the wall of the house, rolled it carefully over the cobbles, and then down through the orchard where I picked up speed and zoomed up and over a knoll and out of sight. Upon observing the departure of the German auto, I returned to the house where Suzanne said that the officers had inquired as to my identity. She'd explained that I was a neighbor boy come to borrow a wheel for his hay wagon, which had been wrecked as the result of a frightful runaway. What a delightful imagination had this girl! She explained that these visitors had been officials of the local German government.

Periodic tours of inspection of all farms were accomplished and a census taken of all cattle, sheep, chickens, rabbits, pigs, children, and other livestock. The latest tallies were matched against those of previous checkups, and the farmer suffered for any deficiencies. For each cow, the Jerries required the farmer to deliver three kilograms of butter each week to the German storehouse in the village: an impossible order, for with a cleaver one couldn't get that much out of a cow. For each hen, so many eggs. New calves were confiscated, as were all crops after harvest.

Anyway, that is the way the Jerries had it doped out: but Vitrice kept his new calf staked out in the forest, and Robert had four of his pigs stashed away elsewhere. About a tenth of all butter churned went to the Jerries, along with apologies that the cows were either tuckered out or running dry. So it was always a game of countless little deals like that, with almost everyone out to screw the Wehrmacht. But four years of occupation hadn't left these people very much.

My friends had little to call their own: a bed and feather quilt; three chairs and a plank table, hand-hewn. A few chipped plates with faded hunting scenes glazed into their faces. A bucket and a wash-pan and a well and the roof over their heads. Three tired heifers and a bony mare were theirs, and a two-wheeled cart and a broken-down old McCormack mowing machine held together by an intricate maze of rusty wire. But they had each other, and Suzanne was an excellent cook. She could make a wonderful salade from the stuff in her tiny garden, and there was always a ham hanging in the kitchen chimney: jambon, tender and smoky and salty. And there was plenty of milk, and the plums and cherries were coming ripe in the orchard. Poor in material things they might have been, in heart they were magnificently wealthy.

That afternoon of the wagon-wheel incident, Vitrice noted my restlessness and asked me if I'd not like to walk into the forest with him. He took up a long-handled spade and together we struck out along a faint woodland trail. It was the right prescription, for the wild pine smell and the springy moss underfoot filled me with content and soothed away my reckless ideas. As we prowled, my friend told me of his life before the war: of hunting trips through this same forest, for deer and boar and birds.

For three or four kilometers we walked—with caution—into the dense woods. When we came to a cross-path we followed along it, and I led the way. Vitrice shouted a warning and I halted dead in my tracks, fortunately.

Vitrice came up ahead of me and knelt down, brushing aside the leaves and twigs until there lay exposed a circular steel trap a foot in diameter and complete with gaping saw-tooth jaws. A skillfully camouflaged length of chain fastened the trap securely to a deep-sunken "dead-man."

I was interested: what game did Vitrice trap? Quel animal, mon ami? Le cerf ou l'ours, ou le sanglier peut-être?" The stag or the bear, or the wild boar perhaps?

Vitrice laughed furiously and whacked me on the back: "Les Boches!" The downright orneriness of his reply made me grin.

"Combien des Boches, Vitrice?" How many had he taken?

His eyes twinkled. "Cinq soldats!" said he, and he chuckled and slapped his leg. Then he demonstrated with dramatic gestures just how these five soldiers had each taken a shortcut through the forest . . . stepped into the trap of Vitrice . . . rolled in agony upon the forest floor . . . tried in vain to pull up the stake . . . and at last had expired when he, Vitrice, had smashed in their goddam heads with this very spade. Good ol' Vitrice's eyes gleamed as he acted out the manner in which he'd buried the victims and concealed their graves.

Embracing him in good Gallic fashion, I clapped him on the back and showered him with genuine congratulations. We headed for home arm in arm, cussing the Boches and complimenting each other on our dirty work. Vitrice was coughing steadily, and I asked him what might be his trouble. He explained that the Jerries had removed one of his lungs before sending him home from the concentration camp.

We paused to roll a cigarette. "Now," said Vitrice, "I have but a few more years," and he chuckled. "But Suzanne, she makes me happy. Monsieur le Medecin has said that to smoke will hasten my death, but it gives me such pleasure that I smoke anyway. Heh heh!" He took a deep drag and passed me the butt. He patted his spade and chuckled again. And after supper, Vitrice said that we'd harvest his wheat in the morning.

For nearly three days we worked in the wheat field. Vitrice mowed with his old machine until he ran out of hay wire, and then we finished the cutting with scythes. In one hard, hot day's work from dawn 'til dark we bundled the wheat, first raking it into windrows, then scooping it into piles: then kneeling the piles into tight bundles, we tied each bundle with a rope of twisted wheat stalks. At dawn of the following day, Vitrice harnessed his old mare to the rickety two-wheeled cart and we climbed aboard and took off for the field. Vitrice, unable to work very hard, would lead the horse up and down the rows of bundles while Robert and I would fork them up into the rick where Suzanne would stack them. With a great top-heavy load aboard, our procession would wend slowly back to the farmyard, where we'd pitch the bundles into a shed and arrange them there, thatched-roof fashion. Then back into the empty cart for a gay journey to the field. And had I a motion picture of some of those trips, my fortune would be assured; for absolutely, they were the most hilarious ventures I've ever been witness to.

It would seem that Vitrice believed his mare to be endowed with human intelligence. He didn't think of his horse as a horse, but rather as someone who had been living on his farm for long enough to at least be able to understand the wishes of M. le Patron, and to be able to interpret his every mood. Up into the cart we would clamber, and Vitrice would take over the controls.

"Allons!" he would shout to his horse, and we'd lurch forward. Vitrice would turn to me and smile as though to say, "Look at that! Ain't she a dandy horse?"

Now the trail to the wheat field ran diagonally across a bit of a meadow, made a 45-degree port turn, and followed along a little footpath, through a gate, and so into the field. The old mare—her name was Flora—realized that she had to make a turn to some different heading, but she could never quite figure out which way to go, and generally she'd plod off to starboard, jouncing us about as the cart would bump over the hummocks of the meadow. Vitrice would shout, "Halt! Halt!" and the mare would dribble down to a stop; whereupon Vitrice would leap to the ground, march forward, seize an ear of his horse in either fist, and cuss a blue streak—which I could translate roughly: "Stupid beast! Great dumb animal! I told you to follow the path! Good God! A thousand Good-God's! Three thousand Good-God's! Monkey! Clown! Sonuvabitch! Name of a name of a name! MERDE!"

The longer Vitrice would curse at poor Flora, the more flushed would his face become: the veins of his forehead would swell and throb and he would belabor the beast about the head with his clenched fist. Then, with a final warning to Flora, Vitrice would turn to climb into the cart. Sometimes, on further thought, he might again turn to his horse and shout: "Eh bien! Now take us directement to the field of wheat or tonight you do not eat!" Underlining the threat with a boot to the ribs of the old mare, Vitrice would climb into the cart. From his high perch he would shout, with ruffled dignity, "Allons!"

Another fifty yards, and the critter would make another wrong turning. "Sacré bon Dieu!" would shout Vitrice, leaping from his cart to bludgeon the beast again. One time he became so incensed that he bit Flora on the ear. I tried not to laugh but that was impossible, and Suzanne was no help, for she giggled continually at her husband's furious arguments with his horse. Had the harness been equipped with reins, things might have gone more smoothly.

Each morning Vitrice would milk two cows while I painstakingly drained the crankcase of the third. Slinging the brimming pails onto a circular spreader-yoke, we'd lug the milk a kilometer across the meadows to the farm of Vitrice's parents, where we'd run it through an antique deVilbis separator. Vitrice's mother was a prune-faced old gal of about seventy-five years, and she had joined joyfully into her son's conspiracy to hide me. The governor bell on the machine was broken, and the old woman would watch my arm go around and around, and should I turn the crank too slowly she would peep out: "Tink-tink-tink!" And one morning the old lady and the old man came trudging across the fields to Suzanne's with a gift for the American aviator: a crock of sweet butter. The good dame pinched my cheek and said that I must eat all the butter by myself, because I was poorly.

At frequent intervals from dawn 'til dusk German soldiers would stomp into the farmyard, dusty and tired and thirsty, and carrying jugs and litre bottles to be filled with cider. If I happened to be handy, I'd fill their canteens then hold up five fingers, dumbly; whereupon they'd fork over five francs. Suzanne would tuck the money into her apron pocket. Sometimes I'd hold up five fingers and the Jerries would just snatch up their cider and take off without paying.

I was all for bumping the ante to ten francs, but Suzanne said that then none of them would pay off: besides, she smiled, the stuff we were peddling to the Wehrmacht was strictly bar cider, and not the best in the house! I found this life of collaboration to be entirely interesting. Should the Jerries hang around the farmyard making themselves comfortable and making me the opposite, I would always find many little chores that needed doing. While Suzanne made small-talk with the soldiers, I'd putter about the house. I'd rip up a basketful of grass and stuff it into the rabbit hutch, watching the delicious white hares gobble down the tender shoots. Or if the situation became particularly embarrassing, I'd slip into the tool shed and create an atmosphere of rural industry by pounding spikes into the walls or sharpening a spade with a rusty file.

One morning as Suzanne and I sat at the kitchen table, there came a clatter of boots and a trio of soldiers appeared in the yard. They sounded a polite knock on the door and Suzanne hollered, "Entrez!" And three young Jerries entered—rookies en route to their first combat, I'd say—and they joked and laughed and winked at Suzanne.

I collected their flasks and drew them full of green cider from a barrel in the barn and took their money. I sat at the table drinking good cider, and the young soldiers sat on the floor and flirted with Suzanne in the bits of French they knew.

She slipped me a wink and slyly went to work on the boys. She said that they were mighty young to be soldiers, and they replied that they were eighteen, twenty-one, and twenty.

"You look so tired!" said Suzanne. "You have come far today?"

"Ah, oui, mamselle. All the way from Paris since last evening."

"Tsk! Think of that!" said Suzanne. "It must have taken many trucks to bring you all so far."

"Oui, mamselle. A long column of forty trucks and eight tanks and twelve-hundred soldiers!"

Suzanne gathered up their now-emptied canteens and sent me out to refill them, this time for free. When I returned she was saying, for my benefit: "You leave for Mortrain at sunset to attack the American army there, eh? Well, bonne chance!"

Each question received a bragging answer, and after each answer Suzanne would look at me with a grin and a wink. The affair was becoming so obvious that I feared that the rookies would wise up and I tried to bring the interrogation to a grinding halt, but Suzanne paid no heed to my frantic gestures and so continued until tired of the game. When the soldiers had thanked her for the cider and had gone their way, I breathed easier. Had their commander overheard the information they'd been spilling so freely, the trio would have been drawn and quartered.

And the rascal Suzanne thumped the table with her fist and laughed: "Peut-être I make the good espion, non?"

I whispered a weak, "Mon Dieu!" and wiped my forehead and had a shot of applejack.

Each evening we would sit together on the grass in the orchard to admire the flaming sunset and watch the countryside go to sleep. We'd sit in the gathering dusk and have a cigarette, and when the birds had quieted down and darkness had at last settled over the farm, Suzanne would black out the kitchen window and light up the candle and we'd sit down to a merry supper. Afterwards we'd lean our elbows on the table and nibble on the jug and talk: I'd tell of America, of the farms and crops and people, drawing sketches to make clear my points.

But striking discord into this gentle life were always the sounds of warfare: of soldiers voices, of crackling brush in the fringe of the forest, of rifles clinking against helmets, of tank and truck engines; and always at night the rattle of iron wagon wheels jolting over nearby gravel roads. And frequently the monotony was relieved by a little aerial activity.

One evening a dozen P-47s cruised in from the west, low over the treetops in a weaving formation, their pilots essing and rolling over so as to see beneath their wings. The leader spotted something and the boys spread out into a wide Lufbery directly over our farmhouse. The ships peeled down in strafing runs, and for a moment I feared that we had been selected as practice gunnery range; but the 50s chattered and streamed smoke and the ricochets snapped and whined around us. The 500-pounders blasted and shook the ground under our feet, and as the ships banked and chandelled low overhead I could see the pilots crouched in their cockpits. It made me feel mighty homesick.

After the show, Vitrice sneaked down the line to the target area. He reappeared in a state of high glee: "Quatre chars et six camions! Cent Boches mort!" Four tanks and six trucks, flaming and blown up! A hundred Boches lay dead in the ditches!

Knowing Vitrice, I cut the score in half, but we broke out a bottle of vin rouge and toasted les aviateurs Americains.

Unable to sleep one midnight, as I paced the orchard there appeared high overhead a train of heavy bombers. A neat row of brilliant yellow target-marker flares was dropped to hang in the sky some fifteen or twenty kilometers east of the farm. Even where I stood, the light of the flares cast sharp and steady shadows. I gave a shout, not wanting my friends to miss the fireworks.

Just as Vitrice and Suzanne stumbled from the doorway clad in long nightshirts, there came a terrific blast: a sheet of white light and after a slow count of twenty seconds a mighty push of air and then a thunderous roar hit us, setting us onto our heels. The British had either used some damned big bombs or had laid a few small ones into an ammo dump, for it was a highly satisfactory explosion. Suzanne, frightened by the uproar, let out a wail when a bomber streaked vertically earthward, wrapped in a flaring shroud of high-octane flame.

August 11. Seven days had I spent at the little farm, and now the rumors flew thick and fast. An American strafing plane has killed General Rommel! "C'est bien!"

"Ha! Les Americains are but ten kilometers away to the west!"

"Non! The Panzers have defeated them at Mortain!"

"You are mistaken, for the battle is at Vire and Vassy to the northwest!"

"Ah, non! Much closer, at Flers and Briouze now!"

"Mortain is liberated by the Americans, and Mayenne! Soon they fight les Boches at la Ferte-Mace. Then Carrouges, but ten kilos! Liberation tomorrow!"

Liberation tomorrow! Ten days! Next month, peut-être. Well, the Jerries were still pouring troops up the blacktop road to Carrouges to the northwest, so I knew that some of these rumors had foundation. What the hell. My patience was trickling away. By now I was shrugging and waving my old arms and cussing French along with the best of 'em. I wanted to talk to an American and I wanted to burn down twenty American cigarettes one after the other until they were all gone. I was mighty restless. Suzanne, watching me pace the floor, started talking me out of leaving even before I'd said anything about it. She told Vitrice to take me out into the forest for a while.

He knew his woods, that one. This trip out, I caught on the wind a peculiar odor—one that I couldn't identify but had smelled once before when I'd crawled into a distant cave for a nap. So I asked Vitrice. He sniffed and whiffed and cocked his head. Like those of a hound dog, his ears and nostrils twitched as he savored the faint, rank odor.

"Ahhhhh!" said he, holding up a forefinger. "That is the wild boar. Trés sauvage!" All of which lends weight to the theory that if it's dark enough, it doesn't make a great deal of difference what a guy sleeps with.

On the thirteenth of August things began to pick up. The tempo of our little war increased to such a lively degree that I knew the Jerries were desperate. They put their tanks and trucks out on the highways in broad daylight, and as the long mechanized columns roared over the roads and through the brush, prowling Thunderbolts were cutting them to ribbons. From all directions came P-47s, rolling over and down upon countless targets that were hidden from our eyes. Their 50-caliber guns, talking business all up and down the countryside, were delivering into the eager hands of the Valkyries more dead types than had been seen in Valhalla in a coon's age. Certainly there was no meat shortage there. Now and then a little light flak would track a fighter across the sky for a ways, then would cease abruptly as our boys spotted and eliminated the nuisance.

Countless files of Jerry infantrymen streamed into the forest, headed mostly west and north toward the distant sounds of battle. And today for the first time, none of the bastards showed up in our kitchen looking for a handout.

I was jumpy as a cat now, with senses sharpened and cautions deliberately redoubled. Should I relax at this stage of the game with my goal almost in view, I had a sinking feeling that a stupid mistake could be made. But Vitrice and Suzanne and I were infecting one another with the ill-concealed excitement that each of us felt.

For my two friends—as for all French patriots—these days meant approaching deliverance from the grinding slavery, mortal fear, and complete humiliation that had been theirs for five bitter years. It would be the radiant light of freedom displacing the sinister shadow of brutal Nazi occupation. Hopeless for many a moon, today these French could sense that freedom was near. The grim bête-noire was being lifted from their shoulders.

Vitrice dashed aimlessly about his little farm, now and then pausing to embrace Suzanne or to point wildly toward the strafing Thunderbolts. "Beaucoup Boches mort! Ha-ha!" Many Jerries dead today!

Suzanne was happier over his happiness than she was for herself, and I was happy for both of them. For myself, knowing well of the dirty double-crossing tendencies of the fortunes of war, I was withholding my moment of frenzy until I'd taxied into the hangar and cut the switch. When I was drinking a Scotch-and-soda with the squadron back in England, then I would congratulate myself on having accomplished an adventure.

That night Robert came to the house with news that American soldiers were fighting near Couptrain, some twenty kilometers to the west. In a gay mood for the first time, Robert said that come the liberation we would drink his best Calvados until nobody walked!

"Tomorrow the liberation!" he shouted. With that, he hopped onto his bicycle and whizzed down the back road in a cloud of dust. To further brighten our evening, Vitrice once again furnished a moment of rare comedy.

The warped and weathered wooden windlass over the well had finally given way. The first I heard of the tragedy was the unique sound of Vitrice—stooping way down inside the ancient well—shouting bitter, echoing profanity after his drowned water bucket. I found a length of chain and fashioned a grapple to one end, and after much maneuvering of the dangling hook we snagged the pail and fished the damned thing back into the light of day. Vitrice cursed it hysterically, shook it a couple of times, and hurled it violently to the ground. What a character.

Sleep was out of the question on a night so pregnant with possibilities of action. Afraid I'd miss something, for a long while I sat against a tree in the orchard listening to the varied sounds coming in on the night wind. I prowled around and hid out near the highway, trying to make some sense out of the Jerries' confused maneuverings.

Motorcycles and staff cars, tanks and trucks and horse-drawn stuff rolled frenziedly along every little trail. Blackout headlamps burned dimly, twisting and turning through the dark countryside. Most of the vehicles, many of which towed artillery, were headed away from where the front was supposed to be. But weary infantry reinforcements cycled the roads and trudged through the brush, west-bound. The best I could make of it was that they were intended to delay the Americans while the guns and heavy tanks were withdrawn to be regrouped for another stand elsewhere. The ditches were littered with fresh carcasses of vehicles and men, and the wind that rattled the pines carried with it the stink of death, for our strafing fighters had done a dandy job in the past couple of days.

At sunup we had our bread and milk in the kitchen, then Vitrice and I went to the edge of the forest and cocked our ears: a few distant rifle shots, then the far-off sound of many rifles and the frequent short bursts of a single machine gun. The nearby crackle of underbrush. A shout in German.

When the cows were milked, Vitrice gave a gay flourish and told me to throw the milk to the pigs. Whistling happily, he walked to the kitchen. I picked up the pails and headed for the pigsty—which was mighty handy to the house, being right in it. And as I stumbled along over the cobblestones skirting the front of the farmhouse, there hit my ears a sound that spurred me to instinctive, lightning-fast activity.

A high-pitched whistling whine of extreme urgency, and nobody had to tell me that a high-velocity artillery shell was about to rendezvous with me. The milk pails went clattering. A burst of speed took me to within range of the coffin-shaped stone water trough that stood by the well. A flying, headlong leap and a mighty splash and I lay full length in a foot of scummy water, with half-foot-thick walls on four sides. Simultaneous with my arrival there came the final shrieking crescendo of the incoming shell: a sharp and violent blast, a whine of fragments, and a lot of miscellaneous crap flew about for a while. I shook the water from my eyes and peered over the rim of my shelter.

The back wall and a small portion of the roof of Vitrice's house were in need of repair. A tree had been felled across the gate. Great clods of earth lay about the farmyard.

Worried about my friends, I ran for the kitchen door to the tune of another inbound shell. I hit the stones at the base of the kitchen wall as number two whined in to explode at the end of the house. Scampering inside, I found Vitrice with his arms around Suzanne. They were huddled in a corner of their bedroom, wild-eyed and paralyzed, and I hollered, "Allons!" as a shell burst closer to us than had the others. Plaster plunked down from the ceiling. I hauled my friends outside and we made a break for the orchard where there was a ditch. But halfway to safety, Vitrice skidded to a halt, clapped his hand to his forehead, and hollered, "Mon Dieu! The money!" And he twirled Suzanne about and sent her dashing back to the house! In a moment she reappeared, packing a tiny rattling tin box. Hoisting her skirts, she ran like a deer and we lay with our noses in the dirt for perhaps ten minutes as a series of shells howled in. All landed in our immediate vicinity, neatly spaced as though one gun were doing the dirty work while an efficient crew fed in the shells, like clockwork. Things were in a helluva turmoil.

Puzzling was the fact that the shells came from the southeast, while our latest rumors had the Yanks coming in from the opposite direction. Maybe we were involved in a sub-pincers attack, a trap within a trap. Maybe it was Jerry artillery. What the hell, I didn't know what was going on.

After a while, all was relatively quiet again except for some noises from the forest that sounded like stuck pigs squealing in German. The farmyard was a disorderly mess of twigs and branches, rocks and dirt and shell fragments. And Suzanne began to weep, for her house was in sad shape indeed: the door dangled from one bent hinge and a few shards of glass remained of the windows. The roof was holed in several places and the poor old gate was finished. Flopped crazily out of the edge of the forest were the splintered remnants of a dozen pines. In the yard, a chunk of shell casing had ripped through the rabbit hutch spreading the occupants messily about, and their bright scarlet blood trickled onto the green grass below.

Taking the tin treasure chest from the weeping Suzanne, I asked her to rustle up a little grub. She smiled and began to putter around the kitchen while Vitrice and I swept the tumbled plaster into a corner. I didn't want to waste time eating, so I took a long pull from the jug of applejack and went back outside and took up a stand down in the meadow, from where I could gaze into the valley.

Shells were whining again, but this time flying at right angles to the farm. Across the valley to the south there rose a massive timbered hill, and about every ten seconds up on the crest a shell would burst with a pure white puff, beautifully visible against the gloomy background.

I tried to spot an Allied uniform in amongst the scuttling Jerries, and I was delighted to note that the vaunted War Machine was performing in a highly erratic and obviously confused manner: troopers in singles and pairs, threes and fours were scampering through the hedges, popping into the forest at full speed, and then darting out again even faster. Some were running north and some ran south, and an equal number of soldiers dashed east or west—depending, I suppose, upon individual preference. German tanks were passing German tanks, driving on opposite headings at maximum throttle. From the forest came the tortured howling of engines and the ponderous crash of trees and underbrush as some of the harassed and bewildered tanks lit out for the Fatherland on a cross-country course.

I caught a familiar whistle of wings and the high whine of superchargers and a distinctive staccato exhaust, and I scrambled to the roof of a shed in hopes of seeing Mustangs from my own squadron, but they were flashily-painted strangers. Then a lone Messerschmitt 109 snarled down the valley, weaving frantically and leaving behind him a trail of clipped branches as though the devil himself were in hot pursuit—which was very likely the case, too.

Artillery fire was intermittent, but the crackle of small arms was fairly steady now, and now and then I'd hear the wicked "ZZZZT!" of a burp-gun getting off a short burst. Hot damn! For sure, I—along with ten thousand frenzied Jerries—was in the relentlessly tightening loop of the assaulting Yank armies.

I began to shake the hell out of a plum tree in the orchard, and ripened fruit as big as lemons was dropping to the ground like hailstones. Suzanne came along and was filling her apron when three flights of Thunderbolts barreled overhead from out of the west. I froze in my tracks, cautioning Suzanne to move not a finger for fear that that one of the trigger-happy types might sight in his guns on us. The dozen ships were right on the deck and they rolled into a steep climbing turn, swinging out into a Lufbery circle with the farmhouse in the center. And when the leader peeled off and dove directly at us, I half-tore Suzanne's arm from its socket dragging her across the orchard where I then led her in a fast dive over a scrawny hedge and down into a deep-sunken trail. No sooner had we hit the dirt than the squadron leader unlimbered his eight 50-caliber guns and a pair of five-hundred pound bombs; and, at the very least, I believed that the world had come to an end.

The target seemed to be the crossroads some two hundred yards from where we lay huddled, and as the attack got under way the earth beneath us bounced merrily and ricochets snapped through the hedges just overhead. Each blast sent a shower of leaves and twigs and clods of dirt down upon our shoulders, and stones and fragments whistled through the brush.

As each ship pulled out, it would chandelle above us and I could see the grinning faces of the pilots as they checked back over their shoulders to observe their target. With one bomb hanging, the squadron leader circled the target area while the rest of the lads took their own sweet time, picking their targets with deadly care and deliberation. Making precise passes at low airspeed and delivering concentrated bursts where they'd do the most good, the bastards had a right to grin, for my old outfit had never had it so good: this sort of cold-turkey attack was not at all like the frantic days when we'd strafed airdromes deep in Germany, with five-hundred-and-a-quarter on the clock in an effort to outrace the murderous sheets of flak.

That husky Thunderbolt fighter had been my ship before the slim little Mustang, and now as I cringed on the ground on the receiving end I felt like a motherless child. I was led to believe that in this attacking squadron were a few hot-shot training-command types—come over lately to soak up the gravy—for there were a couple of wild bombs that gave me the idea that I was about to be abruptly and permanently liberated.

After the fourth or fifth ship had bombed, I'd just about regained my natural poise and charm and was beginning to feel happy again when along our footpath from the direction of the crossroads came seven German soldiers—and a sadder-looking bunch one could not imagine. They came on the run, crouched down, with three or four rifles between them, and only a couple had helmets. Their uniforms were torn and caked with gray dust and spattered with not enough blood, and the boys were fully equipped with terror-stricken faces and ghastly eyes. The bastards couldn't have kept on traveling, either, but instead they had to flop down across from Suzanne and me, joining our cozy tête-à-tête.

One of them croaked out, "Tous les comrades kaput!"—me pals have all been clobbered! Suzanne clucked her sympathy and I assumed an expression that would have done credit to any wealthy undertaker. Quickly shifting position, I sat on my feet so as to hide the great obvious GI shoes, which had suddenly come to feel as though each were wrapped in a little American flag.

Over the uproar of the continuing strafing attack, the soldiers babbled on: their troop convoy had been surprised at the crossroads by the "Jabo-fleugers." One of our dapper companions had been freshly blown out of his Tiger tank and was toasted and bleeding to some extent, but not yet feeling any pain. So these Jerries sat in a miserable row across from us, their heads swinging in unison as they followed the flight of each strafer as it roared past us after its pass. And I was experiencing a series of chills as I realized what would happen should one of the pilots glance down into our little international pow-wow: in one moment, instead of one numb French girl and one sad American throttle-jockey and seven sorry members of the Wehrmacht, there would be a great bleeding stack of twitching arms and legs. As though reading my thoughts, one of the shabby soldiers—looking at me as though I were der Führer, or at least a glass of cold beer—asked me where he and his comrades might hide from the Americans.

Now that was a poser. But overlooking the element of humor in the matter, and seizing the opportunity to be rid of these outnumbering foes, I pointed and hollered: "Courez au forêt! Au forêt! Vite! Vite!"—run into the woods, chums, and be quick about it! And the seven tattered troopers leaped to their feet, dashed up the trail, and faded into the forest amidst the downpour of falling debris. I was so goddam pleased with myself that I jabbed Suzanne in the ribs and chuckled. But she just gave me a sick smile in return.

The last Thunderbolt dove down and squirted a very generous shower of incendiaries over the entire target area. The flights reformed and the squadron droned back toward its field. And I for one was happy to see their tails, for they'd made things downright unhealthy for a while.

"Okay, Suzanne!" I announced. "Fini l'attaque!" And I scrambled to the top of the bank for a looksee, arriving there just in time to receive the full blast of a delayed-action bomb, which puffed me to an awkward position midway across the sunken trail, where gravity took over and let me down hard, flat on my back. With ringing ears and spinning head, I looked startledly at Suzanne's worried face and remarked, "Mon Dieu!" And she, taking one look at the expression I wore, screamed, "Ah-ha-ha-ha-ha-ha! Fini l'attaque! Ha-ha-ha!"—laughing until the tears rolled down her cheeks and plopped into the dust.

I leaned against the dirt bank and rolled up a smoke and thought that this was turning out to be quite a day. All this, and not yet noon! Upon recovering from her fit of mirth, Suzanne murmured that if the Jerries didn't get us, my American comrades would. And I didn't disagree.

Chapter I I

YANKS!

◈

I tilted a chair against the kitchen wall and absorbed a slow trickle of applejack while Vitrice raved on. Come the liberation, a grand fête to end all grand fêtes! Turnabout! When all the Boches lay dead in the ditches, then it was time for the Frenchmen to sing, dance, and drink brandy until the world whirled! To interrupt this merry soliloquy came a spatter of rifle fire. We poked our heads outside to take a look around, whereupon the fire became quite heavy.

We stood in the wheat shed until a bullet splintered the wall. Fearing for Suzanne, Vitrice bounced up and down indecisively, then dragged her to the doubtful shelter of the tool shed. When splinters flew from those walls, he rushed her across the cobbles to the pigpen, booted her through the low doorway, and dove in behind her. They had a good thing there, but I hated to miss the show.

After the past ten bucolic days, these fireworks were highly acceptable. Always in Occupied France was the exhilarating spice of lurking danger, but here and now was a little visible action. With my carefree innocent-bystander status, I thought it a rare opportunity to observe the development of this skirmish. But intriguing as had been the varied phases of this process of liberation, I still felt that the eager gun crew had gone a bit too far. Skirting the tool shed, I climbed to a vantage point atop a stack of cordwood and cast a thoughtful eye out over the valley.

In a corner of the wheat field a Jerry machine gun chattered incessantly, spraying great quantities of lead at invisible targets. A furious sputtering of rifles and sub-machine guns sounded from every point of the compass. There was every indication that I was in the middle of a running gunfight, but I couldn't see anybody outside of an occasional crouching Jerry slinking along a hedgerow. Everyone was sneaking around. It wasn't much of a feud, and I felt cheated. I was looking for something along the lines of that fine painting of Custer's Last Stand, copies of which hang in many of the better saloons in the States.

Up the valley a ways—where most of the shooting had progressed—there appeared a bold aeronaut with a little Maytag-Messerschmitt strapped to his butt. As I watched him wheeling lazily over the treetops and meadows, I wondered why some Jerry wit didn't lob up a rock and claim one Cub destroyed.

Clicking suddenly into my flak-happy mind came the fact that for the past half hour, I'd been dimly aware of numerous pleasant little humming sounds—the last few of which had penetrated my mental fog to register with more of a snappy zing than a soft and faraway drone. Perhaps it was that the earlier shelling and state of proximity to the dive-bombers' target had rendered me scornful of the great power of small bullets. As fast as gravity would permit I faded from my kibitzer's perch and sat on the ground, a husky chopping block at my back. I rolled a smoke and figured that had it been a Yank sniper, I'd have been hit. So it must have been some Jerry out for a last free shot at a Frenchman.

A suspicious lull fell over the countryside. The birds—who had tucked their heads beneath their wings during the shooting match—now took courage and were winging once again. No Jerries were to be seen. No Americans came dashing up the valley waving their hankies at me. No strangers of any type were in evidence. So I gave up trying to analyze the local situation and sat in the orchard eating delicious plums while chatting with Suzanne. In a couple of hours we heard tanks on the highway and Vitrice went whooping off through the underbrush. He returned in a few minutes, shouting so excitedly that I could just make out the fact that he had seen the machines, but never before had he seen anything quite like them. He was positive, at any rate, that they were not German tanks! Upon filtering out this bit of intelligence, I lit out for the road with Vitrice and Suzanne doing their best to keep up, but flying a poor second and third position.

Halted on the highway was a column of Sherman tanks—a dozen of them, with engines idling throatily. Pushing dusty goggles up onto helmets and wiping sweat and gun smoke from their eyes, their crews were leaping down into the open arms of a hundred country folk who had materialized, as though by magic, from out of the desolate timberland. A wild and poignant affair on that lonely country road, with the anguish of the long reign of terror now dispelled by a sudden joyous embrace. And the unchecked tears of citizens and soldiers alike flowed nearly as fast as did the gifts of long-buried bottles of wine and cognac flow down the parched throats of the liberators. As Vitrice hopped to and fro in an erratic, frantic attempt to pump the hand of every man of the tank squadron, Suzanne stood and sobbed, her face buried into the grimy neck of a smiling gunner who patted her shoulder with compassion as he watched the scene about him.

The men of the leading tank were squatting alongside their machine running fingers over a map they had spread out on the highway. I ran toward them, stumbling as the sole of one shoe flop-flopped on the hot tar. What a moment! What joy! Hot damn! Yanks! And I tapped the shoulder that bore the most brass: "Howdy, neighbor! Where the merry hell you been keeping yourself?"

The tank men looked up at me blankly. Then they looked at one another with shrugs and lifted eyebrows, and their leader jumped to his feet, hand on pistol-butt. He cocked his head and regarded me with narrowed eyes.

"Que dites?" What say?

I took another gander at their tank. Painted upon the turret were a Croix de Lorraine and a tricolor flag. Below that was the name "Madeline." What the hell. It looked like everybody but me had been liberated: this was a Fighting French squadron, and nobody in the whole danged outfit could speak a word of English. So for me, it was back into the tired old song-and-dance again. I gave a sad shrug and with a wave of my arms began to explain: "Je suis aviateur . . ."

But Vitrice came dancing along to save the day, and he sputtered away with the French soldiers. "Ha-ha! I! Me! Vitrice! I, all by myself, have saved this officier Americain from les Boches! Is that not so, mon lieutenant?"

When I had gleefully verified his modest confession, Vitrice's stock went way up, for then to the soldiers he wasn't just another liberated hill-billy but was a comrade-in-arms. The commander of the tank shook hands with the smiling Vitrice and told him gravely that he had indeed done a brave thing. And the soldiers showered my happy friend with compliments and loaded him down with cigarettes.

The tank outfit, it developed, was just an isolated, roving column that was spending the day charging around through Jerry territory. The commander—a colonel and a reckless type—shook my hand and laughed. My face, he said, had been "tragique" when I'd found only Frenchmen in these American tanks. "Have patience, mon ami," said the colonel. "Your countrymen will be here today!"

With that, he blew a blast on a whistle. He and his exuberant warriors mounted their machines and the engines revved up. Atop his tank, Tommy-gun in hand, the colonel shouted down at me: "Let's go! Climb aboard!"

"Where are you going, mon colonel?" I hollered back.

He pointed dramatically up the road: "To battle!" I thumbed my nose at him and waved him on. Bouquets of wildflowers soared up into the cockpits of the tanks, and a veritable deluge of cigarettes and rations sailed down in return. The colonel tossed me a fresh pack of Camels and spoke into a microphone. The whole column roared forward, clanking as fast as it could clank on up the highway toward Carrouges, and in a moment the squadron was swallowed up by the forest.

The natives faded back into the brush. The highway was quiet and it was difficult to believe that the armored column had really been there. But in my hand I held the evidence in the form of a pack of American cigarettes. I broke out three and when we lit up we made a little toast. Closing my eyes, I took a deep and hungry drag. When I looked around again, the trees, the road, and the sky began to tilt and whirl. Ha ha! Tobacco again! Off-balance, I tottered across the road. Vitrice became wracked by coughs. Suzanne snuffed out her cigarette, murmuring disappointedly, "Trop forte!"—too strong. But I smoked mine down to a nubbin and lit another from the butt of the first.

Sending Suzanne back home, Vitrice and I sortied out to see what we could see. Wreckage still burned at the crossroads strafed by the P-47s some hours earlier. A careening staff car, well-riddled, had made a spectacular high-speed plunge from the highway and lay on its side in a meadow with flames still licking over it. A trio of well-done Jerries lay inside, and a fourth rested lonesomely in the weeds. His Luger pistol was soon at my hip.

Three massive tanks lay ditched and burned out, and alongside one lay a body, on its chest a fancy medal that I plucked for a souvenir. With professional interest, I conducted a post-mortem of a row of smoldering machines, some still blazing, that had been hauling Twin Bofors guns. All was kaput. Upon tracing the course of a single furious projectile, I observed that it had efficiently removed the head of the truck driver, carried away half the steering column, and torn hell out of the instrument panel to then penetrate the firewall and blast away a sizeable chunk of the engine block. Just one slug out of the four thousand per minute delivered by the eight roaring guns of a single wicked Thunderbolt.

Perhaps fifteen skeletonized troop trucks littered the bloody crossroads, and a satisfactory number of Wehrmacht types lay tumbled in the ditches —all in fantastic states of disrepair and in amazingly awkward positions. Quite a few of them were already barefooted: for many a moon, these local Frenchmen had worn rough wooden sabots and coarse burlap stockings. Now, without giving a corpse a decent chance to quit twitching and cool off, some ridge-runner would pop out of the brush and jerk off the boots. Before long, Vitrice was stepping high and handsome in a gleaming black pair, which fit him well.

Pistols in hand, we prowled the heavily strafed back roads, salvaging Jerry equipment and hiding it here and there along the way: coils of rope and wire, tins of fuel and rations, tools and blankets, and a goodly assortment of items valuable to Vitrice. Upon arrival back at the old homestead, we gave our thumbs a gleeful lick and split the take of francs deftly requisitioned from the wallets of many an unprotesting Boche. While frisking these characters, I'd noted that quite a number of them, instead of carrying pinup pictures of over-developed females, had queerly enough treasured the neatly framed photos of pretty American actors. I tucked the bulky wad of francs into my poke and thought it damned obliging of the Wehrmacht to refinance my expedition.

Vitrice led the way on a circle tour of neighborhood farms, letting the local folk in on his big secret. Each farmer, in proper response to Vitrice's gay flourishes, dug out his best wine and my head was soon spinning under the impact of the countless toasts consumed. At the end, we strolled arm in arm up to the roadside house of Vitrice's aged parents, being met there with a large crock of cherries soaked in apple brandy. Delicious booze, that, going down the throat like warm honey to rest in a smoldering puddle at the pit of the stomach.

The old lady whispered to Vitrice. He in turn gave me a wink and we left the kitchen and walked to the lean-to that was tacked onto one end of the house. Flat on his back in a sticky patch of congealed blood and dust lay an extremely dead Jerry. Vitrice braced a foot in the victim's crotch and removed the boots one at a time and with a grunt for each. The old lady apologized: right after the American fighter planes had flown away this morning, this Boche had come crawling into the shed, croaking almost immediately. Vitrice took the arms and I took the legs and we hauled it to the roadside ditch—downwind from the house—and returned for another nip of that slow-burning brandy.

Feeling unliberated and slightly forlorn, I stood in the hot sunshine at the edge of the road. In the distance could be heard rifles and what could have been a brief duel between a burp-gunner and a Tommy-gunner. I peered into the brush. I gazed off into the blue, wondering what to expect next: Jerries, French, or Yanks. Then, with a spray of gravel and a roll of dust, a jeep zoomed up over the brow of the hill and I didn't make a move.

When I saw the right-colored uniforms, I gave a whoop and a holler but the machine whizzed past and in reply to my shrill cries, the four men aboard raised weary fingers in a casual V-for-Victory. Brought from the house by the commotion, my friends joined me at the roadside just as the American Infantry appeared in the wake of the jeep: a single file of Yanks on either side of the road, a half dozen paces between men!

Robots, they were: flesh and uniforms of one gray shade, caked with chalky dust. Expressionless faces etched by fatigue. Sunken eyes blank, and the deliberate quality of their stride was painful to behold: long, slow, dragging paces. Men in a dream, marching solely by habit. The files wound downhill and the leaders were out of sight around a bend, but still they kept stringing on past us, moving now in a choking pall of fine dust that hung over the road. The lump in my throat kept me quiet, and Suzanne stood weeping, dabbing her eyes with a hanky and holding my arm tightly. But Vitrice, quite delirious with joy, dashed in and out of the moving files lugging a tin pitcher of cool cider and pouring out a glassful to any and all who held out a hand to him.

As the tag-end of the outfit came into sight, the column halted and the men tumbled into the ditches close to the cover of the hedges where they lay sprawled flat out. But for an occasional movement amongst them, they closely resembled the ditchful of their opponents who were installed back at the crossroads.

Things were too damned quiet to suit my fancy, so I shoved my hands into my pockets and wandered down the road a piece until I stood before a couple of Yanks. I stared deadpan at them, knowing I wouldn't have long to wait—and I didn't.

One husky gent, looking slantwise at me, whispered to his buddy for a moment. Spitting the dust from his throat, he spoke up:

"Hey Monsieur!"

"Oui?" said I.

"Cognac?'

"Certainement, soldat!"—for two hundred francs per litre, cash on the barrelhead.

As the spokesman translated this happy news to his pal, six or seven of their comrades came crawling over to lie in a cluster, hanging on each word and running dry tongues over dusty lips. The first soldier hunted around in a pocket and came out with a fistful of francs. Another dug out his wad, and another, and I accepted all offerings with glee. Then one of the more recreation-minded lads growled at me: "Femme? Femme?"

With curving gestures, I constructed out of thin air the body beautiful. A sly smile and I furthered the illusion. "You are in luck, Messieurs," I said. For it so happened that I did have one sister: just seventeen years had she, and a vision of loveliness she was. And this belle petite demoiselle, I told the wolves, did love American soldiers like nothing else in this world.

Weariness seemed to have become a thing of the past. There arose a series of coarse and brutal remarks that were not intended for my ears.

"Vous are okay, Pal! Bringez yer cognac and trot out this filly of seventeen young and tender years!"

"Un moment, soldats!"—this would require beaucoup additional francs!

"Combien?" they howled in chorus. Money was no object.

I leered. Seeing as how it was them, they were in for only five thousand francs. With a vulgar rustle, cinq-mille francs were quickly produced and thrust into my hands. Expectantly, these high-minded types looked at me. Mon Dieu! What evil faces!

"A helluva thing!" I remarked, forgetting to speak in French: "Try to get into me sister, wouldn't ya? You bastards been taxiing around with yer flaps down. I've had this country liberated for three months!"

This sudden outburst, spoken in low American patois by a shabby French bum, caused an immediate reaction that left nothing to be desired. I savored the stunned silence until my grin went all out of control.

"Yuk-yuk-yuk!" I chuckled.

The first soldier picked up his jaw and turned wearily to his comrades: "Well I'm a sad sonuvabitch if it ain't the friggin' air-corpse!" And they snarled at one another as they sorted out their money, each accusing his partner of having been deceived by my corny disguise.

This was such a good thing that I could hardly stand it. After very little urging by the first suckers, I taxied on down the road to accost a second bunch. The same routine achieved the same hilarious results, for these braves spoke just barely sufficient French to cover the minimum essentials of combat life: booze and females. When the whole outfit was wise and the feeble joke had been run into the ground, my jowls ached from laughter. My pockets were loaded with smokes, which I burned up as fast as possible. I was even throwing away the butts—something I'd sworn to do never again.

It was purely delightful to sit in with this rangy, hard-bitten crew and to talk and listen without having to work at it. Pretty soon a jeep came along and a sergeant flagged it down to introduce me to his commanding officer, Captain Ford of the 357th Infantry, 90th Division, Third Army.

The captain took a look at the wings and insignia on my blue velvet jacket. Suspicious-like—and rightfully so—he asked me where in the hell I got 'em. From force of habit, I was about to spin him a good yarn when I remembered that I'd just been liberated, so I told him the truth—which was not accepted as such. But after I'd named the first ten presidents of the United States, he shook my hand and invited me to join him.

What with all my social obligations, I explained, that would have to wait until morning; but I accepted his thoughtful offer of escort back to the farm. For like he said, his boys always got a little trigger-happy come sundown.

But the turmoil of this reckless day must have been too much for Suzanne and Vitrice, for I found them to be sound asleep in their half-wrecked house. I took a blanket and settled down in the meadow and the night, for a change, felt friendly and not at all hostile.

When the sun awakened me and the day was full, I headed for the American encampment. The bivouac was on a rising meadow that terminated at the edge of the forest, and I picked my way through a network of foxholes to a tumbledown stone hut that was tucked into a fringe of the woods. Everybody was hollering "Howdy, flyboy!" at me, and when I poked my head through the doorway the captain grinned and told his sergeant to rig up his trick stove and brew up some coffee. He tossed me a couple of boxes of rations, which I found to contain a veritable treasure of cigarettes and canned meat and tins of greasy egg-stuff. As I polished off the last of the second carton, the hush that had fallen over the little gathering was broken when the sergeant yelped: "Christ Almighty! He likes that crap!" When I told 'em that it tasted like fried chicken, the captain suggested that I try it three times a day for three months and then tell him what it tasted like.

The captain was wiry, serious, friendly, and his eyes had seen too much, and over our cups of steaming coffee we swapped many a lie. His outfit had been in constant action since D-plus-2, having begun combat with 1,200 men. Fifteen hundred replacements had since been required, and of the original officers, only Ford and the company chaplain survived.

Dave Graf, a captain of the 343rd Field Artillery Battalion, joined the party then and together we looked over the charts of the local area. Ford sighed as he stabbed a finger at the map to indicate the forest through which I'd navigated. To clean out those woods, he said with some bitterness, was the next dirty job for his outfit, and for that mission he'd received no intelligence whatsoever. When I explained that I had a nodding acquaintance with two-thirds of all the trees in that damned forest and could offer some information as to defenses, numbers, and disposition of Jerry troops and tanks concealed therein, the captain seemed quite happy and made notes of what I told him.

Our liberation, I learned, was the result of a major pincers movement that was still under way. The American Third Army, said the captain, had covered hundreds of kilometers in a swing to the south of Alençon and had then driven northward through Alençon and Sees to Argentan. Montgomery's forces were to have spearheaded straight south out of Caen, meeting the Americans at Argentan and so closing the trap on a quarter-million Jerries. But The Master, with rare cunning, had called off his dogs and had settled down near Falaise, some six or eight kilometers from where he'd started. His failure to close that gate of the corral left a narrow escape corridor through which the Jerries were now stampeding, hell-bent for the Fatherland. But the weather was good and thousands of Allied fighter-bombers were having a field day, and a massacre was taking place to the north of us.

Seeing as how we were having a critique of higher strategy, I accused the artillery captain of having blasted my friends and me out of the old homestead. He chuckled and said that had it been his men doing the shooting I wouldn't have been sitting there to tell of it. He did concede, however (and because of that, I think he was guilty), that there had been rumors of a Jerry observation post up that-a-way.

At this point a soldier poked his head through a window and said that some crazy Frenchman was giving the sentries a bad time. I ran down the slope to see if my guess was right. It was.

"Bonjour, Vitrice!" I hollered.

"Allons!" he shouted impatiently. "Let's go! Gotta find more boots! Gotta get me a German gun!"

The two of us circled through the brush to find great quantities of dead people but nary a fusil: it appeared that the natives were fully equipped for the revolution. So I took Vitrice up to meet the captain and acted as interpreter.

Amused at the wild ways of my reckless friend, the captain nevertheless questioned him with grave courtesy. Upon learning of his concentration-camp troubles, he called for the company surgeon who unbuttoned Vitrice's shirt and poked around to verify the fact that the Frenchman's health was indeed precarious. But Vitrice's apprehensive expression changed to one of happiness when I reported that Monsieur le Medecin had found him to be in excellent condition.

Vitrice whispered in my ear: could I ask Monsieur le Capitain if there was a spare rifle that he, Vitrice, could have for to hunt the deer in the forest?

The captain said to his sergeant, "Get me that gun I've been savin' for myself." And Vitrice was presented with a brand-new Mauser along with a box of shells and the admonition that he was not to fire a single shot until after the war. Delighted, Vitrice shook hands with every Yank in a fifty-yard radius.

En route back to the farmhouse, I made up my mind to take off. I couldn't wait around for the long-planned grand fête. At long last there was a narrow liberated corridor through which I could flee. I'd fly low on up to the beachhead and from there to London I'd make my way. I wanted to tell the right people about some ripe targets I'd blundered across. I wanted to be back with the old squadron. I wanted to send a cablegram to the home folks, for I knew danged well that mother, wondering where in the blue-blazes might be her wandering son, would have just about now run out of hairs to snatch from her graying head. Aside from all that, my heels were itching uncontrollably. After the extended trek through the bush, the bright lights were calling and the great roll of francs lay smoldering in my pocket.

So I told Suzanne that I'd been ordered to report to the big general at Alençon: le grand chef. She let out a wail, but to no avail: Il faut partir. I had to make tracks. To her I bequeathed my beat-up old flying jacket—Vitrice could skin a rabbit and make a collar for it. I printed a fancy letter of commendation and gave it to Vitrice, for the best use he could make of it. We set out for the old folk's farmhouse.

As we trudged through the stubble field, Vitrice looked around sadly: "The Americans, they will come and take my wheat?" He said it not as a question, but as an acceptance of fact, and I told him gently that he was a free man again: all he had harvested was his own, to keep or to sell, for never again would invading soldiers confiscate his crops. He pounded his chest and waved his hat and hollered to the skies: "Haha! Vive l'Amerique!"

I hope I told him right.

The old lady of the little house on the highway brought out her delicious brandy and we stood in a circle and clinked our tiny cups. Saying goodbye was difficult, but I told them that they were the bravest of the brave—the best of good patriots, and that to them I was forever indebted.

So I said au revoir to Vitrice and shook his hand. I said au revoir to Suzanne. She turned on the waterworks and kissed me and slipped into

my hand a silver coin of twenty francs inscribed: "Liberté Egalité Fratér-
nité—Republique Français."

I opened the gate and smiled and waved and walked down the gravel
road. I was leaving this valley and I didn't feel happy about it. A hundred
paces and I looked back to see Suzanne waving her hanky and Vitrice
swinging his battered hat in great circles about his head. My heart told me
to go back, go back; but I waved and walked on.

And that was my last sight of my good French friends of the little farm
at the edge of the forest near St. Nicolas des Bois.

Chapter **I 2**

A THOUSAND MEMORIES

◆

Back at the command post I found the captain buckling on his gun
belt. "Howdy!" said he. "Latch onto a carbine and tag along. We're
just fixin' to reconnoiter a patch of your woods!"

I took a thoughtful look into the silent and ominous forest: and the
wise old gremlin who rode my shoulder whispered into my ear a premo-
nition of impending doom, and my scalp gave a reflexive crawl. So I told
the captain that I'd seen the guts of that forest one time and had no desire
to see it again. I'd as soon have taken a carbine and gone pussyfooting
around solo, but I took a dim view of thrashing around through the underbrush with a flock of people whose methods I didn't savvy. There wasn't
any future in it. So as the patrol set out on the old warpath, I waved them
a fond farewell.

There was a courier due to leave for battalion headquarters somewhere
around Alençon, which had been liberated for a day. I was content to sit
around on my haunches shooting the breeze while sweating out the ride.
One of the lads fixed me up with a gas-impregnated field jacket and a pair
of old combat pants, so I discarded my old flea-bitten costume in favor of
my new makeshift uniform. The company cook unlimbered his chuck-
wagon and fried up a panful of bacon and eggs, and I probably gained five
pounds in as many minutes. A master sergeant from Tucson—Parker by
name—hauled out his Graflex and snapped my picture, promising to send
me a print someday. The time passed swiftly in such good company.

When the patrol returned in mid-afternoon, there was no merriment in the outfit: their beloved captain had been cut down dead by a short burst from a burp-gun in a little skirmish deep within the forest. I left the encampment quietly, heading down the road in the general direction of Alençon, against warnings that snipers were active in the woods that bordered the highway.

Overhead the sun was a ball of fire in a brilliant sky. The tar of the undulating road was soft underfoot, and I followed my nose through truly lovely country. Wherever one might glance there was a gay profusion of wildflowers and, if one knew where to look, on the shady banks there could be found succulent strawberries.

In its round black leather holster rested a fine Luger pistol, which at each pace delivered a reassuring thump against my thigh. In one leg-pocket was stuffed a rapidly diminishing supply of good American cigarettes, and the other bulged with its wad of kindly donated francs. And before long, I felt free and reckless and happy as a lark and in no mood to take anything from anybody. Soaked with sweat in an hour or so, upon hearing the drone of an overtaking jeep I stood in the center of the road with my hands hoisted up into the blue to forestall any unfortunate misunderstanding.

Then I was traveling first-class. The sergeant at the controls was en route to battalion HQ to deliver a pair of very glum Nazi officers who were perched without dignity upon the hood of the jeep. With a nasty chuckle of glee, I accepted the sergeant's Tommy-gun and jabbed it into the spine of the nearest passenger. The driver, well aware of snipers, kept the throttle up against the firewall. Little freelance groups of Jerry stragglers were in the habit of ambushing solo vehicles as they traveled the lonely stretches of country road. Sometimes they would mischievously string a cable across the highway at windshield level for the purpose of decapitating unwary tourists. It occurred to me that it would be rather comical should our two prize hogs up on the hood lose their heads over a little thing like that. Perhaps they had something of the sort in mind, for they kept their eyes strained out ahead of our careening jeep.

When we jolted into the bomb-spattered outskirts of Alençon, I let out a triumphant howl. Revenge! Just about a fortnight before this fine day, I'd jounced along over these same cobblestones a hungry, desperate prisoner of war trapped in the hind-end of a Jerry truck and staring into the business end of a burp-gun. Now, a perfect turnabout!

The good citizens of Alençon—liberated now for some thirty-six hours—were blowing off steam in great style. A whoopin' and hollerin' celebration, with joyous gangs clubbing the daylights out of various blood-stained types who must have said a jolly "Bonjour" to a Boche at one time or another during the long Occupation. With shouted insults and curses, folks lobbed showers of rocks at the pair of Jerries who crouched grimly upon the nose of our jeep. We had to assume that the rocks were intended for our passengers; for these French were miserable deflection shots, failing entirely to calculate in the correct lead for our moving vehicle. So between dodging sticks and stones and acknowledging the V-for-Victory signals that were thrust at us from all sides, the sergeant and I were kept quite busy.

Four naked queens dashed yowling past us, beamed right down the main drag of town, and the pack in full cry was hot on their trail. These career girls, what with their hysterical screechings and being shaven stark raving bald, resembled nothing more than a frenzied quartet of fugitive baboons. I shook with laughter. For having worked nights and slept days and never having been out of bed during the entire Occupation, those girls could still run pretty good.

We prowled around in a bit of a woods beyond Alençon and finally located battalion HQ. I bailed out and trudged up to a big tent, thinking that perhaps someone could expedite a quick trip to London.

A lot of colonels and one-star characters were there, rubbing their chins with cupped hands as each scowlingly drew a maze of red lines to and fro across his own individual chart. Spotting a sign that read "Intelligence," and in hopes of finding some there, I taxied over and plunked a dog tag onto a table behind which sat a gloomy colonel.

"Howdy, Colonel," I said. "I'm an old broken-down fighter pilot, and to whom do I spill my secrets?"

"Hmmmmm!" replied the colonel. "Better send you up to Regiment, I s'pose." He handed me a fighter pilot's helmet and goggles that had been found in Alençon Gestapo HQ. They bore three initials, which he suggested I have traced. The colonel wrote out a pass and I took off.

I thumbed down another jeep. This ride was far more wild than the last, involving the fording of several creeks with mighty splashes and a sputtering engine, a tilting flight over a rickety pontoon bridge, and a careening cruise through another forest where we at last came upon regimental head-quarters. This tent was more elaborate than the last, with awnings and neat rows of carefully selected and whitewashed cobblestones to mark out the headquarters area. Strategically deployed on the lawn beneath the trees were a dozen or fifteen deck chairs that contained a lounging assortment of Yank and Limey brass—the latter soaking the inevitable moustaches in the inevitable teacups.

I moseyed up to the tent and peered around a totem-pole-type sentry to focus my eyes upon a covey of elderly citizens who puttered, bobbing and weaving, before a great plexiglas-covered map. Fascinated, I gained the illusion that here was a row of demented musicians each—with loving skill and flourish—wielding as a baton a red or blue crayon to conduct his own secret symphony. The setting was the sky of a clear summer's night, there were that many stars twinkling from collars and shoulders. Since my sorry-looking uniform had already drawn a number of hostile glares, I decided that I was in the wrong pew and executed a strategic withdrawal, shaking my assigned escort en route. Had I mixed with that crew, I'd be there yet.

Retreating via the back roads into Alençon, I slunk into a musty base-ment bistro to plot and plan. I shuddered. In the short course of a few hours, I'd shuttled from the farmhouse to Company HQ, to Battalion HQ, to Regimental HQ, and all the time I was getting farther away from Lon-don. The hell with it. Division HQ, I figured, could get along without me. I'd go as far as I could tonight and then have a party. I'd head for London tomorrow.

A quick couple of jolts of Calvados restored my sunny disposition and I picked up a conversation with a much-liberated Frenchman, asking him what had been the fate of the prisoners of the Boche Bastille outside of town. Between hiccups and belches, he told me that all had been evacuated two nights before the liberation to a prison beyond Paris. Upon learning that I'd escaped from Alençon, my friend set up a jug of wine—which was what I'd had in mind all along. As we sat chuckling over this and that, a tipsy Yank sergeant drifted in and joined us, and pretty soon all was rosy. For the good sergeant was en route—via all pubs—to Division HQ near Le Mans, and he invited me along.

I accepted with delight, despite the fact that Le Mans lay some fifty kilometers south of Alençon and that much farther from London. No matter what the direction of travel, a day's walk accomplished in a forty-five minute jeep ride was not to be sneered at. Anyway, once in Le Mans, I'd be poised for a flight up along the liberated strip left in the wake of the Third Army spearhead. The sergeant promised to steer me clear of Division HQ, to protect me from all high brass, and to deliver me to a place suitable for my long-planned wingding; and a gift bottle of red wine clinched the deal. We took off.

The sergeant—with a "So yer a fighter pilot, hey?"—gave me the full treatment on that nerve-shattering flight to Le Mans. I was unhappy until our jeep ricocheted off the curbing in front of the Hotel Moderne. "Classiest jernt in town!" cried my daring chauffeur, spitting clear up over the windshield. "Goddam officers got it, nacherly!" I bailed out, all eagerness, for it looked like I'd hit the jackpot again. Over the doorway was a little sign: "AAF Intelligence."

The sentry at the main entrance got a little snotty. Not caring to bandy words with the likes of him, I went around to the rear and muttered, "Counter-Intelligence!" to the corporal on guard—and with a respectful salute, he let me pass. I pulled a bead on the bar. What a lovely thing it was: mahogany, curved and carved and tended by three entirely charming barmaids.

Mon Dieu! A dream come true! I was a starving urchin in a candy store clutching a newfound nickel. I was Dangerous Dan just in from the creek with a rusty old load in his poke—dog-dirty and loaded for bear! I swirled a little brandy in an eggshell glass and inhaled the sharp fumes as I savored the delights of civilization. This celebration was not to be undertaken with clumsy haste, and I sketched out a rough plan of action: first, I'd have quarters assigned, then a hot bath. I'd shave and untangle my hair and maybe borrow a decent uniform. Then, by God, I'd do me a victory roll or two!

So I tracked down the Billeting Officer, who was also Club Officer and whose tertiary or spare-time duty, it seemed, was that of local Air Corps Intelligence Officer: a glaring misnomer. A pimply-faced, four-eyed, incompetent jerk of a Second Lieutenant who didn't know which way was up, this character said—as he peered down his nose at my raunchy costume—that the hotel was full, old boy (the sonuvabitch had probably spent a weekend in London) and anyway I'd have to go to a special place for quarters. He handed me a little ticket with a number printed thereon and told me to catch the army truck outside. It would take me directly to where I was to go.

Shoving past the sentry and climbing into the truck, I found myself in the company of a bunch of critters who probably found me to be as strange as I found them: a few Russians in shreds of civilian clothes, a few pockmarked Frenchmen, and sundry other crummy types. After a fast ride across town, our bus halted before an imposing gate. Walking past two Zouave sentries—each a good seven feet tall—I headed along a pathway toward a big U-shaped four-story building that obviously had been constructed about the time of Christ.

Within I found a bored English leftenant who, in exchange for the ticket I slapped on his desk, assigned me quarters: third floor, Room 10. Up and up I trudged, dreaming absent-mindedly of tile showers and soft white sheets. Up and up.

Third floor, Room 10 was a completely filthy stinkhole: barred windows, a foul-smelling honey-bucket in one corner, a litter of moldy straw in another. That was all. I approached terminal velocity during the peel-off to the ground floor, my rate of descent increasing to keep pace with the murderous rage I was acquiring. Upon arrival at the bottom of the staircase, however, I wired down the safety valve and walked over to the leftenant's desk: "Nice place you got here, Jack, but what the hell do you call it?"

With a show of irritation, he explained that this was an ancient French prison. During the Occupation, the Gestapo had kept local political prisoners here; and now various Allied prisoners and unidentified persons such as I were being held here. "And," added this royal jerk, "you will be detained here until our investigators get around to your case."

"Funniest thing I've heard all day!" I said, hauling my liberated Luger from my belt. "Leftenant, I'd tell you what to do with your hotel, but I kind of doubt if it'd fit."

He halfway rose from his chair, but before he could say anything I hollered, real mad, "You say one more goddam word and I'll strafe ya, but good!" The leftenant sat down and kept his trap shut, so I left, pausing at the doorway to add that should there be a fuss at the main gate, he would be short two black soldats.

It was a long haul back to the bright lights, and I cussed every step of the way without repeating myself, enlarging both my vocabulary and philosophy sufficiently to cover the awful incidents of the past hour. By the time I'd arrived back in the center of town, I was once again my own cheerful self, and I slumped wearily to a bench beneath a statue only to spring into the evening air and let fly a string of oaths that startled the passing French people. In amazement they beheld a tattered, fugitive-type Yank shaking his fist at their favorite piece of statuary, all the while muttering bitterly, "You're the bastards that got me into all this!" For Fate's limber finger had dealt the final, ironic goose of the day: the happy, smiling faces of Wilbur and his brother Orville Wright gazed down at me from their perch atop the monument commemorating their historic flights in Le Mans back in the year Ought-Nine.

Hell's Bells! This haywire day was wearing away and I had a grand fête to get done, so I headed back toward the Hotel Moderne. Unable to orient myself in this big city, I inquired the way of four or five jolly innkeepers, pausing with each to exchange a few francs for a nip of wine.

Once again at the cozy bar of the hotel, I had a little pow-wow with a likely looking combat captain. He cocked a sympathetic ear to my sad cry, led me to his quarters, donated a shaving kit, soap, and towel; and in very few minutes I skipped merrily back into the bar, now fresh like the daisy and raring for mischief. As for a place to shack up, well to hell with that. I'd ponder the question when it might come up. Now wheee! Time was a-wastin'!

Yvonne, Yvette, and Marie: three angels making with the old cognac! What scenery! What luxury! What luck! A smoky old joint complete with beauteous barmaids, crystal chandelier, and plenty of booze of excellent quality! Retiring to a dark corner, I tallied my wad: somewhere around twelve thousand francs, courtesy of the combined efforts of the Wehrmacht and that hot-shot dive-bombing squadron.

At the moment, Yvonne—a delicate, dark-eyed creature of rare charm —was tuned in on the frequency of a finely feathered paddlefoot, listening with patience to his no-doubt depraved murmurings. I would cut his type out of the traffic pattern, so I taxied over, winked into Yvonne's sparkling eyes, and riffled my attractive roll of francs under her saucy nose, like so: "Ffftttttttrrrrrr!"

This subtle maneuver sufficed. Yvonne and I retired to a secluded corner table. I let out a whoop.

"Hey, Marie!"

"Oui, Monsieur?"

"Champagne, mignonne!" I said.

"Beaucoup champagne!" quoth Yvonne, the darling.

And we vive'd la Belle France. We vive'd Amerique. We vive'd Le Mans and Tayo and Yvonne and la sack until that jug and another just like it was all gone.

"Ha-ha! Marie! Deux bouteilles du vin rouge!"

And with the fine red wine of Bordeaux sloshing about behind my belt, I was cruising at 4,000 rpm and drawing about four yards of the old mercury. Was I havin' fun! Now there joined the party a quartet of French Canadian outlaws, saboteurs of an OSS outfit who were celebrating their lucky return from a daring mission behind the lines. These reckless raiders brought over a couple of litres of rotgut Calvados that passed around from hand to hand until empty. A Yank cavalry officer latched onto the party, a Grade A character, about six-foot-six and bony, wild eyes and sharp cheekbones, stringy black hair and a drooping handlebar moustache mounted halfway up a gaunt, weather-beaten face. He wore an old-time western gun belt with a brace of pearl-handled six-guns. This thirsty apparition obtained numerous bottles of booze for to help keep the jamboree afloat.

"Yeeeow, Marie!" And a bottle of anisette and another of some bitter emerald-colored booze appeared on the scene. The poppety-pop of corks. The musical gurgle of fast-poured wine and the clink of glass upon glass. Gleeful, off-key harmony with Yvonne, in her piercing soprano, la-la-la'ing a hole right through my eardrum. Between verses she would sink her dainty choppers into my benumbed neck. There was no mistake about it: this was developing into a dandy party. The joint was coming apart at the hinges, and I was justly proud of having been the instigator of such an affair. Hot damn! Hadn't had so danged much fun since the day my old Aunt Nell got her starboard tit caught in the wringer!

There came dim and insidious rumors to the effect that the bar was about to close down, so I made my way to the cellar and purchased four bottles of wine, two red and two white, for future reference. With great cunning and shrewdness, I cached them away in some dark corner and returned to the party. And what a party! Zonk!

I opened an eye . . . wiggled an out-flung hand . . . dusty, bare planks, and my face was resting quietly thereupon. I heard faint voices and sat up in a hurry, relaxing again upon realization that it was English being spoken. A very chilly, dark, bare and bleak hallway in France, and I didn't know why or how I might have come to be there. I had, however, slept well and soundly. I leaned my back against the wall and chuckled as dim bits of the hilarious evening filtered through my head. I took inventory.

My Luger had been liberated for the second time. No francs remained in my pockets, but in my shoe there was still tucked a thousand-franc note—placed there with remarkable foresight. All else was missing in action, including a silver skull-and-crossbones I'd removed from a dead Gestapo officer's hat somewhere along the line. But in my coat pocket was a bottle. I fished it out and it was half full of red wine, so with a shrug I forgot my losses and took a long pull on the jug, and it was very good wine.

Tiptoeing along the hallway, I opened a door to discover that I was in a rear entryway of an outbuilding of the Hotel Moderne. The sun was just peeking up over the horizon and the sky was still dim, and there was a golden line of sunlit clouds in the eastern sky. The breeze was fresh and cool and dewy, and it was a beautiful day in Le Mans!

I bummed a smoke from the sentry at the curb and leaned in the doorway of the hotel, smoking and nipping at the plasma and watching the sunrise, and I felt happy and eager to prowl through another day. In the kitchen I found sitting the shameless wench Yvonne, and she turned her big black eyes on me and smiled slyly and flapped her curly eyelashes a few times. Indeed, she looked so exceedingly tender that I didn't have the heart to accuse her of having rolled me. She rustled up a couple of eggs and some bread and jam, and I sat on a box and had breakfast. Then I told her that I thirsted for a bottle of vin rouge, adding pointedly that I couldn't pay for it. Flashing a roguish grin, she ducked into the bar, returning in a moment with the goods; and I sat in the warm kitchen chatting cheerily with Yvonne and a fat old cook while working on the jug. After a while, along came the Air Corps paddlefoot—the gentleman who'd so graciously assigned me quarters in the local penitentiary. I asked him, quite nastily, how went the war.

He appeared to be a bit startled to find me sitting there in the kitchen making free with the private stock. And then—in all seriousness—he gave me the word that I was supposed to be under guard, but being as how I was here I could stay until nine a.m., at which time an army truck was to leave for Rennes with a load of suspicious citizens for the concentration camp there. The Lieutenant said that at Rennes we would be investigated and interrogated for a minimum of ten days. With a straight face I nodded and bowed and agreed with him: I'd be sure to be aboard the truck at nine sharp. I even signed somebody else's name on a paper to that effect. Imagine that silly bastard wanting to play games!

When he had gone away I sashayed out the rear, sailed over a fence, and scuttled down an alleyway to the street where I spied at the curb a jeep, and a young captain was throwing his luggage aboard. I asked him if perchance he might be heading in the general direction of the English Channel. Said he with a grin, "Climb aboard!" There were no foolish questions at all, and in a moment we rolled out of Le Mans leaving behind us a fine hotel, an excellent bar, one sweet thieving rascal of a barmaid; plus one rear-echelon Intelligence Officer, the sole aim of whose miserable life was to spin about me his spiderweb of red tape. I was grateful, however, to have met that nincompoop: for the encounter served to dispel any lingering wistful notions that I might have entertained about being received by the likes of him with open arms and shrill cries of gladness. Anyway, I was a bit tickled to know that my days of shifty ways were not yet over. I was London-bound now, and nonstop.

Handcuffed to the rear seat framework of the captain's jeep was a prisoner: a furtive French Nazi who had about him the air of a man on his way to being guest of honor at a necktie party—which in fact he probably was. To him we paid no heed as we cruised westward out of Le Mans, but just basked in the gentle early sunlight, swapping lies and passing the jug back and forth. Some eighty kilometers later when we pulled into Laval, the jug was bone-dry, and the captain and I were great friends. He gave me a pack of cigarettes when I bade him adieu.

I legged it on uptown and took a good squint down the narrow main drag; and right then and there was born Operation Bistro. Speckled conveniently along either side of the street were innumerable tiny cafés, and I resolved to sample the wares of each just for the hell of it. So I zigzagged through Laval savoring the fine wines and brandies and enjoying the generous hospitality of the recently liberated and highly exuberant townspeople. When I at last emerged at the city limits on the far side of town, I was slightly boiled. My feet hurt, for the streets were hot and my shoes were sole-less. And my thousand-franc ace-in-the-hole was dwindling.

The road out of Laval angled north and west toward Fougere and Avranches, and it was the express pipeline supplying the Yank blitzkrieg that was tearing across France. "The Red-Ball Highway," they called it, and an amazing variety of military machines roared along at full speed in a never-ending stream, almost bumper to bumper. Trucks full of gasoline and ammunition, tanks, ambulances, prime movers, rolling machine shops, all whizzing toward Paris unmolested beneath the clear blue skies. I was happy in the knowledge that the sole reason for this freedom of movement was our terrific fighter superiority. One squadron of Messerschmitts could have thrown a helluva cork into this Red-Ball bottleneck. It even made my mouth water to see such juicy targets. We'd knocked the Luftwaffe out of the skies and strafed what they had left on the ground. And when that job was done our fighters had chopped the Jerry supply lines to small and bloody bits. Evidence of the past three months of merciless strafing was wherever one might look—the ditches were full of wreckage. I looked at this smooth flow of traffic along the Red Ball and thought of the Jerries' frantic horse-drawn nocturnal stumblings.

Intending to journey in style to Fougere, I flagged down a truck and jumped into the cab. After a few kilometers I revised my plans, for the dark-complected lad at the controls sang boogie-woogie, drove with no hands and fewer brains, and knew only one throttle position, that being full forward. I bailed out at the first little village, found a little café, and had a jolt of eau-de-vie to steady my shaking knees. I would walk to Fougere, I decided, figuring that after having come this far intact, it would be a bum joke to be knocked off by some unconscious, feather-brained, throttle-jockey.

So I acquired a bottle of wine and started walking, taking my own sweet time and admiring the beauties of nature and quenching my thirst from time to time with a long, gurgling swig. But pretty soon I looked through the bottom of the bottle and saw the heat waves shimmering up from the tar road, which seemed to extend for a thousand kilometers ahead of me. I resigned myself to another chance with a boogie-woogie driver.

But the empty trucks whined past one after another, ignoring my waving thumb. After a moment of concentrated thought, the solution to my problem appeared and I retreated to the place where I'd tossed away the empty wine bottle. Retrieving it, I waved it enticingly at the first truck to come along. The way those hydraulic brakes started operating, one would have thought that charmed bottle to be a washed-out bridge. I jumped into the cab and apologized to my thirsty chauffeur for the ruse; and so I rode on into Fougere, arriving with all nerves vibrating like banjo strings at a Kentucky barn dance.

Fougere was a shamble of buildings shattered into rubble. Bleak walls and solitary chimneys broke the skyline. Dead tanks and strafed vehicles blocked the streets. It was past noon now and there was a little weasel gnawing around behind my belt buckle, and in Fougere there were no restaurants anymore. A Yank MP was profanely directing traffic at a battered intersection, and I asked him civilly enough if he could tell me where I might get a bite to eat.

Obviously startled to hear his own language coming from beneath a black beret, the MP scowled belligerently and asked me who in hell I thought I might be. When I replied truthfully that by this time I was a little doubtful myself, I was forthwith escorted to the guardhouse, shown to a room, and told that I'd be investigated by the commanding officer, who was at the time somewhere out in the countryside tracking down spies or gathering daisies or something of the sort.

Smiling up into the town MP's face and rubbing my hands together, I waited with patience for this amateur gumshoe to finish his jabbering and leave me alone. When he left, locking the door behind him, I counted to a hundred, smashed a chair, and used a leg of it to rip the bars away from the rotted wooden casement. I left town by the back way, highly amused at the wonderful ways of life.

A few kilometers beyond Fougere, I lurked alongside a bomb crater in the highway that forced traffic down to a crawl. Before long I made a flying leap into the rear of a canvas-covered truck and found myself to be in good company, for a change. I'd landed in the center of a group of a dozen combat infantrymen who were en route to a rest camp up near the Channel. They were well equipped with booze and rations, and I filled up on both to the tune of many a good war story. It was a merry party, and when the truck wheeled into the outskirts of Avranche I fell out—literally—into the middle of the street and the truck rolled on. The awful din of the cargo of drinking, singing soldiers soon faded in the distance.

Having again met some decent Yanks, my morale—grown slightly frazzled and threadbare—was once more so high that I could hardly live with it. I peeled off into a sagging-floored café for a nip and immediately latched onto a trio of Air Corps Engineers who lounged at one table. They soon invited me to accompany them to the Channel Coast. To Bayeux they'd take me, and from there they claimed I'd have no trouble smuggling myself aboard a vessel bound for Merrie Olde. With that cheery thought in mind, I dug out my remaining francs and purchased a litre of good Bordeaux rouge, which I resolved to refrain from uncorking until I was back with my old squadron.

It was late in the afternoon, and we were traveling the winding back roads of the rolling Bocage country near the coast when we saw, framed in a notch of the forest, the delightful and unbelievable sight of a castle that towered right up out of the sea. Mont St. Michel it was, and we paused for a smoke and a chat and to feast our eyes upon the fairy-story beauty of the ancient fortress. And then there came to my ears the distant sound of an aircraft engine revving up. A couple of kilometers away there arose a swirl of brown dust.

An air evacuation strip, explained the engineers, with C-47s flying ambulance service to England. "Thanks, boys!" I hollered, and bailed out to take off across-country, dogtrotting toward the beacon of prop-blown dust. Hot damn! I'd flown into France and be damned if I wasn't about to fly out! Ten sweaty minutes later I came to a tiny, dusty, sun-drenched meadow.

Six inches of powder-fine dust lay underfoot, billowing up at the slightest movement to settle over a pair of drab C-47s amid the dozen ambulances that were queued up on the wide cargo doors. Aside stood a couple of oven-like tents, and around them milled a little group of tired, dust-caked people. Observing the glitter of oak leaves on various collars, I just crawled under the closest ship, pausing en route to kiss a darling dimple in the oily metal belly. Amazing that I should feel such affection for a lousy transport—but she was still a flying machine and I rubbed a gentle hand over her flaps, then poked a grinning face up into the open cargo door. The pilot was puttering around up in the cockpit.

"Achtung!" I cried. And he whirled about to regard me darkly.

"Lookit, Buddy," I said in a pitiful voice. "How's about flyin' a refugee fighter pilot outta this goddam country on the sly, eh?"

But before he could make answer, there appeared from around the edge of the navigator's compartment the lovely tousled head of a starlet-type American flight nurse. "Tut-tut, flyboy!" she said sweetly. "Ladies present!"

She slim-hipped down the length of the ship. I quit scratching my armpits. Blowing my likker-laden breath into her face, I apologized for my raw talk and told her that she was absolutely the most beautiful thing I'd ever seen in all my wide travels. I added that this was the first time I'd ever seen a flying suit that looked like a négligée. I showed the pilot my green tarnished dog tag. But the nurse wrinkled a pert nose and laughed at me. She remarked to her pilot that I had all the earmarks, and could be nothing other than what I claimed to be. So the pilot held out a helping hand and hoisted me up into the ship. He looked me over for a moment and grinned. "Lay low up in the cockpit, friend, and we'll be airborne as soon as we pick up a load!"

I crawled into the pilot's seat and looked around, chuckling like a fool; for it was old home week! An excellent assortment of clocks, gauges, dials and cranks, levers, toggles, switches and buttons! I laughed inside when I flicked back over the day and a half of wheeling and dealing that had taken me from St. Nicolas des Bois to finally lodge me where I now sat!

Eighteen broken soldiers were lifted gently into the ship and their stretchers made secure. The cargo doors banged shut and the pilot came forward, and I slid into the co-pilot's seat. Switches on and the props turned over. The engines caught and coughed, then took hold and roared and we bumped along a fence-line to the end of the meadow. To my high-speed eye the runway looked suicidally short, and I sweated a little while the pilot ran up his engines and poured on the coal. But then we were sluggishly airborne and I was back in the Twentieth Century!

Off the port wing to the west, the sun hung low over the Channel and the long, sharp shadows emphasized the bold features of the jagged coastline below us—the same coastline I'd buzzed on D-Day, but there'd been some changes made. The villages weren't in such good shape anymore, not nearly as quaint as they'd been. Bomb and shell craters dotted the countryside, and overall was a twisting maze of tank tracks that wove strange patterns over the fields and farms.

From my cockpit window I gazed out past the shimmering prop and past the trembling wingtip. I looked out over the rugged Bocage country: over the black forests and sunlit hillside meadows, over the faint, thin lines of countless hedgerows to where they gave way in the gathering dusk of the eastern horizon to the hazy country through which I'd struggled; at the still-occupied France where good friends of mine even now were fighting in their own ways against the hated Boches, with every move still governed by fear of Gestapo reprisal. I strained my eyes in an effort to penetrate the quickly darkening horizon, for somewhere there in the mysterious haze lay the River Orne and Caen, Dozulé and the prison camp at Bonnesbocque; and out beyond in the beautiful coastal hills lay Pont Audemer and my comrades of le Maquis César. Engulfed now in a thousand memories, I didn't want to leave.

In the murk off the starboard wing lay the Invasion beaches, fringed with rusting debris and with hundreds of tiny vessels riding at anchor just offshore. Now Cherbourg slid past to the west, and at first I wondered why the pilot wasn't taking a bit of fancy evasive action—for the flak there had once been deadly.

Taking over the unfamiliar control column for a moment and sensing the faint vibrations of the ailerons as they came trickling through to my hand, I had a great urge to crank this clumsy old boxcar through a slow and easy barrel roll. Already bored with straight-and-level flying, I retired to the radio compartment and browsed through a Yank magazine, catching up on war news. And when I turned to the back page, my howls brought the flight nurse forward. For some sorcerer had sketched my picture and placed it in this aircraft for me to find!

The scene was a musty old wine cellar where a tattered Frenchman, with simple grin on face and tin cup in hand, reclined against a dripping hogshead. Over this contented citizen there stood a brawny Yank Tommy-gunner, shouting: "I've come to Liberate you!"

Well, that about did it. Swamped by alternate surges of triumph and nostalgia, I stood in the cockpit and watched the coast of France dwindle and fade from sight. Ahead lay only the English Channel, vast and calm and twinkling in the slanting light of the setting sun.

It was only a flight of a couple hundred miles but it seemed inter-minable, for my thoughts were running wild. I looked at my shabby cos-tume and then looked at the instrument panel: 180 miles an hour toward England! And not daring to believe my luck, I sat and rubbed that dusty bottle of vin rouge as though it was Aladdin's favorite lamp. I'd be in Lon-don damned soon, and I'd cable home first thing. Then, to the right people, I'd unload some of the hot information I'd picked up in my travels: an underwater bridge across the Seine . . . locations of several Jerry headquarters and ammo dumps, and a wealth of other items of general interest. And then I'd head for the little flying field at Bodney for a roaring squadron reunion!

Then landfall over England, near Southampton, and down to a gentle landing at a RAF airdrome there. I was primed for action and short on patience. I'd rolled fast for a long time, and with that inertia still with me I hit the ground running and rounded up the local Intelligence Officer. I should have known better.

After whispering a few hoarse words of advice to this dummy, and after thanking him for his total lack of cooperation, I bowed out of his office figuring to hit the highways and make my own way into London. I'd be there by dawn by hook or by crook. But at the main gate I was met by a Tommy-gunner who turned a deaf ear to my shrieks of pain: the airdrome was closed, for a major airborne attack was being readied for dawn take-off. No one—not even the bloody great king—was permitted either entry or exit at this airdrome at this time. I was trapped, and I mulled over that news while grinding my molars to a powder. I could leave anyway, without too much trouble, but I was weary of eluding people with guns. Now it didn't seem quite worth the risk. After all, twelve hours before I'd been gulping wine and playing patty-cake with Yvonne clear back in Le Mans in the middle of France. The truckload of suspects dispatched back there by the jerk lieutenant was most likely only about halfway to the concentra-tion camp at Rennes. And what the merry hell! I was in England after a fast and hilarious trip and—despite the fact that I'd immediately become involved in another feud with another fathead who'd been weaned on red tape—I was happy. So I gave up the ghost and finagled a little room behind the kitchen of the Officer's Club.

I combed my shaggy head and licked my thirsty chops and pulled a bead on the bar, intending to maneuver a little bit of Reverse-Lend-Lease and run up a terrific bar bill. I'd just hooked a rundown heel over the brass rail and shouted for Scotch-and-soda when a blimp-type Limey paddlefoot tapped my shoulder and said, "My word! You cawn't be in here dressed like that, ol' boy!"

Insult to injury! I left quietly, without a word or a struggle, before I should find myself tagged as Exhibit A at a local murder trial. Back in my quarters I smoldered a while, considering the fence and a quick trip to London, but unable to resist the lure of the sack I tumbled in and was soon unconscious.

At the crack of dawn I stood at the edge of the runway and watched the aircraft and troopers getting squared away for their mission. The gliders were racked up at the end of the field and the paratroops—armed to the very teeth—tumbled aboard. The poor bastards. The troop-laden C-47s groaned and moaned and thrashed the chilly air with their props as they laboriously hauled their awkward trailers up into the blue. Where they were going I didn't know, and cared less. Before long the sky was full of aircraft and the airdrome empty, and I sought out the highest-ranking officer I could contact.

As a result of several minutes of weeping upon this gold-plated shoulder, I found myself strapped into a tiny Cub en route to London. The weather grew increasingly foul, and my pilot seemed to take high delight in coming as close as possible to the many barrage balloons that would loom up out of the quarter-mile visibility. I was unhappy until I set a shaky foot upon the concrete runway of the RAF base near the big town.

A jeep and driver were donated: but now—so near to the end of the long trek—I hated to give up my freelance status. So I asked my driver if he wouldn't enjoy a day off. In reply to his quizzical look I proposed a little deal, suggesting that he deliver me to the nearest Tube station, give me ten shillings cash, and ask no questions. I would go about my business and he about his own. No sooner had I spoken than we screeched to a halt in the suburbs, and I pocketed my stake with thanks. The gaily whistling driver smoked his tires on takeoff, intent no doubt upon immediate rendezvous with the queens up at Ma's Nifty Rooms.

With my great ruined clodhoppers parked comfortably upon the green plush, I rode in solitary splendor through the blitzed outskirts of town. Then the train ducked underground and rattled along, and I bailed out at

Piccadilly Circus feeling very jolly, to trudge unchallenged past the horde of white-helmeted MPs. They figured, I suppose, that here went some old saloon-swamper heading for Soho: a jaunty character with a piece of filthy parachute for a shirt, beret sloped over an ear, shoes without soles, and a bottle of wine tucked into a coat pocket.

It would be fun, I thought, to run across some of the boys from the squadron, so I checked a few of the lower Piccadilly brasseries. Nobody there. I tried the Regent Palace bar, but the doorman spoke unkindly to me. I snarled at him and drifted up the road to Oxford Street and drank ale in the American Bar.

And then I was broke again, so I jumped into a taxicab and rode in style to a hush-hush address on Brook Street. I pounded on the portals. The door squeaked open and I slid inside to surrender to AAF Escape & Evasion headquarters. My duty was done. Everything was legal, and the lieutenant at the door had to take care of the cab fare.

The owner and operator of this efficient little Escape headquarters was a courteous and exceedingly thoughtful young captain by name of White. Over his desk was a sign: "The Air Corps Looks After Its Own!" And people set about proving it to me. The captain put my jug of wine into the safe. He lent me five pounds and before anyone could catch me, I ran out of the building and down to the cable office to send the first message the home folks had received since the "So sorry" telegram from the War Department some months before. "Well and Happy. Love, Ted."

I was introduced to a two-pound slab of beefsteak, rare and sizzling, which went into my belly to the sloshing tune of a half-dozen cans of cold American beer. Then, gently but firmly, a sergeant escorted me to a bathroom where I was exposed to a bar of poisonous yellow soap, a scrub brush, and a bathtub. I chiseled away the clothes I'd worn for so many moons, and they crawled under their own power from the bathroom whereupon they were snatched up in tongs and hurled into the furnace. After beating to a turbid froth four separate and distinct tubs-full of steaming water, at last I sat exhausted in a bath of water that remained comparatively clean. Now there appeared a flight surgeon proudly bearing a mug of his own miracle medicine, which he guaranteed would drive away the tenacious, maddening scabies and other small and nibbling animals which were wont to join forces with wandering airmen.

No sooner had I finished killing bugs than in strode my no-good whisky-drinking squadron commander Willie O. Jackson who—in response to a teletype—had jumped into his Mustang and flown to London to identify me and welcome me home. And I breathed easier upon learning that a goodly percentage of my old sidekicks were still flying low over Piccadilly. Mac had sent his regards along with a handful of pound notes. Parchesi-Joe had sent his best uniform. I put it right on, and felt then as though I'd never left home!

After spilling my pack of lies to various undercover types, I was set free for the evening with carte blanche to a fancy hotel. And when the sun went down and the fog rolled in from the Thames, then took place my introduction to the buzz bombs!

I'd watched a hundred of the lethal little rascals take off from Nazi France to growl away toward England; but now, on the receiving end, the goddam things were terminating their mischievous flights all about me! Their incoming routes were well marked, for as they howled in from the Channel to slip through the balloon barrage, they were picked up by the more distant of the thousands of flak batteries that dotted the rooftops and parks of London. The blasting of the guns would grow louder and louder as the flak marched across the city, until the batteries in one's own block would pound and flash, and then shell fragments would rain down into the streets. Searchlights would sometimes catch the robots as they bored in low over the chimneypots, and the unmuffled, staccato roar of the jet engines would fill the sky until the fuel gave out. There would be a few awful moments of silence as the bombs would plunge earthward, and then would come the terrific explosions. Glass would splinter, plaster would sift from the barroom ceilings, and people would get up from the floors, brush themselves off, and resume their interrupted conversations.

The damned robots that first night seemed to hold a personal grudge against me. Dodging the bastards, I hopped about London from pub to pub like a flea on a hot skillet. Nevertheless, a dandy party was had, and when I hit the sack we weren't at all bothered by the roaring guns and swooshing rockets and the intermittent crash-landings of the buzz bombs.

I journeyed through the rain the following afternoon to a colossal suburban paddlefoot resort known as Wide Wing, where I observed at first hand the rugged wartime hardships that some of the boys were enduring with commendable fortitude. Placed with cunning strategy amongst piles of beefsteak and a surplus of beautiful waitresses were more flak batteries than the Jerries had used in Happy Valley during the merriest days of the air offensive. Huge camouflage nets protected mountainous stacks of crated beer, spare staff cars, female majors and captains and lieutenants, and quantities of other stateside goodies. And all about were tall towers topped by shiny sirens that yowled fiercely at the whispers of distant robots.

Tact was not with me, but I finally left the area with two pockets stuffed with back pay, with full flying pay thrown in for good measure. Sadly, most of this treasure was forever lost in the maze of lower London's lower bistros.

Still full of the old zip and charging around from sheer momentum, the next morning I delivered a long-winded and slightly alcoholic lecture to a few hundred local Intelligence officers who had gathered in a London theater to hear my story and others like it. I took a dim view of the proceedings, but—like I told them—talking to my own countrymen shouldn't be so tough after making small talk with a roomful of Jerries.

Orders at last, releasing me to my outfit. Retrieving the jug of wine from the safe, I scampered down to Liverpool Station and rode the slow train up the crooked rails through Cambridge and then to Thetford. There was as usual no one there to meet the train, and I was forced to goose the old goblin up the highway until I came upon the little grassy flying field at Bodney. Once past the sentry, I was so damned happy that I couldn't keep from breaking into a run. And the faster I ran, the faster I thought, and the faster I ran. After a slight delay I'd completed that last, long flight and my one-hundredth mission was just about done. I'd flown out of this field by Mustang and come back by horse-drawn still, Maquis automobile, Jerry trucks, farmers' hay wagons, Yank jeeps, trucks, tanks, recon cars, DC-3, Cub airplane, subway, taxicabs, dinky train, and on foot. I'd sworn to never walk anywhere again, but here I was—running! By hook and by crook, I'd come to the end of the trail.

I wandered into the Club and it was just suppertime. I swaggered into the dining room and took a grinning look at the long table where sat the reckless remnants of my infamous squadron, all stuffing their ugly faces with Spam & Sprouts.

"Ha ha ha!" I cried. "I bin everywhere!"

Archy-the-Gremlin threw his fork to the table and hollered in great disgust: "Hey, you guys! Lookit what just walked in! Death, warmed over!"

Bottle-Arse Leo tore himself away from a trough-full of swill just long enough to growl: "Christ Almighty! The gawdam Jerries won't even have him!" And he bucked his head down and flailed away at his supper with a fork in either hand.

Parchesi-Joe, poking a chunk of cut-plug into a cheek, muttered: "Ya sonuvabitch, why'd you have to come back? Things was just gettin' peaceful around here!"

And my old partner McKibben yowled, "C'mon Faro! Leave us have a goddam party!" And with that he bounced from the table and scuttled into the bar.

When the bottle of Bordeaux Rouge was dead and each of the outlaw crew had had a nip, Archy let out a groan.

"All right, start talkin'," he said resignedly. "But whatever you tell us, it's a goddam lie!"

It looked like I was back amongst friends again.

Hot damn!

ACKNOWLEDGMENTS

◆

Dad's one and only visit to the Continent began on D-Day+2 and ended in August 1944 when he was reunited with his squadron. He never returned to Europe, but he maintained contact with those who'd befriended and protected him: The Flea, César, Vitrice, Suzanne, Helene, Maurice, and others from these pages. Conditions in post-WWII France were challenging, with widespread inflation, unemployment, and food shortages. Meanwhile the States prospered, and Dad never forgot those who gave him refuge. In the post-war years, he and his mother sent food parcels, the always-cherished American cigarettes, and a few Yankee dollars to his French comrades. This book is a continued expression of gratitude to those French warriors and their progeny to whom I am bonded but have yet to meet. To those in his squadron who knew him as "The Joker," to those of the Maquis who knew him as "Tayo," thank you. Without the support you offered him at great risk to yourselves, your friends, and your families, Ted Fahrenwald might not have made it to the most noteworthy chapter in his life, in which he was able to fulfill his most significant and glorious mission: becoming "Dad."

I had a tremendous amount of ongoing help and encouragement from Dad's flight mate and best pal in England and afterward—Don McKibben, or "Mac" as he was known in C Flight of the 486th Fighter Squadron in the famed 352nd Fighter Group. After Dad's death in 2005, Mac supplied every kind of support to help me realize this project, from facilitating the scan of the original manuscript to contributing his Photoshop, writing, proofreading, business, and extraordinary networking talents at every step of the way—not to mention his prodigious memory. Mac, thank you for stepping up to the plate again and again: I wouldn't have done it without you.

Dad's sister Caroline Price, her husband Clark, and daughter Becca Price were always available to proofread, cheerlead, and offer ideas and new perspectives. Thanks to David Salm for being a great editor, advisor, and supporter. My niece Jessica Simkovic did beautiful design work for the cover and cleaned up the decades-old photos. And last but far from least—Jay Stout, author of *Fighter Group: The 352nd Blue-Nosed Bastards in World War II*, discovered the book through his research on the 352nd and carried the manuscript right to the publisher's door. Jay, there's no way to adequately thank you for your generous efforts at the final hour and the magic you worked!

I'm grateful for all these contributions, because without this foundation of support, Dad's fantastic story would continue to be known only within our circle of family and friends.—Madelaine